THE HOUSE OF MACMILLAN

THE HOUSE OF
MACMILLAN
(1843–1943)

BY

CHARLES MORGAN

"We have commenced quite in
a small way. . . . If the business
should prosper, we shall, both of
us, do our best to realise some of
our ideals. . . . We feel, however, that the world can go on
without us, or our ideals ; and,
in the meantime, we shall strive
to do the work that lies nearest
us in the best manner we can."
Daniel Macmillan, 1843

NEW YORK
THE MACMILLAN COMPANY
1944

PRINTED IN THE UNITED STATES OF AMERICA

TO

DANIEL AND HAROLD MACMILLAN

" A thousand thanks for your obligingness. You certainly
are a most pleasant person to deal with, and please God you
will have no cause to regret it."
Charles Kingsley to Alexander Macmillan, 1856

FOREWORD
To the American Edition

MR. GEORGE BRETT'S *wish to publish this book in his own country, although it is not principally concerned with the firm over which he presides, gives me an opportunity to write a note of grateful acknowledgment. Publication in the United States is, on this occasion, more than ever welcome for two special reasons: first, that it enables me to continue without a gap in the series a happy association of my work with the imprint of Macmillan's of New York; secondly, that it illustrates one of the book's principal themes—the solidarity of the Houses of Macmillan throughout the world.*

What is told here is the story of the London house. How the American organization began, how the Macmillan Company of New York came into being, how it grew, and how, in its independence, it is related to England has been briefly indicated; but the tale of its independent growth until it became the great organization that it is to-day is properly the subject of a separate history to be written by an American author and published in 1946, when the American company will celebrate its own fiftieth anniversary.

CHARLES MORGAN

PREFACE

OTHER writers, unquestionably, have known in their childhood that they would write when they grew up, but who else, I wonder, has been so vilely precocious as to choose his publisher at the age of seven ? In my father's library, so many of the books, from *Alice* to Tennyson and from Pater to Matthew Arnold, bore the Macmillan imprint that I began to consider it a hallmark. It was noticeable, too, that the Collected Works of the Giants usually wore a green binding with gold letters on it, and this I came to regard as the decent dress of authorship. Nothing, I resolved, would content me, when my time came, but Macmillans on the green.

I had to wait until 1929, when *Portrait in a Mirror* was published. Three years later *The Fountain* unaccountably slipped into a blue coat. Since then the colour has been as constant as the imprint, and, in face of Byron's remarks on Barabbas, it is as well that an author should declare himself content. It was good, therefore, to be asked by Daniel Macmillan to write this book. From his own point of view and from that of his brother, Harold Macmillan, it is the courteous dipping of an ensign as their ship continues, after a hundred years, her long voyage across the world ; from mine, it is an opportunity to make the salute.

Paper being rare and for gentler reasons, they and I felt that this was not an occasion to produce what George Moore would have called " a tombstone in two volumes." In any case, the work that I have now to do permits me to write little, and even this essay, slight as it is, could not have been completed, could not have been begun, without the help of Thomas Mark and those older members of Macmillan's staff, past and present, who have lent me their memory and experience. I wish also to acknowledge my general debt to Thomas Hughes's *Life of Daniel Macmillan*, to C. L. Graves's *Life of Alexander Macmillan*, and to *The Letters of Alexander Macmillan*, edited by George A. Macmillan; and to thank Trinity College, Cambridge (for Sir J. G. Frazer's letter); the Trustees of Thomas Hardy's estate; Mr. Guy Morley; Mr. G. Bernard Shaw; Dr. C. M. Ottley (for Walter Pater's correspondence); and Mr. H. G. Wells for having generously allowed me to reproduce letters of which they control the copyright.

If one may not write stories, it is something — an exercise at least of the old craftsmanship — to give the bits and pieces of life to writing in a different kind. What follows has, then, been written happily and with care — happily because with care—but the year is late, this is a centenary volume, and I allow the manuscript to go, as I should not let go the manuscript of a story, in the knowledge that, if I were to put it aside for six months and come again to it, I might eliminate some of its faults. The reader must pardon them, for I do not. He will, I think, do so the more easily if he understands that what is offered to him is a note on the personality, rather than the history, of a great publishing house; a glancing impression, not a formal discourse. Though he like nothing else in my book, he will find, on turning to the title-page, that there is great merit in its imprint.

CHARLES MORGAN

CONTENTS

PART TWO : SCIENCE, " ALICE," AND THOMAS
HARDY (1863–72)

CHAPTER FIVE

CHAPTER SIX

PART THREE: END OF THE OLD ORDER (1872–90)

CHAPTER SEVEN

CHAPTER EIGHT

Contents

PART FIVE: CONTINUITY THROUGH TWO WARS
(1914–1943)

CHAPTER TWELVE

CHAPTER THIRTEEN

THE HOUSE OF MACMILLAN

PROLOGUE

ON the tenth of November 1843, two young booksellers, Daniel and Alexander Macmillan, published from Number Fifty-Seven Aldersgate-street, in the City of London, the first book to bear the Macmillan imprint. This at any rate was the day on which the volume reached the British Museum, though there are wise men who remember having seen at Simpkin's a record, which cannot now be traced, of its having been issued a month or two earlier. Both young men were Scottish peasants from the island of Arran. Daniel was thirty and Alexander twenty-five years old. The competition upon which they entered was fierce, for the Victorian tide was rising strongly. Gladstone, Darwin, Thackeray and Dickens on the elder side, and Charles Reade, Trollope, Charlotte Brontë and Jowett on the younger, were all within four years of being Daniel's contemporaries. Froude, Clough, Charles Kingsley, George Eliot, Herbert Spencer and Matthew Arnold were within the same range of Alexander. The giants were putting out their strength. Eighteen forty-three was the year of *Past and Present*, of *Martin Chuzzlewit*, of *Modern Painters* and Macaulay's *Essays*, of Mill's *Logic*, Liddell and Scott and *The Bible in Spain*. The wealth of the period in scholarship, imagination and controversy makes a modern observer rub his eyes. Alexander was destined, during his twenty-ninth year (1847), to see come from firms other than his own a group of books that may well challenge any twelve-months' yield in the history of publishing : *Tancred*, *The Princess*, *Jane Eyre*, *Vanity Fair* and *Wuthering Heights*.

Meanwhile, all that the House of Macmillan had to offer was a foolscap octavo of ninety-two pages : *The Philo-*

I

sophy of Training by A. R. Craig, Barford-street Institution, Islington, late Classical Master in Glasgow Normal Seminary (Private Department). Sugared descriptions, now called blurbs, were not even then unknown, but the conscientious young men of Aldersgate-street would have none of them. They were deeply interested in education, having lacked it themselves ; they had published an educational book and were proud of it. The work was described as embodying " suggestions on the necessity of normal schools for teachers to the wealthier classes, and strictures on the prevailing mode of teaching languages." The Macmillans were at the time setting up business in Cambridge but their next book still bore only the London address. It was no more magnificent than the first, being of pocket-size and containing but a hundred and twenty pages. But they were pleasant pages bound in sober, dark-brown covers, stamped with the figure of a pilgrim in gold, and the title was, in its way, as full of social implications as *The Philosophy of Training*'s concern with the improvement of the wealthier classes. *The Three Questions : What am I ? Whence came I ? Whither do I go ?* (by William Haig Miller) suggest that the Macmillans had their ear to the ground. Newman had left St. Mary's, Kingsley was in the offing, *The Origin of Species*, Mill on Liberty, and *Unto This Last* were all less than two decades away. In one form or another, scientific, religious, sociological or aesthetic, these three questions would be asked with fervour and anxiety for the next half-century. In fostering the books that asked them, the Macmillans would serve their God and make their fortune, because, as it happened, they believed in both — in their God with the earnestness of their up-bringing but with a remarkably unsectarian freedom of spirit, and in their fortune with that mingling of confidence and modesty, as an opportunity for good rather than as a means of gain, to which the great Victorians had the key.

Prologue

" I have just read Carlyle's new book, *Past and Present*,"
Daniel wrote in a letter dated " April 29, 1843." " . . . I felt
it do me good ; felt very strongly the truth of what he says
with regard to the Mammonism of our time. Mammon
the god ; riches, or success, heaven ; poverty, or want of
success, hell. This is putting the whole matter in a very
striking light. It is really worth taking to heart. I often
feel myself falling into this wretched and cursed spirit of
our time. It requires to be watched and kept under." A
few days earlier, this bred Calvinist, who was " rather
vext " by some things in Carlyle which looked " very like
Pantheism " and yet could learn from him and say : " I
think he will do good in our time," had been recommending
to his friend, George Wilson, Mr. Newman's volume of
University Sermons, " if you can lay your hand on them.
You will see that he is no old woman, and that his notions
about God are as sublime as anything you have ever read.
I don't expect you to have much sympathy with the book.
It was most painful to me. Still I could not help admiring
the wonderful power of the man, and feeling that he was
advancing much that was well worth thinking about, but
which was too much neglected. Above all, it seemed most
absurd to pretend to despise such men."

Daniel preserved his own judgement but was alive to
wisdom in men who differed from him. Seldom has a
man without classical education, indeed a self-educated man,
been at once so eager for the truth and yet so balanced in
his quest of it. When Scots are tolerant, they make even
of their tolerance an act of conscience ; it is stalwart, not
loose ; and Daniel Macmillan had in him an integrity that
exempted him from imprisonment by cliques. " Newman,"
he wrote, " is a true product of the nineteenth century — a
genuine steam-engine ; and yet no one is more conscious
of the weakness and self-sufficiency of ' our enlightened
age.' When he indicates this feeling some might think him

an atheist ; he seems to make the solid earth shake beneath you " — and he did, indeed, send many lesser men than Daniel scurrying for refuge into the deepest recesses of their prejudice. But Daniel stood his ground : " And yet I think he is a good man ; and he has great faith in goodness. One may learn many things from him, but I should be sorry to make him, or any of the class of which he is the most powerful member, my guide in spiritual matters."

These are hints of the man. Another letter throws light on the merchant at the outset of his career : " We have commenced in a small way. If a large tree grows from this small seed we shall be grateful. If not, we shall be content ; we shall feel that it is as it ought to be. We are determined that it shall not fail through indolence or extravagance. If business should prosper, we shall, both of us, do our best to realise some of our ideals with regard to what should be done for the craftsmen of our land. We feel, however, that the world can go on without us, or our ideals ; and, in the meantime, we shall strive to do the work that lies nearest us in the best manner we can."

The seed has spread. From it there has sprung up in the United States one of the great publishing houses of the world, independently directed and managed by Americans under the presidency of George P. Brett (Junior) but still in the effective ownership of the British Macmillans ; and branches of the original tree in London are to be found in Toronto, Melbourne, Bombay, Calcutta and Madras. As such things do not happen by chance, it would appear that a policy of some kind, a principle or character, has borne fruit, and it will be of interest to discover, while following the Macmillans' history, what that policy has been in its relation to the trade of publishing, to the art of literature, and to the changing times. That the policy can be sharply defined is improbable ; that it ought not to be is certain. There is an opportunism in trade, as there is in art and in soldiering,

4

which defies the text-books. Nevertheless, an artist has his
style, a great firm its character, the betrayal of which is a
damning, and always in the end a destructive, self-betrayal.
The highest opportunism — the same which distinguishes
a statesman from a die-hard on the one hand and a turn-
coat on the other — consists in preserving a style or a
character by developing it within the altering pressures of
circumstance.

There are two principal aspects of publishing, the idealistic and the commercial, and the character of a firm must
largely depend on its reconciliation of them. You may put
out books because you believe someone will buy them, or
you may put out books because you believe it right that
they should be available to the public, or you may put out
books for both of these reasons. If the motive of goodness,
as distinct from the motive of gain, enters at all into the
process, it may do so in several forms. It may, for example,
be a fanatical desire to convert the world to your ideals,
or a more humane wish to give opportunity to good writing
and honest thinking wherever they may be found. Evidently
fanaticism had little part in the founder who wrote as he
did of Newman and Carlyle, and though there were then,
and have been ever since, an impetuousness in the Macmillans' blood and a pulse that could beat high with their
determination to be masters in their own house, none of
them, in his capacity of publisher, has been stiffly exclusive
of ideas not his, or so convinced of his own virtue as to
deny other men their cakes and ale. In brief, though their
House was formerly an important part of the Broad Church
movement, their interest and sympathies extended even
then far beyond it ; they published Huxley in the early
days, Frazer in the later, and have never been publishers
to a party or a sect. At the same time, they have exercised
both their taste and their conscience. If this is paradoxical,
it is at least a paradox which, until the ideologies smote the

world, was familiar in England and in parts of Scotland. " If business should prosper " — it is a shrewd proviso — " we shall, both of us, do our best to realise some of our ideals." There is a glorious moderation in that, and, after a hundred years that have brought us to what we now are, almost a saving grace in what follows : " We feel, however, that the world can go on without us, or our ideals." Read, as it is to be read, in a context of faith and not of indifferentism, it might well serve as motto, not only for a pair of Victorian booksellers, but for our improbable new world. Some time may, however, pass before the new world sees the profoundly permissive idealism of it.

PART ONE

THE FOUNDATIONS
1813–63

CHAPTER ONE

Macmillan Origins

Childhood in Scotland—Daniel's Apprenticeship

HE Macmillans appear to have come originally from the coast of Argyllshire whence they migrated to the island of Arran. There, amid a superstitious countryside much given to witchcraft, Malcolm Macmillan, tacksman of the Cock farm and described by Tom Hughes, Daniel's biographer, as " a sort of ' chief peasant,' " was an Elder of the Established Church, a sternly conservative upholder of Christianity among the witches. When the Haldanes, revivalists of that day, came to Arran, Malcolm disapproved of their new-fangled ways, but did not positively forbid his children to attend their meetings. The children went, among them Duncan, the sixth of Elder Malcolm's ten children, who had been born in 1766 ; so did Katherine Crawford, daughter of a more progressively minded Elder, William Crawford, a Lowlander whose fore-fathers had come from Renfrewshire and the holder of a small peasant farm neighbouring the Cock. The revivalists, who estranged the Elders, drew the young together. Near the end of the eighteenth century, Duncan married Katherine, and succeeded his father-in-law on the little farm of Upper Corrie. He had twelve children, the tenth, Daniel himself, appearing on September 13th, 1813. Some three years later the family moved to Irvine in Ayrshire, and here Alexander was born on October 3rd, 1818. In the summer of 1823, his father died. The report of those who knew him, gathered before it was too late, preserves a pleasant picture of " old Duncan." At Irvine, he was a crofter ; he kept a few cows, pastured on the burgh moor, and cultivated a few acres of the town's land. He was a carter, too, and as his cart returned from carrying coal from the neighbouring pits to the harbour of Irvine, it would fill with children, some of whom remembered, as late as 1896, having enjoyed a " hurl." Evidently he had a way with children. His own revered his memory, though Daniel had not been ten or Alexander five when he died, but the strongest influence on both their lives, particularly on Daniel's, was that of their mother, Katherine. Her eldest son, Malcolm, a schoolmaster about twenty-five years old, was now head of the family ; he contributed to their support and came to be regarded almost as a second father by his brothers and sisters ; but Katherine Macmillan was the background of their life and the solace of its hardships. She was, it will be remembered, of Lowland stock, and Daniel describes her as " a Teuton," thanking heaven for this balance of steadiness and composure in his otherwise Celtic nature. Soon after his father's death, as it was urgently necessary that he should be put in a way to earn his living, his education abruptly ended, and on January 1st, 1824, being then three months beyond his tenth birthday, he was bound for seven years as apprentice to Maxwell Dick, bookseller, of Irvine, at a salary of eighteenpence a week, to rise each year by a shilling. He served so well that when he was fifteen he was left in charge while his master went to London, and the relationship between them was throughout cordial and prosperous. From Mr. Dick he learned to bind books and sell them and buy them, to groom and ride horses, to stain and varnish wood, and many things not specified in his indenture, for his master, he remembered long afterwards, was " a queer, queer man." Mrs. Dick was kind but " a wee daft," and from her he learned all her love affairs before he was twelve.

One fiery incident is recorded of his Celtic nature's revolt against its Teutonic control. Mr. Dick was rash enough to accuse his apprentice unjustly. Daniel protested with indignation so hot that Mr. Dick struck him, to learn, as others have learned since, that there are moments in the lives of all Macmillans when the Lowland lid fairly leaps off the Highland kettle. The boy seized his cap from its peg and the day-book from its desk. The first he clapped on his own head ; the second he hurled at his master's ; and vanished for ever. At any rate, he did not go home, his mother missed him with alarm, and what had become of him Mr. Dick could not say. He did not know what appears to be true, that, in the emotional crises of their lives, Macmillans take to the water. Daniel had marched six miles to Saltcoats and taken passage in a fishing-smack to Arran.

Meanwhile Alexander, though smaller, had been contributing to the tradition. At the Irvine Academy, he was vigorous in snowball fights and " stane-battles," but, when challenged to throw a somersault into the river, hesitated.

" You're frichtit ! "

" That was never telt of a Macmillan yet ! " cried Alexander, and took to the water with such impetuosity that he knocked the wind out of his body and had to be dragged ashore.

Daniel returned from Arran more peacefully, and life at Irvine continued. Old Duncan was there no longer to read the Bible in Gaelic or to improvise prayers in the same language ; but Katherine, having done all the work of the household with her own hands, kept the fireside and sang to them all at the long day's end. She was a reader, too, and in her old age was found sitting up in bed in her black mutch reading Cary's Dante ; but in the 'twenties she had a sweet voice, a great stock of ballads and hymns, and her singing was her sons' reward when work was over. Daniel, when he wrote of Celt and Teuton, knew what he was talking about. It was by her nature, even more than by her teaching, that she gave balance and humour and open-mindedness to the boys' character. " Puir body, he has nae room in him," she would say of zealots, and she told the inhabitants of Irvine that, to her thinking, such of them as had the good fortune to reach heaven would have to put up with the company of many Romanists there. Daniel knew, and never forgot, her quality. Years later, when she was dead, he found it unbearable to be in an Irvine that was empty of her, and in 1833, writing from the exile of Glasgow to his brother Malcolm who had dared to ask " What are you, or your father's house, that you should be ambitious ? ", he gave a defence of his father's house which showed that Katherine Macmillan was, for him, its corner-stone. " I know her as well," he said, " as ever a son knew a parent, and my persuasion is that she is the most perfect lady in all Scotland. . . . Few appreciated her, but no one could despise her. . . . I think she has one of the *finest*, I mean the most refined, minds I ever came into contact with, and yet she is far from being deficient in strength — a most strong and deep nature, yet a woman's nature. No one could be more deeply religious than she is, and yet how little she talks about it ! . . . If ever I saw any one with the same tenderness, strength and calmness, the same joyousness of heart, with the same depth, I should instantly fall in love with her, that is —" and here a wariness characteristic of the writer when on the subject of ideals asserted itself — " that is," he added, " if there was any chance of its ever coming to anything ! But at present a grave seems the most likely place for me. Pray send mother to Glasgow. I want her to cheer me. No, I can cheer myself. . . ."

Daniel's health had failed. At the beginning of 1831, when his apprenticeship to Mr. Dick ended, he had gone as a bookseller's assistant to Stirling where by this time Malcolm was the minister of a Baptist congregation. But, as Tom Hughes says, " the place was too small and the boy too big." He had chafed against the confinement of it and suffered " a most violent brain fever." As soon as lancing and leeching had cured him of this, he had gone to the shop of Mr. Atkinson in Glasgow, full of ambition and hoping for a partnership in the business. In his eagerness, not only had he worked in the shop from seven in the morning until midnight, but had regularly sat up until three or four in the morning reading, because they seemed " valuable for the purposes of business," the chief weekly, monthly and quarterly periodicals of the time. Illness had followed. His mother, hearing that he looked as if he were dying, had bidden him come home, and he might have gone if Mr. Atkinson had not chosen that moment for a long visit to London that should leave his assistant in charge and prove his worth. Daniel had held on and proved his worth so well that Mr. Atkinson, returning, had rewarded him with " a handsome present. A fortune seemed glittering before me," Daniel said. " I was full of hope. I strove with all my might against the weakness of my body. But it was no use. I could bear up no longer." So on June 15th, 1833, he wrote as he did to Malcolm, asking that his mother should come and in the next sentence unasking it. Two days later, his journal has : " The doctor looked very grave to-day. What does he mean ? This is a bad cough. I don't like this blood-spitting. I don't like this weakness in my limbs. Byron said, ' Death laughs.' But I daresay he found it no joke to fall into his hands. . . . But death is not all, *after death the judgment*. A serious matter that."

It was time that his mother should come. She bore him home to Irvine. After blistering and a week in bed, he was up again, trying, against the doctor's order, to write to Malcolm and beginning well enough, but : " My hand gets tired. I will write by and by. Kate promises me a ride on their pony every day when I get better."

As soon as he could think of himself as convalescent, he began to look for work. In Glasgow he had made friends with another young shopman, James MacLehose, afterwards to become a great man in that city, and, shortly before Katherine Macmillan had rescued her son, MacLehose had gone to London as an assistant in Messrs. Seeley's book-selling shop in Fleet-street. Daniel asked what the prospects were. " What kind of gents are S. and Son themselves ? . . . Are you hard wrought ? . . . What are your hours ? Are good lodgings easily had ? Are they expensive ? " MacLehose sat up until two in the morning to write six sheets of detailed answer and offered Daniel half his bed while he was looking round. There must have been Scots who failed for lack of industry, or of Scottish friends, or of a good mother. The biography of one of them would be unique.

CHAPTER TWO

Struggle and Independence

Invasion of London, 1833—Seeking Employment—Early Days in Cambridge—Two Clerks at Seeley's—Their own Bookshop

ON his way to London, Daniel stayed in Edinburgh with the Wilsons. Mr. Wilson was a wine merchant there who, with his wife, befriended the young Macmillans continually, from the year, about 1830, of their first acquaintance, which may have sprung from an introduction by Mr. Maxwell Dick. Daniel admired Mrs. Wilson next to his own mother. One of her sons, Daniel, afterwards Sir Daniel Wilson and President of Toronto University, was to be spoken of by Alexander as his oldest friend ; but a younger son, George, who was Alexander's age and was to end a life of sickness as Professor of Technology at Edinburgh, had an even more intimate part in the affection of the two brothers. He occurs repeatedly in their letters and in such a way as shows that he was even more often in their thoughts. C. L. Graves, Alexander's biographer, describes him as having been crippled by the amputation of a foot, racked with rheumatism and enfeebled by repeated haemorrhages, and yet as having preserved " an unconquerable gaiety of heart." It was he who saw the traveller off at Leith, when, after his stay with the Wilsons, Daniel embarked on a sixty-three hours' voyage to London. There he arrived on Tuesday September 7th, 1833.

The " little English ladies " who kept MacLehose's lodging in what was evidently, for Daniel, a deeply foreign land seemed to eye him with suspicion. They had not been warned of his coming and, unversed in Scottish hospitality, were reasonably astonished by his claim to a half of Mac-Lehose's bed. Moreover, though he appears not to have guessed it, they understood him at first little better than he had understood his father's Gaelic prayers, and sent for MacLehose's fellow-lodger, presumably a Scots interpreter, for, says Daniel, " he put them quite at ease."

When he had washed and been given tea, Daniel set out for Fleet-street. Another man — almost any one of us — after such a voyage as he had made might have been content to await his friend's coming home from the office, but Daniel was revived by strong tea, walked abroad at once, and found MacLehose in Seeley's. It was seven o'clock. They went out into the Row — the Paternoster Row which was then the actual, and always the traditional, home of the book trade, until the Germans wiped it out. Daniel was in the Promised Land. He wanted " to see all the Houses," whose names were already familiar to him, and called at Longmans' to see " a young Glasgow man, named Murray, brother to Murray of Glasgow." A little to his surprise, for it cannot yet have been much past eight, Murray was gone. " He was not in. He had gone home." So Daniel and MacLehose went home too. " I spent a very pleasant night with him."

The following days, while Daniel fired off his letters of introduction, were filled with hope deferred and the kicking of heels and much sickness of heart. Mr. Dyer, for example, gave him " a little religious advice " and the way he gave it dangerously roused the Macmillan blood. " There is a great deal of humbug about religious people. I wish they would . . . give up using slang phrases. These disgust me." William, Daniel's next brother after Malcolm, had — seemingly in earnest praise — spoken of Mr. Dyer as " the prince of the Baptists," but Daniel was unpersuaded. " He treated me as if he really were ' the prince of Baptists,' the King of the Cannibal Islands, or something equally grand."

He passed his visitor on to Mr. Wightman who knew of no situation in town but thought that, if Daniel called again next day, there might be news of something in Cambridge. Murray, the " brother to Murray of Glasgow," was good-natured, but firm in his belief that there was no vacancy at Longmans'. Daniel was as firmly resolved to present his letters, and, after a tour of the trade (for Murray was that very humble employee, a collector), he found Mr Green available at one o'clock. " All I can say to you, Mr. M., is that you may leave me your address and a specimen of your penmanship, and if we should require anyone I will send for you, but at present I see small chance." Young Mr. Longman, to whom Daniel carried a most flattering letter, would not be at home until Friday.

Daniel went out into the streets and prayed and wept, but his prayers were not at once answered. Orr and Smith were not in, nor was Mr. Macrone, of Cochrane and Macrone, though Daniel had toiled as far as Waterloo Place in hope of him. Back he went to Simpkin and Marshall in the Row, but they were too busy. Half an hour later, he tried them again and was told to call next morning. Tegg was not at home, but away to the west Mr. Macrone was at last run to earth — a pleasant man, who said that if Longman and Simpkin yielded nothing he would write to all his friends in the book trade. We may be a little suspicious of Mr. Macrone, but Daniel was not. It was now seven o'clock. After returning to the Row and taking tea with Murray, he called it, as indeed it was, a day.

The next was worse. Mr. Marshall, of Simpkin and Marshall, with an alacrity that must have seemed ominous, offered him £60 a year, living in, on condition that he would engage for a year. " They were very much troubled with young men coming for a month or two and then leaving." Thus warned, Daniel resolved to find out what the conditions were before engaging, and set to work then and there, making out invoices. He did not like what he saw. In an interval for tea, he visited Mr. Wightman again, hoping for news of Cambridge, but was too late ; Mr. Johnson of Cambridge had come and gone, but would come again next morning. Daniel returned to Simpkin's and liked it even less than he had. They worked that night until ten. On Friday they would be four or five hours later ; from Saturday, they would work through until six on Sunday morning. Daniel went out at ten, understanding why Mr. Marshall's young men left him, but with no other work in prospect. " The idea of living in Simpkin's was intolerable. It almost crushed me through the earth. . . . All the way from Stationers' Court to Goswell Road was sprinkled with tears." (This account was written on the following afternoon.) ". . . At that hour the passers-by could not notice me. I certainly did not notice them, except when I was stopped and spoken to by the poor and unfortunate. These I could have taken and pressed to my heart." Dickens was within a few months of Daniel's own age. Hood's *Song of the Shirt* was to appear a decade later, in the year when Daniel became his own master.

In the morning, Mr. Johnson of Cambridge offered him a half of the Simpkin salary and board with the family. Daniel did not return to Simpkin's, not daring to as it was already eleven o'clock, but consulted MacLehose, who was strong for Cambridge ; but the petitioner himself was a romantic, the great name of Longmans' dazzled him, he could not bear to leave London with this glorious prospect unexplored, and to Longmans' he repaired. Young Mr. Longman received him and read Atkinson's glowing letter. He believed they had no openings, no vacancies. But this was Magazine time ; he was busy and had not leisure to be sure. Mr. Macmillan might call again on Monday.

Mr. Macmillan wandered through the streets. Old sins kept stalking before him and he was miserable. If only he could postpone the Cambridge decision — supposing always that Mr. Johnson himself should decide in his favour, for even this offer had not been firm ! If only he could gain enough time to give Longmans' their chance ! At last he reached his lodging, wrote part of a serial letter home, and was in bed before MacLehose came in. MacLehose wakened him to read a letter in which Mr. Johnson said yes. Daniel was to call on Mr. Wightman for further particulars, and on Saturday Mr. Wightman gave him until Monday to decide. Still, it might be Longmans' ! While waiting for the fateful hour on Monday morning, Daniel kept his nerve steady by continuing his letter home. Then broke off : " However, I must not talk about these things now. I must go to Longmans'. I hope God will lead me in the way that is right. Lead me to seek the kingdom of Heaven ; whatever be my troubles, whatever painful things I may have to endure. I must just put down my pen and think of this for a few minutes before I go out."

When Longmans' had disappointed him, he was, and did his utmost to feel, submissive to the will of God. " I ought to feel quite submissive, quite pleased, deeply grateful . . ." but it was hard ; he was far from home and Longmans' would have been a compensating glory. He made the best of it, resolved clearly for Cambridge, and, it being but half-past eleven in the morning, went out with a friend of MacLehose's " to see all the lions of London." He went to the Coliseum, to the Zoological Gardens and into the dome of St. Paul's. " I like this London." But he was homesick and still very young. When he sat down to write an end and, it seems, a new beginning to the letter finally dated " September 13, 1833," he remembered that this was his birthday. " I have just been saying to myself, ' What a pity it is that we must separate thus ; that I am to

17

have so few of the pleasures of home. I am not twenty yet
(yes, just twenty — I shall be twenty by the time I have
finished this letter), and now I have been sent adrift again.
I have bid home farewell.' "

The three years spent at Cambridge were an interlude,
but an important one, seen in the light of after events, for
he became known there. Learned men came to Mr.
Johnson's shop, a little to Mr. Johnson's chagrin, because
the wise young Scot was good — and perhaps amusing —
company when they were in quest of books, and the reputation he won then stood him in good stead when he set up
for himself in Cambridge ten years later. He was happy
in the Johnsons' house, for they were " nice folk, so pleasant,
so kind, so pious, so everything I could wish," but once
again, as in Stirling, the place was too small, the boy too
big, the dream of Longmans' stayed with him, his work from
7.30 A.M. to 7 P.M., though long enough, was not charged
to the tension of his ambitious mind, and he hankered
after the Row. Nor would he have been of his period if
he had not been of a troubled conscience, the trouble
taking a secular as well as a religious form. Hitherto an
admirer of Byron, he now cast him away " with indignant
contempt . . ." for he had read Moore's *Life*, and saw
him as the writer of letters in which " the never-ceasing
witticisms, the everlasting tittering and smirking, is most
loathesome. . . . What sympathy," he wondered, " could
Shelley's sincere and holy nature have with Byron ? " Not
that Shelley himself had " solved the dreadful enigmas of
life," but he had at least believed that Right would at last
prevail, and this Daniel wished to believe. But he hesitated
to join a church ; " the very fact of there being sects " con-
fused him, until, after three or four months of domesticity
with the Johnsons, he joined their Baptist community. This
gave him a niche and cleared away what he called his Calvin-

istic cobwebs, but did not make a partisan of him or prevent his devouring Jeremy Taylor, Landor, Gibbon and Voltaire. Challenged on politics, he was equally forbearing. He was, he supposed, a Conservative — " Conservatism and Toryism being entirely distinct," but, in truth, to write to him of politics was a waste of time, for " I can't comprehend them," and, though England was still in the rough waters of Reform, he " scarcely ever read a newspaper."

At the end of his first year, he tried to get back to London but could find no vacancy there and stayed at Cambridge. At the end of his second, during which his mother died (August 1835), he signed on again at a salary increased from thirty to thirty-five pounds, but at the end of 1836 broke free. He went back to Scotland as he had come, by ship plying between London and Leith. Exposure on the voyage made him invalid for three months and Mrs. Wilson nursed him as if he had been " her own and only son." Perhaps his ambition was reduced by sickness ; certainly he was lonely and wished to be near the Wilsons, whose home gave him ground under his feet ; in any case, he came near, at that time, to settling in Leith as shopman to a stationer. From this he was rescued by an offer, through MacLehose, of work at Seeley's in Fleet-street at £60 a year.

Settled at last and with fair prospects, he took upon himself at once an increased share in the maintenance of his own people. Falling sick in 1839, he went to Scotland to recover his health, and, when he returned, meditated upon his duties. He was, in effect, head of the family, for William had died in the previous year and Malcolm was failing. Alexander was in his twenty-first year and had not prospered. There had been work enough, but little reward. He had been an usher in small schools, had kept shop for a chemist in Glasgow, and in September 1836, driven by some impulse of adventure or despair, had, in accordance with the Macmillan habit at a crisis, taken to the water. His voyage was longer than Daniel's to Arran but he had returned, like Daniel, in calmer mood. One journey to America before the mast — described by him afterwards as " a somewhat foolish attempt at being a sailor " — had cured him of sea-faring and landed him penniless in Glasgow — poorer than even his brother had ever been. " If I had been offered a good porter's place at 6s. a week I would have taken it." Instead he had become an usher again and had lived for nine months on 5s. a week until he moved to what seems to have been a scarcely more prosperous place at Nitshill, near Paisley. His sister, Janet, kept house for him, contributing a little from a sewing-school of her own, but they were very poor, and Daniel rescued them.

The Seeleys were persuaded to give Alexander a start at £60 a year. It is completely irrelevant, and yet of a kind of superstitious interest to lovers of coincidences and anniversaries, that, whereas Daniel went to that famous interview with young Mr. Longman on his twentieth birthday, the thirteenth of September 1833, Alexander arrived in London on his twenty-first — the third of October 1839. He lodged with Daniel at the boarding-house of the Misses Nutter in Hoxton. He was happy, promised well in his employment, and it might have been supposed that the two brothers would, for a little while, have rested content. But there was something in Daniel's conscience that was for ever bowing his shoulders to the burdens of the world, and it came into his mind that he ought to bring Janet and a niece from Scotland. For once the Scottish passion for education led him astray. Poor Janet's " education was very deficient " and her ingenuous brother, diving perilously into the feminine temperament, " fancied that she might improve it if she put herself under the care of the Misses Nutter." She came on November 2nd, and evidently did not like being improved by the Misses Nutter. Daniel's fraternal duty lay heavy upon him. " It is scarcely time for me to be an old man yet," he had written in October at the prospect of his sister's and his niece's coming, " but few fathers feel so serious. Were I to die or lose my health, or be thrown out of my situation, why we should all be reduced to beggary in a very short time." And now that Janet was come, they must all be uprooted. The boarding-house could not hold them, furnished lodgings were too expensive; even unfurnished lodgings for them all would cost £30 a year. They had no furniture and Daniel possessed but £10 in the world. Nevertheless the prospect of having a home warmed his heart. He borrowed £60 and, with the help of " an earnest socialist, a most disinterested man," bought the furniture. When all was settled in March, the rooms, at 26 Bartlett's Buildings, " looked very pleasant." The pleasantness did not last. Janet was not strong ; she proved uneconomical and " rather awkward in her management " ; they were not living within their means, and must make haste, as honest men, to cut their losses. Janet was sent back to Scotland. The furniture and Daniel's beloved accumulation of books were sold to pay off debt, and the brothers went into another boarding-house at 8 Charter-house-square.

Alexander, though he had had a smattering of Latin, was less well-read than his brother and now set out to remedy that defect. Daniel helped, introducing him to the works and the lectures of Carlyle. Alexander's duties required him to rise at six. While he breakfasted and even while he dressed, Daniel read to him, and what he read — or one of the books he read — was *Sartor Resartus*. Alexander, independently, devoted himself to Shelley, and made a selection from his work of such poems or passages from poems as pleased him and could, at the same time, be " safely recommended " to the young. He added a biographical sketch, published the little volume anonymously with George Bell, and kept his secret.

During the autumn an event occurred which may be thought of as the Macmillans' first emergence from the sedate life of bookselling into the jungle of authorship. London Fields lay open, and one summer's day, while the brothers walked there together, they fell into discussion of a book Daniel had been reading : *Guesses at Truth by Two Brothers*. He admired its style. Every sentence appeared to him to have an " exquisite finish and clearness," but what held him was the healthiness of the writers' mind, his sense that the guesses they made on religious subjects would be of peculiar value to young men of his condition, if only the Two Brothers' writings could be made accessible to them. He recommended the book to his friends, watched its effect upon them, longed to seek out the authors and tell them what was on his mind. But there was a tradition of privacy in those days ; a reader did not write lightly or without good cause to an author, least of all to an anonymous author, whom he had met only between the covers of a book ; and Daniel hesitated. At last, feeling that the authors might be almost unaware of the existence of the young men whose need of guidance was reflected in his own, he wrote. Archdeacon Hare courteously replied and for nearly two years there was no more correspondence between them, but it arose again when Daniel sent to the Archdeacon two pamphlets by Alexander Scott which, he thought, might interest him. Hare was enthusiastic. His friend, F. D. Maurice, the author of *The Kingdom of Christ*, had praised Scott, and the Archdeacon himself confessed that " hardly anything he had read since Coleridge had taught and strengthened and delighted him so much as these lectures." They were, " indeed, a consolation under the grief for the loss of my noble-hearted friend Arnold." Men had not lost the habit

of letter-writing ; archdeacons and booksellers' assistants
who rose at six in the morning and worked until late at
night were still able to compose long, thoughtful letters
with what seems to have been an unhurried pen. It was a
habit that neither Daniel nor Alexander ever lost, and, on
this occasion, it led to a productive friendship — to multi-
plying friendships. Daniel was invited to Hurstmonceaux.
" It may be as well to let you know," he wrote with his own
special dignity, " that I am only one of the clerkly species,
whose singular and unfortunate position with regard to
spiritual culture was the cause of my first writing to you.
I have no learning, can read no language except English,
speak none except a partly intelligible Scotch-English
dialect. I mention this so that you may know that I don't
belong to any of the learned professions." Nevertheless, to
Hurstmonceaux he went by train and coach in September.
The large, comfortable Rectory, every wall of which was
lined with books —and books, too, as he observed in their
markings, which had all been read ; the Archdeacon himself, " not at all stout " with an eye " large, soft, swimming ";
the fact that Landor himself had been there a week earlier
and Arnold not long before his death — all these things,
together with the freedom and ease of the conversation,
delighted Daniel. He stayed three days, and afterwards in
London developed his friendship with Maurice and went
to his house. Maurice had written for the *Encyclopaedia
Metropolitana* a " History of Moral and Metaphysical Philosophy " which Daniel thought should be published separ-
ately. He called on the proprietors and said so, but they
shook their heads ; it would injure the sale of their *Encyclopaedia*. Daniel knew it would do nothing of the kind.
His publisher's genius was denied and he indignant. " These
wretched men — these publishers ! What fools they are ! "

Maurice was to become one of the Macmillans' closest
friends and their most prolific authors. For them he was a

" Prophet," and, when business prospered, they " did their best to realise some of their ideals " in publishing him. In after years, Alexander was to say that he was prouder of publishing Maurice than of his appointment to the University of Oxford, but was to say also : " had we had only such books as his we could not have lasted three years." The two sayings, taken together, give character to the firm's portrait, of which the preliminary forms had begun to appear in the two booksellers' assistants who, in that autumn and winter of 1842, were so near to their chance of independence.

They made their plan boldly and yet with care. By this time Alexander had £80 and Daniel £130 a year. It followed that, if they were to establish a shop of their own, the fall in their joint income would be less if the elder remained bound to Seeley's while the younger went free. This decided, they looked for premises. In the West End, there was nothing to be had for less than £150 a year and £200 for the " coming-in " or premium. A place in Aldersgate-street was less far beyond their reach : rent £45, fixtures £100. Mr. Burnside of Seeley's, the same whose earlier loan had been repaid by the sale of Daniel's library, offered to lend them what they needed. They did not call upon him, for the landlord knew Daniel and accepted his bills. " We thus commenced without capital. We were able with ease to pay this £100 as it became due."

This was in February 1843. The shop just paid its way and no more. The Archdeacon became a regular customer and sent his friends, but it was clear to Daniel that Aldersgate-street was too far from the book-buying public and that he must move when he could. Anxiety to sell books never prevented him from loving them and did not check a stream of literary correspondence of which a man of leisure, in the quiet of a private library, might have been proud. It was now that he discussed Mr. Newman's volume of University Sermons, and Carlyle's *Past and Present*, and Coleridge's

philosophy and " a strange man named Borrow, who has
written a book called *The Gypsies in Spain*, and *The Bible
in Spain.*" A new edition of Maurice's *Kingdom of Christ* is
found by him " a book that I could not live without. . . .
For calmness, for candour, for insight, I have never seen anything on the same subject to equal it." The range and the
warmth of Daniel Macmillan's reading is, in the circumstances of his life, an evidence of his quality. Meanwhile,
he was presumably in treaty with his own first authors,
Mr. William Haig Miller, about to ask his *Three Questions*,
and Mr. Craig who, in the Barford-street Institution at
Islington, was preparing his " strictures on the prevailing
mode of teaching languages."

In June, the Macmillans heard that there was an opportunity to acquire Mr. Newby's business at Cambridge and
informed the Archdeacon. What, the Archdeacon inquired
on August 22nd, was the chance of its being profitable ? He
and his brother might lend the necessary money. Daniel
answered at once and in detail. The prospects were good ;
his only security was a bond upon the stock ; he had been
examined with a stethoscope and believed that he might
live to be an old man. Hare accepted a bond for five hundred
pounds at four per cent interest, and Number Seventeen
Trinity-street, Cambridge, was bought at once. Daniel went
there to open the new business, Alexander held the fort in
London, and on the tenth of November the British Museum
acknowledged the receipt of their first publication. Cambridge was bitterly cold and Daniel worked single-handed.
Suddenly a violent haemorrhage stopped him. Alexander
travelled on the outside of a stage-coach to bring him aid,
and, on arrival, was himself so ill that he had no power to
give it. " I am ordered not to write," Daniel wrote to the
Archdeacon on February 27th, 1844, " but I cannot help
thanking you for your great kindness in writing to my brother
and myself. We have resolved to follow your kind suggestion.

As soon as my brother can leave me he will go to London to get rid of the shop."

Daniel Macmillan was thirty years old. He had worked in the book trade for twenty years and had thirteen to live. He would never have health again and was heavily in debt ; but he had published a book.

CHAPTER THREE

From Bookselling to Publishing

*A Basic Principle—Trinity-street, Cambridge—Friends and Anxieties
—The Maurice Controversy—Marriage—" The dangers of
prosperity "—Charles Kingsley and " Tom Brown "—Daniel's
Death*

To one who looks back, with a century's endowment of perspective, on the period in the firm's history which intervened between their going to Cambridge and their re-establishment in London, it is clear that they received their character then. So different were the conditions of that time from those we now live in that it might seem futile to attempt to draw any conclusions applicable to modern publishing from the days when works of theology commanded the widest of all markets and *Westward Ho !* was passionately provocative in three volumes at a guinea and a half. For that very reason such principles as do appear, appear in the stronger light. They may be left to emerge from the narrative itself, but one, which is perhaps a summary of them all, is worth remarking : that a publishing house is deeply and inescapably personal ; only the devotion and the individuality of its chiefs can make or preserve it ; there is a part of their task that cannot be delegated, and it is that part which gives the firm its life. It will be said that this is true of other businesses, but it is not true in the same sense, and a reason, among others, is that authors are children, some full of outward confidence, some easily cast down, but all, except those who are plain hacks, responsive to kindness, to the steadiness of a judgement they have learned to trust, above all to an imaginative care for their childish projects. One might have supposed that

Charles Kingsley of all men was able to look after himself, but he poured out his heart to his publishers about what he called his " Micawber's purgatory," he sent outlines of projected books for their comment, he invited Alexander to Eversley and sat up with him over " considerable pipes and beer " to discuss a novel he was planning, and there is a little note, dated " May 22, 1856," which may not mean much to other folk but, to the ear of a writer, has a note of feeling in it : " A thousand thanks for your obligingness. You certainly are a most pleasant person to deal with, and please God you will have no cause to regret it."

But the time for this was yet far off when the brothers took over Number Seventeen Trinity-street. Kingsley was a pupil of Maurice's and, though it may seem almost a slight on Alexander's memory to say so (for Alexander had no doubt of " The Prophet's " greatness), to a later generation of readers the Rev. F. D. Maurice himself will have to be a little explained.

In the early days at Number Seventeen, Daniel's mind was full of publishing schemes. He himself had no capital except the little he had borrowed and the Cambridge system of long-credit tried him hard, but, if he could as yet do little of himself, he might nevertheless act for others, and when the labour of cataloguing his stock was done and he was settled in his new premises, he wondered, in a letter to Archdeacon Hare, why Cambridge did not " republish the writings of the best of her sons " — Jeremy Taylor or Fuller or Barrow, perhaps. Donne, Henry More, John Smith, Cudworth, might follow. A good edition of Milton was wanted " and it might be so edited as to be for the good of the Church." And why not some good Cambridge tracts to lessen the mis-understanding between rich and poor ? If such a thing could be set a-going he would be glad to undertake the management of it. But this, for the moment, was dreaming, though he did publish, in the early autumn of 1844, with money not his own or, as publishers say, on commission, William Law's old answer to Mandeville's *Fable of the Bees*, the point of the reprint being that F. D. Maurice would write a preface to it. For himself, he dared risk nothing as yet. The first year's trading was good, but the brothers' capital was out, they had too many creditors, and were anxious.

Towards the end of the next year, a chance came to them which was disturbing but which, if they were to pursue their ambition, they could not refuse. A bookselling business, established in Cambridge in the middle of the eighteenth century, had been taken over by Thomas Stevenson in 1822 and was now offered to the Macmillans. The opportunity was too good to miss, though to seize it would cost £6000 and the money was not to be had without their taking a partner, a wholesale druggist of Farringdon-street who neither knew about books nor would leave them to those who did. There was an occasion, some years ahead, on which this gentleman, having obstructed Alexander's purpose to acquire the right to publish the translation of a foreign work, suggested, as an amiable compromise, that they should offer £10 for the right to publish if the author should become celebrated — an example of commercial intelligence which may excuse Daniel and Alexander for not having suffered the druggist gladly. But they were compensated for what they endured. The house at Number One Trinity-street, to which they moved, was the corner house in which the business of Messrs. Bowes has so long flourished ; it faced west towards the Senate House, and Daniel's bedroom looked south to St. Mary's ; it was, in every way, better than the house they had left, and here they were to live while they were bachelors and Ellen Stead, " kind, diligent and scoldy," looked after them. It was to be the scene of great occasions — none, perhaps, so great in their eyes as Wordsworth's visits to Number Seventeen when he told them that he had tried in *The Excursion* to bring out the spiritual life of Scotland, but it was at Number One that Kingsley showed them the manuscript of *Alton Locke* and Thackeray lunched with them in November 1851.

The great names have been thrown out as an indication of what was happening, but they do not in themselves represent the less dazzling but solider truth of it. Daniel had worked in Cambridge before and was already a little known there. Now, partly through Hare, partly through Maurice, but much more by the brothers' power to win always the respect and nearly always the affection of those they met, they were making friends, and because in friendship, as in all else, they were unswerving and untiring, they did not lose them. W. H. Thompson, Master of Trinity, dropped in from Olympus. W. G. Clark, who made their acquaintance then, was described by Alexander sixteen years later as being " genial and manly as ever " and as coming in " to have a pipe and a chat." Todhunter of the Calculus and Barnard Smith, Westcott, Lightfoot and Hort were of the booksellers' clients who became their guests, their friends and often their authors. But dons move slowly, under-graduates are a vanishing stream, and it appears that at Cambridge in those days the great and learned had often surprisingly little contact with their pupils except on duty — and at Number One Trinity-street, which, whether or not the great and learned happened to be present, became a little college in itself. The manner of it may be suggested by an instance. One of these undergraduates, Sebastian Evans, who afterwards wrote an account of Alexander quoted at length in Mr. Graves's biography, was loitering in the shop one day while a friend of his was trying to persuade Daniel to undertake a translation of Comte. He had come upon a copy of Berthelet's edition of Gower's *Confessio Amantis*, and was deep in the story of Rosiphele when he became conscious that someone beside him was leaning forward to look over the book : " ' Ye love the black letter ? ' he asked in the sweetest of Scots Doric." Evans replied that he did but that the story was worth telling in any letters. " We eyed each other tentatively," he says, " much as a Scots collie and a dachshund puppy might on a casual first meeting, both desirous of manifesting good will, but each a little uncertain how his advances might be received." Now why is it that men of learning and taste — for Dr. Sebastian Evans had both — who were undergraduates in '51 and who, at the beginning of the present century, could see with their mind's eye anything as good as that collie and dachshund, were yet " desirous of manifesting good will " and could not simply " wish to show it " ? The question is to the point, for soon Daniel came out from the back of the shop, and he and the Comtist and the collie and the dachshund were locked in conversation about Broad Church principles and " young regenerators of science and philosophy " and " the noblest workers of to-day," and one would give one's head to have at least Daniel and Alexander's share of the dialogue in the plain Scots Doric in which they spoke it. But no : we have to take the story as Dr. Evans tells it, and, except where six syllables are made to do the work of two, he tells it well. " So we talked, half in jest and all in earnest, till it was time for me to go back to hall. . . . Such was the beginning of a warm and intimate friendship " — the more remarkable when it is grasped that Dr. Evans believed in no dogmatic theology and that Alexander regarded his opinions " as virtually subversive of all morality as well as religious faith." But Alexander, stern though he was against what he considered to be error, never shut out men because he disagreed with their opinions. He had a " distinctive faculty of teaching or rather of advising," and though men like Evans, with Clough in distant support, felt that, in the long run, the Carlylean gospel of " work,"

the constant putting forward of " useful and helpful labour "
as in itself almost a spiritual end or at any rate a spiritual
appeasement, led only to the wilderness, even they came to
him with their problems, for they, like authors, found that,
though he might not give the counsel they hoped for, he had
an imaginative care for their childish projects, which enabled
them to counsel themselves. Not for nothing was Alexander
a reader of Plato and a student of the Socratic method.

The moral seems to be that to be a good publisher you
must take children and artists seriously, and that is a hard
moral, for how does it differ from saying that to be a good
publisher you must be a good man ? It helps no tradesman
at a stock-taking, unless it be the last.

Many of the allies thus earned among the senior and the
junior members of the University came to the Macmillans,
in the first instance, because they were booksellers. They
had assistants, but they themselves attended to the shop,
and, as Daniel wrote to an applicant for a job, made
their " assistants attend to most of the details." These
young men who, from 1846 onwards, included Robert
Bowes, a nephew of the partners, came to work punctually
at seven o'clock every morning. " From seven till nine we
expect you to put all things in nice order : to see that the
boys clean windows and so forth . . . and work separ-
ately, that is, if one is working down stairs let the other work
up stairs or in the back-shop or in a different part of the
front shop." In the intervals of keeping the boys apart,
the assistants kept the accounts together, sent out orders
and saw that the " posting " was done daily. There were
two day-books. Yesterday's day-book was posted up to-day,
and to-day's day-book would go into the counting-house
to-morrow. With this echo of the *Pervigilium Veneris* in
their minds, the assistants " pressed forward in the day "
so that when the shop shut at eight on a winter's evening
there might be, as their masters wished, little outstanding ;

but what was outstanding they stayed to do. In summer, the shop closed at seven, and for three months the assistants were allowed " to get away alternately at three o'clock, that is unless any pressing business should hinder." The Macmillans worked harder than their staff. Daniel's illness came upon him again and again ; for several months in several years he was drawn by it from Cambridge to Torquay, and Alexander carried the business on his shoulders. Even at that distance, nothing was done without discussion between the brothers, and long after other men's working hours, Alexander would sit up over a gigantic correspondence, written always not as we write but with the spacious courtesy and the moral heaviness of that age. The letters to Daniel were kept to the end that they might be mellowed by a leisurely pipe and never betray weariness or impatience. When Daniel advised his brother to take a wife, Alexander gently replied that he had no time to look for one. Very seldom is there even a hint of a frayed nerve in these wonderful letters. Daniel had a habit of embedding long, long messages, intended for others, in the text of his, and his brother had to dig them out, and copy or summarize them, and send them on. If only Daniel would write them on separate sheets ! And there was a bleak moment in the spring of '55 when Daniel, borne down by his ill health and the anxieties of the business, spoke of reducing his midday meal to a single chop and dragging himself back to his brother's rescue. " Now take two chops to-morrow or I shall think you a goose," Alexander replied. " I really am doing as well as I know how in every matter. . . . Don't worry yourself and don't be too hard on me."

When Daniel's health made it possible for him to be in the shop, they worked together in perfect balance, full of knowledge of their trade and of the love of books. The old principle of unity between bookselling and publishing had one of its last great exemplars in them, and the men who came into the shop to buy books stayed in the publishing house to write them. Thus they drew on the whole resources of the University and an upper room in Number One became a common-room where young men and old men assembled to discuss books or God or social reform — but chiefly, it would appear, God — before going into four o'clock hall. They drew on Cambridge, which was one world, and they drew on the world of F. D. Maurice, which, though the circles intersected and pretty fiercely on occasion, was another.

The controversies of Maurice are more remote from us than those of Laud with the Puritans, but they are knit with the history of the Macmillan firm and cannot be passed over. It is best to call in the witness of Sebastian Evans, who stood outside the battle. He says that when Daniel and Alexander began to be known in Cambridge, " the decadence of the Oxford Movement had already advanced by leaps and bounds, while the earlier Evangelical movement . . . had become in the hands of Carus little more than a travesty of former enthusiasm. An intellectual renaissance of some sort in the Church was imperative if it was to retain its hold upon the people. An extensive and influential, if partial, renaissance came in the form of what a little later was known as the Broad Church movement, of which a vigorous offshoot was both applauded and reviled as ' muscular Christianity.' Of this movement F. D. Maurice was the best known and perhaps most popular leader, and of F. D. Maurice, Alec Macmillan was the most enthusiastic admirer and exponent. He always spoke of Maurice as ' The Prophet ' " — and here Dr. Evans's tone gives a full echo of the period — " and regarded him as entrusted with a mission to expound Carlyle's profoundly nebulous religiosities to an unbelieving generation in a more systematic and intelligible form." When the great Victorians begin to

34

joke together we are further from them than when they are directly in earnest, but Dr. Evans's tale of the giants is worth repeating : " ' Matt,' stammered Charles Kingsley to Matthew Arnold at one of the Thursday evening gatherings in Bedford-street, ' Alec strongly suspects Tommy Carlyle of being a deeper humourist than Dante.' Arnold snorted, and smiled grimly, but said nothing. The quip was true. Alec looked upon what he called Carlyle's ' message to mankind ' as a revelation of permanent interest, which it would be the task of seers in after ages to interpret and act upon as the needs of their own times might demand."

However that may be, and whatever opinion Dr. Evans may have held of Carlyle, it is certain, and it is just to add, that Maurice was deeply conscious of serving a master other than the Scottish sage. It is no less certain that the Macmillans considered him a greater man than he was. They threw themselves into his Christian Socialist movement ; they became a focal point for the intellectual activity of his Broad Church circle ; and Alexander took upon himself the chief burden of the Working Men's College in Cambridge. When, in 1853, the Low Church lay members of the Council of King's College, London, were struggling to eject Maurice from his Professor's Chair because his views on eternal punishment differed from their own, Alexander, like a good publisher, fought to save his books. On September 17th, at night, he called on the Rev. Charles Clayton, Fellow and Tutor of Gonville and Caius College, " to ask if his interdict [presumably against the use of Maurice's books by students] applied to all Maurice's books." It was a searching question, for the lecturers had recommended his *Moral Philosophy* for the Moral Science Tripos. Clayton " seemed at a loss " and tried to ride away upon the hope that his theology would not be put into such a book. Alexander replied with reason that Maurice could scarcely write the moral history of man without referring to God.

35

Clayton then thought it " would be safer to comprehend all his books " and Alexander said his say : " I told him," he wrote to Daniel next day, " I had read the book through when it was passing through the press and since very carefully, and had felt thankful to God for having raised up a man in our time who seemed so able to stem the tide of infidelity that I felt coming on us, and was utterly staggered to find men who I had every reason to believe had the cause of Christianity at heart denouncing a man who was so nobly vindicating the simple Gospel of Christ's redemption against all gainsayers." And, as a parting shot, this : " I told him I wished him to know that we, in publishing the book and in continuing to help its circulation, were acting conscientiously and, as we believed, helping to vindicate the simplicity of the Gospel from the unhallowed speculations of men of all kinds." It must have sounded even better in the Doric.

Whatever may have happened since to Maurice's fame, it cannot have been a little man who thus moved the tongue of the Covenanters to defend the freedom of the press. But there is a melancholy in the event. The Macmillans believed passionately in him — and published and published him, knowing well that he wrote too much for their advantage. At one time his works — *Prophets and Kings*, *Ecclesiastical History*, *Doctrine of Sacrifice* and how many more — occupied a page and a half in their catalogue, " but could I have guided Maurice's pen I would have published about three books for him instead of thirty. . . . Prophets belong, I fear, to the desert, where one has to subsist." And yet, when the Low Church laymen had their quarry down and Maurice had been dismissed from King's College, Daniel wrote : " He is a grand man ! and must endure like other prophets. The good people of the next age will build his tomb." But they have not built it on the scale that Daniel evidently imagined.

Nevertheless the Macmillans had their reward even upon earth. Through Maurice came Kingsley, but it must not be supposed that even Kingsley, though he gave them their first spectacular success, was the foundation of their fortunes. From Maurice's circle came many others who had something solider than fiction to offer and who, together with the great and learned found elsewhere and the demand of an educated public, enabled a quietly profitable list to be built. A few names will show what the firm was and whither it was going : Trench's *Hulsean Lectures* ; H. B. Drake's edition of Demosthenes *On the Crown* ; J. E. B. Mayor's *Juvenal* ; Edward Thring's books on grammar ; Westcott's *Elements of the Gospel Harmony* ; Todhunter's treatises on the Calculus and on Statics ; Barnard Smith's Arithmetic and Algebra ; J. A. Frere's *On the Incarnation* ; Francis Procter's *History of the Book of Common Prayer*, of which a revised edition is still in the list ; Westcott's *History of the Canon of the New Testament* ; essays by David Masson ; a volume of *City Poems* by Alexander Smith whom Alexander fervently admired and to whom Mr. Clifford Bax lately recalled attention ; George Wilson's *Five Gateways of Knowledge*, the success of which was particularly welcome for friendship's sake ; books by Farrar, Selwyn, C. J. Vaughan, and always books by Maurice. Because Alexander particularly cared for it, the translation of Plato's *Republic* by John Llewelyn Davies and David James Vaughan may claim a special place in the firm's history. The authors fortunately lived long, and their book, published in 1852, was still copyright ninety-one years later.

" No really satisfactory idea," wrote Tom Hughes with his unsurpassed genius for detecting self-evident truth, " no really satisfactory idea can be formed of a man without some glimpse into the sacred recesses of his home life." Even in writing a sketch of a firm of publishers — a task less sacred than the writing of a biography — it is necessary to say that the partners were married — Daniel to Miss Frances Orridge, daughter of a chemist and magistrate of Cambridge, on September 4th, 1850, and Alexander, in August of the next year, to Miss Caroline, eldest sister of his friend George Brimley, librarian of Trinity College.

Hughes makes so great a pother about Daniel's marriage as to suggest some mystery in it. With a coyness of which only the manlier and more vivacious of early-Victorians were capable, he spends a page in asking himself " how far the veil can be drawn back so as to let the man be seen in those relations which most shrewdly test his manhood," and reasonably concludes that much depends " upon what is behind the veil." As, in this case, there is nothing " but what is pure and of good report," he will let the light in freely.

All this because what he has to say, with initials and asterisks, is that Daniel had been previously betrothed, that the girl or her family or both had broken the engagement because he was so sick a man, that he told Miss Orridge that this was so, and that they married nevertheless. They were to have four children. Frederick Orridge, afterwards Sir Frederick and head of the firm, was born on October 5th, 1851 ; Maurice Crawford, father of the present Chairman and of Harold Macmillan, on April 19th, 1853 ; Katherine on April 5th, 1855 ; and Arthur, who was not to live beyond twenty, on May 13th, 1857, in the month before his father's death.

Daniel was so well pleased by marriage that he at once urged Alexander to follow his example, and did not hesitate to suggest whom it would be wise to choose. " I have the completest sympathy," the younger brother answered, " in the high estimate you give of C. B.'s character — but I confess I have not the same confidence in my own power of

answering to its excellencies. My habits and in some degree
my natural constitution . . . so totally vary from all that is
required in married life that I never think of myself as a
married man without something like trembling and fear,"
but by mid-August in the following year he was writing
from Ambleside to say that married life had his heartiest
approval. Of this marriage five children were born:
Malcolm Kingsley (1852) who was lost on Mount Olympus
in 1889; George Augustin (1855); William Alexander
(1864) who died in his third year; Margaret, the eldest,
afterwards Mrs. Louis Dyer; and Olive, who married
Norman, the third son of James MacLehose. These children
were to have a half-sister, Mary, who married James
MacLehose the younger, later head of the Glasgow firm, and
a half-brother, John Victor (1877).

Soon after his marriage, it became clear to Daniel that
the hope he had once had of being cured of his illness must
be put away. " I have only been kept alive by issues,
blisters, setons, till my whole chest is a series of scars. My
life . . . is ' copiously illustrated with cuts.' " As soon as
he began to work in Cambridge, illness would drive him
back to the sea, and the correspondence with Alexander
was added to a vast exchange of letters with the rest of the
world. The year 1852 was a promising one. *Prophets and
Kings* was sold so rapidly at the outset that Daniel believed
for a little while that even Maurice might be popular;
Kingsley's *Phaethon* appeared and Todhunter's *Differential
Calculus* was evidently a solid investment. The retail
business was holding its own, but Daniel had come to
think of it as being chiefly valuable for its bringing about
him young men who would grow into authors, and he told
MacLehose that his great hopes were now in publishing.
What, he saw, was wanted was a London house where men
might " call and consult after leaving Cambridge." This

he wrote in July. Before Christmas he found that the retail profits were being very greatly reduced by the adjustments in booksellers' terms recently made, but felt still that things were moving " very smoothly on the whole," smoothly enough at any rate to require him to be on his guard against the dangers of prosperity : " I hope that whatever we do, whatever our success may be, we shall never get into expensive and extravagant ways of living, but strive to live simply, and without luxury of any kind."

The next year, too, began well. Daniel took up to London with him and put into Maurice's hand a hundred pounds for the first edition of his *Theological Essays*. Thring, a friend made at Cambridge, became Headmaster of Uppingham, and his *Child's Grammar*, " the only book in existence on the subject which is at once the result of profound knowledge, and yet a most clear and simple statement of the laws of speech," filled the Macmillans with so much confidence that they stereotyped it. But now they ran into rough weather. The July stocktaking was bad ; the moneyed partners began to complain and economy was in the air. If he and Alexander had been independent of other men's finance, they could have done well enough. Reverses they could have borne, knowing within them that the business was sound at root, and they would have waited contentedly, for the rewards, when they came, would have been theirs. But it was one of the terms of the partnership into which their need of capital had driven them that, if any partner should die, his share was to fall in to those who remained, and Daniel at Torquay in October knew that he was dying. " If I am to die in this year, or the next," he wrote to Alexander, " all my exertions will be for others, and really I feel no call to such work. I am sure you don't wish me to work myself to death for your sake. As for my wife and boys, their interest in the business terminates with my death. . . ." This is so unexpected in Daniel as to mark a deep despondency. And it was in the same month that Maurice was thrown out of his professorship.

The depression long continued for it was some eighteen months later that he threatened, in the interests of economy, to reduce even his food. Meanwhile, perhaps his chief encouragement was his receiving from Kingsley an outline of a novel. It came to Daniel at Cromer in June 1854, and he was quick to see the possibilities of it. "We are greatly taken," he wrote, "with all you tell us about the plan and characters of your novel. Of course you will not adopt that pseudo-antique manner in which *Esmond*, *Mary Powell*, etc. etc., are written. That style is now getting a bore. The free march of your own style will be much more Elizabethan in manner and tone than any you can assume . . ." — a piece of advice to the prospective author of *Westward Ho !* which is interesting in any case but which does not yield all its savour unless it be understood that the Macmillans were always a little suspicious of Thackeray, though they recognized his genius. What troubled them in him is hard to define — a feeling, perhaps, that he was too much a man of the world. Alexander could not put down *Pendennis* as it came to him now from the press, but in later years (August 10th, 1868) he wrote to Hardy a comment on Thackeray which makes criticism envious by its ease and point. He was giving Hardy an object lesson, because Hardy, in writing of drawing-rooms, was, he thought, guilty of a too "wholesale blackening of a class." Not that Alexander liked the class, but he wanted to show in what way Thackeray was the more adroit in his treatment of it. Thackeray's approach, he said, was, roughly, this : "' Dukes and duchesses and all the kit are humbugs, society is based on humbug, but it's rather pleasant and amusing, when you can get pleasant dinners and nice wines. . . .' That was his tone. . . . I don't think Thackeray's satire did

41

much good ; indeed, I fear it did harm. He was in many respects a really good man, but he wrote in a mocking tone that has culminated in the *Saturday Review* tone, paralysing noble effort and generous emotion. . . ." In other words, Thackeray took no social risks ; like our own politer dramatists, he was careful to criticize society in such a way as to encourage its invitations ; and the Macmillans were always made uncomfortable by the complacency of his satire. Why Daniel should have disliked the historical style of *Esmond* it is less easy to say ; but he did dislike it and said so ; he preferred Kingsley, which — however odd it may seem to us — was consistent with his character. And he succeeded because, being loyal to his own taste and conscience, he made himself publisher to those who, in the widest meaning of the phrase, " preferred Kingsley." There must have been a score of publishers now forgotten who, because they had no fresher judgement or more original taste, were wringing their hands because they had not Thackeray and were scouring London for imitators of him. The Macmillans deserved *Westward Ho !* if ever publishers deserved a stroke of good fortune.

By December, though still incomplete in manuscript, it was being set, and on March 2nd, 1855, Daniel was encouraging the author with news that Mudie had ordered three hundred and fifty copies and that booksellers in Exeter, Torquay and Plymouth might be expected to do their duty. Hort and Martineau had read the book in proof and Hort said it had " more of the vigour and enjoyment of life that the *Iliad* shows " than any book he ever read. Alexander's judgement, formed much earlier when the manuscript was still full of gaps, had been to the point : " It is the right article and no mistake."

The reviews were slow and often hostile, but the sales were steady. Kingsley received in March £300 for a first edition, in three volumes at a guinea and a half, of 1250

copies ; in May, £250 for a second edition of 750 copies ;
in 1857, £300 for a third edition, in one volume, of 6000
copies. By these stages there was built up a total of £1750
in payments to the author by the time a new arrangement
for a ten per cent royalty was made in 1873. Kingsley did
not live to hear of the great sales of the sixpenny edition
from 1889 onwards, though his family benefited from them.

Although *Westward Ho !* must have given him re-
assurance from the outset, its immediate yield was not
great and he laboured to earn more. He had been at work
on *Glaucus* in the early months of the same year, and the
first instalment of *The Heroes* was in the Macmillans' hands
by September. In the first days of October there came
from the indefatigable man an outline of the novel which
was afterwards to be called *Two Years Ago*, to say nothing —
because it came to nothing — of another novel, elaborately
planned, on the Vaudois Massacre. Daniel, too, had had
ideas for this industrious author. He had written to Alexander
that it would be " a capital plan for Kingsley in his next
modern novel to take up Mrs. Grundy, and make the
leading characters very clever, and think and speak in the
spirit of the day . . . one-sided and sensible goosey, but
just what goes down for the height of wisdom and sagacity."
It would be looked on at first as a recantation of Kingsley's
errors ; then suddenly Kingsley was to turn the tables, the
truth was to emerge and wisdom follow. But Alexander
checked Daniel's enthusiasm ; he saw, as Daniel surprisingly
did not, that if this was a book at all it required a delicacy
of touch and a satirical detachment that were by no means
Kingsley's, and the author was allowed to go his own way.

Daniel was fighting for life, but his interest in his work
never flagged. The firm took over all the early work of
F. D. Maurice, and did so for love of the man and with their
eyes open. For example : Alexander having suggested a
cheap edition of Maurice's *Learning and Working*, Daniel

replied : " To make *Learning and Working* answer at 2s., you must have a sale of 8000, and Maurice hasn't such an audience. Besides that, we don't mean to publish ugly books. I would strongly advise Maurice not to publish any more books than those already projected. I know from something he said that he would like to say something about the war, but I took no notice of it. He has quite enough on his hands already. When he is writing on the Apocalypse, he can come out about the war. . . ." But it needed only an attack on Maurice to bring Daniel fiercely to his defence. *Blackwood* offended, bringing against Maurice a series of charges of which Daniel tabulates a dozen. They accused him for instance — and it fairly summarizes contemporary criticism of Maurice by the stiffer theologians of the time — of setting forth " an elegant theology — so different from the Bible — so mild and philanthrophic [*sic*]." Maurice, Daniel thought, might well reply, appealing to the evidence of his own sermons and " bringing out distinctly his faith and teaching," for *Blackwood* and all it represented, those whom Daniel calls, with contemptuous irony, " the religious and respectable people of their day," were in his view the spiritual inheritors of those who had misinterpreted and crucified Jesus. Maurice was battling against the same stiffness of neck, the same hardness of heart. " May we be enabled to help in that good work ! " For Daniel had the spirit of a reformer. Neither in theology nor in anything else was he ever a conscript to the big battalions, and when, during the siege of Sebastopol, the solid journals were hot against *Maud*, he was as hot in the poem's defence. " I have just had a third reading of *Maud*, and really I think all the criticisms I have seen more absurd than ever. . . . I don't wonder at their being angry with him for choosing such a subject, or for the way he lays bare the evils of society . . . but I do marvel at their pretending that the execution is inferior to anything he has ever done. It seems to me if possible more perfect. The way in which the rhythm alters to suit the tone of thought . . ." was for Daniel the marvel of the poem, and it is worth while to remark the balance of mind which could, at the same time, praise Tennyson for his aestheticism and Maurice for his missionary zeal. The comment of Daniel's biographer on the Tennysonian passages in the correspondence is itself revealing. " It will amuse young readers," said Tom Hughes in 1882, " to see how the poet laureate, whose every word is now treasured by the whole reading public, and quarrelled for by competing publishers, was regarded in those days."

It was in those days also that Tom Hughes was preparing his own immortality. In the autumn of 1856, he informed Alexander of the outcome :

10 PROSPECT PLACE, DEAL, *Sept*. 25, 1856

DEAR MAC.

How's yourself, and where's yourself ? My chief reason for writing is, that, as I always told you, I'm going to make your fortune, and you'll be happy to hear that the feat is almost or at least more than half done. I've been and gone and written or got in my head a one vol. novel, a novel for boys, to wit Rugby in Arnold's time. Ludlow is the only cove besides my wife who has seen a word of it, (and mind if you take it or don't I can't afford to have it known) and he thought it would particular do, and urged me to go on with it which I have this vacation and only want the kick on the breech that some cove's saying he would publish would give me to finish it. Shall I send you 3 or 4 chapters as specimens or will you meet me in town next Wednesday, Thursday, Friday or Saturday ? Do come up and we'll have a dinner and nox together with baccy and toddy, and I'll tell you all about our Welsh tour. . . . Kindest regards to the frater. Ever yours fraternally

THOS. HUGHES

The book followed apace. Two months later the Macmillans had begun to print it, and although the death of the writer's daughter early in December stopped his work and there was talk of the story's being finished by a popular East End curate, Septimus Hansard, Hughes came back to his desk, and *Tom Brown* was published, anonymously at first, in April 1857. Eleven thousand copies were sold during the year and Hughes had received £1250 by November.

Meanwhile, Kingsley had been in trouble. Nothing of his had been published in 1856. He was overworked and had put aside *Two Years Ago*. Daniel wrote to reassure Mrs. Kingsley. She had done right to keep her husband from overstrain. "We hope to have two or three small books while the two years' rest, preparatory to the great one, are passing. There is no doubt that a great one will be well received, very much better than anything he has done. We see that Mr. Mudie charges 15s. for second-hand copies of *Westward Ho!* while he sold Thackeray's *Esmond* at 9s. This shows that though Thackeray's book was much more successful at first, because he has been longer in the field, and fought his way to a high place right manfully, yet Mr. Kingsley's book has proved more permanently interesting to the English public." What is interesting to us in all comments of this kind is the evidence they give that the tendency of our own times to draw a rigid line between popular judgement and critical taste is extremely recent. Daniel Macmillan knew as well as any man that popularity was not a proof of merit, but he did not make the opposite error, now fashionable, of supposing that it was a proof of demerit. When he encouraged Mrs. Kingsley in the way he did, he was not writing with his tongue in his cheek, and when he added cheerfully that he would print of Kingsley's new novel, when it came, an edition large enough to yield the author £1000 on publication, it did not occur to him or to Kingsley or to any sane man that it might damage an author's critical reputation to be widely read. The effect on Kingsley was to put heart into him and spur him on. After a short rest, he "finished *Two Years Ago* with a rush." On November 4th only a half was done. Nevertheless, encouraged by Froude's high opinion of what he had seen, he pressed on to such effect that not only was the book finished by the end of the year, but all the proofs, except those of the introductory chapter, were returned by January 9th, 1857. As well as the work of his parish and the reading of proofs, Kingsley must have written over ten thousand words a week steadily for seven weeks or more. It is a Balzacian feat. No doubt Scott, Dickens and Trollope equalled or surpassed it on occasions, but it remains an achievement — no one not a writer can know how great an achievement. The courage of it lies, not in the ten thousand words, but in the seven weeks. Even Stevenson's writing of *Jekyll and Hyde* in one continuing drive is less remarkable, for white-heat will sustain a story-teller for ten, twenty, thirty hours, but only an undaunted courage will carry him for fifty days. Even those of us who, perhaps with imperfect knowledge of it, are now little in sympathy with what has been called the muscular Christianity of the the period and, it may be, have suffered in its often strident and jocular aftermath, can scarcely fail to understand what it was that Daniel and Alexander and their children loved in Kingsley. " The keen eagle-like face lighted up by those wonderful blue eyes, the elaborate courtliness of his manner, his boyish spirits, his delightful talk of outdoor things, the impetuosity of his utterance, which was emphasised by his stammer ; all," said Alexander's daughter, " deeply impressed the childish mind." It is a good portrait, and, in his letters, Kingsley drew his own. He was loyal to his friends : " It will be a very great hit. It is an extraordinary book," he wrote of *Tom Brown* before publication. " I should have been proud to have written that book, word for word as it stands." He knew his enemies : ". . . the *Saturday* will surely snub us," he wrote when

Two Years Ago was coming out, " as will the *Athenaeum*, which hateth me with a perfect hatred." And he knew himself and what he was aiming at. Daniel had suggested to him " a common life novel " and Kingsley had pointed out their falseness — " the insipid respectability (utterly untrue to life) of their personages." No : *Two Years Ago* was as near " common life " as he " cared to get " — as near as he could get. " Let me go on, doing what I have always done, from *Yeast* and *Alton Locke* till now ; shewing how much of the heroical and tragical element, supposed to be dead, buried, and whitewashed over, survives in modern society, ready to assert itself for evil and for good the moment a great cause or a great sorrow appears. I am the prophet of the coming convulsion ; I cannot cry peace, peace where there is none. I see all things in Christendom drifting toward the hurricane-circle of God's wrath and purifying storms. . . ."

Two Years Ago more than fulfilled the publishers' expectations of it. After their recent set-back, the Macmillans were on firm ground. The balance-sheet of 1856 was the best they had ever had and, to Daniel's unspeakable relief, the problem that had so vexed him had been solved by the last of their partners' willingness — a final proof of his folly — to be bought out. The two brothers were once more in undivided possession of their enterprise. To this Kingsley's renewed success was added. The first edition of *Two Years Ago* was scarcely out when Daniel had to busy himself in preparing a second and in bringing out Hughes's book. In the midst of this double triumph, he was struck down by pleurisy but recovered from it. On May 13th, Mrs. Macmillan bore him a third son, and early in June was attending her husband again. There was little more she could do for him and on the 27th he died. It may be said that he was denied the fruit of his labours, but at least he knew that the tree was bearing. His wife and four children were at once taken by Alexander into his own household and thenceforward the two families lived as one. Alexander had never had his brother's Puritan suspicion of even a moderate and restrained success, and, after Daniel's death, his personality expanded. He was less of an ascetic than " the grave black man," and his love and respect for him had imposed such restrictions on his own vital development as are sometimes imposed by the love of father and son. Daniel was almost too powerful while he lived, but Alexander, though freer for his going, never forgot or ceased to value him. He felt that, under God, everything he had had been given him by his brother, and asked himself again and again in after years what Daniel would have thought, what Daniel would have done. As success was added to success, he referred it to Daniel's memory, almost as if the senior partner were still alive, and he, Alexander, acting in trust for him. Reading the letters and records of the firm, one has a strong sense, as Alexander unquestionably had, of a continuing partnership. The impression continues to this day. " My brother and I," said Harold Macmillan to George Moore during a dinner-party at the Garrick Club in 1931, " depend very much upon what our grandfather did. I hope our successors will live by what we are doing now. A publishing house is a long-term business. It doesn't live from hand to mouth."

CHAPTER FOUR

The Years of Building

Tobacco and Tennyson—Alexander at Work—Macmillan's Magazine —The Golden Treasury—Copyright and Production—Leaving Cambridge

OON after Daniel's death, Alexander gave effect to a proposal often discussed between the two brothers — the opening of a branch in London. A branch it was — at 23 Henrietta-street, in Covent Garden — for the headquarters of the firm remained at Cambridge for another five years. Robert Bowes, the Macmillans' nephew, who had been employed by them since 1846, was given charge in London, and every Thursday Alexander would come up for the night, and, in two adjoining rooms of the premises in Henrietta-street, was " at home to all and sundry, when tea and stronger fluids, with occasional tobacco, were going on." These were the Tobacco Parliaments which, becoming something of a legend, drew poets, historians, men of science and story-tellers to the same table, where, by all accounts, Alexander was never a conspicuous host but had the art to dissolve himself into the company. At Hughes's suggestion a round table was made for these occasions by a member of the Working Men's College. It stands to-day in the Chairman's room at St. Martin's-street and the signatures of some who attended the Tobacco Parliaments are to be seen on its bevelled edge. David Masson was always there, Tom Hughes often. Old friends appeared from Cambridge. "Science, art and letters," Alexander wrote in the summer of 1860, " are fairly represented in the course of the year. Holman Hunt comes occasionally, Woolner and Alexander Munro, sculptors,

often. Tennyson and Kingsley have both been when in
Town. Henry Kingsley is often there. Huxley, Sharpey
and others of the scientific world come." Any attempt
to recapture the atmosphere of those parties is made difficult by the tendency we have to allow the names of those
who attended them to conjure up a picture of greybeards
at a feast. In fact, they were for the most part young men.
Young Edward Dicey was not long down from Trinity and
ten years and more from his editorships of the *Daily News*
and the *Observer*. Alfred Ainger, another Trinity man,
long afterwards to be Lamb's biographer and Master of the
Temple, was in 1860 twenty-three years old and ordained
to his first curacy. He was already a friend of three years'
standing, having been a haunter of the shop in Trinity-street
when he was a freshman and having become an intimate of
Alexander's Cambridge household. Masson, the Aber-
donian who was to be the first editor of *Macmillan's Magazine*,
though eight years had passed since he succeeded Clough in
the chair of English Literature at University College, was
still in his thirties. Palgrave had gone to Balliol with a
scholarship in the year in which the Macmillans had published their first book, and, after an interval during which
he was assistant private secretary to Gladstone, had returned to take a first in Greats in '47. He held a post in
the Education Department, was Tennyson's friend and
Alexander's junior by six years. Coventry Patmore, whose
first wife's death still lay ahead, and Rossetti's friend,
William Allingham, the Irish poet, were almost of an
age with Palgrave, and at twenty-five Richard Garnett,
an assistant in the library of the British Museum, was
eleven years younger still. Maurice unquestionably, as
the husband of Archdeacon Hare's half-sister and as " the
Prophet," was felt by Alexander to belong to an old generation, though he was not yet fifty-five, but the great men
of science and philosophy, Huxley and Herbert Spencer,

were in their early prime — Huxley, at thirty-five, wrestling with *The Origin of Species*, which had appeared in the previous year (1859), and Spencer, at forty, sending out the syllabus of that *Synthetic Philosophy* which was not to be completed until the century was almost out. Even these few names, chosen almost at random, suggest that the members of the Tobacco Parliament in Henrietta-street were a remarkable company to be gathered now, week after week, about the man who, but twenty years earlier, had come from his obscure schoolmastering at Nitshill to serve Messrs. Seeley for five pounds a month.

The talk, not surprisingly, was of " Darwin and conundrums with general jollity pleasantly intermixed," though perhaps, when Tennyson came, even Tom Hughes rode his jollity on the curb. Not that Tennyson was a cheerless man, but he was a sensitive one. Five years earlier, when he had let himself go in *Maud* as never before or afterwards, and had risen, as Edmund Gosse justly said, " to heights of human sympathy and intuition which he reached nowhere else," criticism had bludgeoned him for his " rampant and rabid bloodthirstiness of soul," and he had withdrawn from the world. Not until 1859 had the first series of *Idylls of the King* appeared, and now, as a consequence of it, Tennyson was in a blaze of fame with few parallels in the history of poetry. Alexander, it will be remembered, had stood by *Maud* in the dark days, and was proud of his discerning ear. " The question of rhythm," he wrote to Professor Shairp in 1863, " is one that cannot well be discussed on paper. I have this element of critical faculty in measure, that it gives me great delight, and I was able to master the varieties in *Maud* more quickly than most of my friends." When the *Idylls* came, Alexander was not left to prophesy in a wilderness. Ten thousand copies were sold in a month, and the poet who came to the Tobacco Parliaments was as celebrated as ever Scott or Byron had been. " Tall and broad-shouldered as a son of Anak, with hair, beard and eyes of a southern darkness," a man dedicated to the art of poetry, combining splendour of appearance with a delicacy of spirit of which his concessions to popular taste may well have been a defence rather than a betrayal — as a pursued traveller throws meat to wolves rather to divert than to sustain them, Tennyson was the strangest admixture of self-confidence with shyness, of discernment with naïveté. Evidently at Henrietta-street he found something to his liking, something necessary to him, and it can scarcely have been the company of Tom Hughes. One night in the spring of 1860, having attended a gathering which had included Woolner and, inevitably, Hughes " and a dozen other good fellows," he stayed on pertinaciously until the good fellows began to vanish, until the exploits of the boxers, Sayers and Heenan, no longer " occupied one half of the conversation," and then, as Alexander reported, " had a nice chat on other subjects." By midnight all the guests had taken their leave except an Edinburgh advocate, Francis Russell, and Tennyson's moment had come. Alexander, back in Cambridge a few days later, described the event in a letter to James MacLehose. " He repeated a long poem in an impossible metre — the subject Boadicea. Its roll was wonderful." The Laureate stayed until half-past one in the morning.

From this it does not necessarily follow, though it is a fair presumption, that Tennyson valued Alexander's judgement of poetry. Writing is solitary ; to imagine is to travel in a world which, when the sun dips, turns suddenly to ice ; Balzac would wake a companion in the middle of the night to hear what he had written. The desire for companionship in that frozen and emptied world is not vain desire for applause, but the need of a seaman for bearings. And if Alexander could listen and genuinely cared to listen, if he could so far give Tennyson his bearings that he would stay for them into the small hours, Alexander possessed, in that power alone, one of the rare qualifications that distinguish a great publisher from a tradesman. Artists are not providers of raw material to a factory. What happens at the retailers may appear to flatter, but does not content them. They try to be reasonable. When they talk like fools of sales and contracts and reviews, even of advertisements, they believe that they are throwing meat to the wolves. But they live between a rapture and a desolation, and there only are they themselves to be found. A great publisher finds them there, remembering that though all the gas-light of fame be turned upon them, they may be lost in the dark.

None of this may be applicable to Tennyson's reading of *Boadicea*; he may have displayed that toy twenty times; but it does apply to Alexander Macmillan and to his relationship with authors. Never did a man take a steadier or a less cynical interest in them. He was his " own taster "; he was tired but never bored; in gigantic, honest letters, to chosen and rejected alike, he discussed men's work as they would have it discussed. How he wrote to young Mr. Hardy will be seen presently. Meanwhile, Tennyson at the height of his glory came to Henrietta-street and stayed to be alone with him, having already that day gone in his company " to see Holman Hunt's picture " — presumably " The Finding of our Saviour in the Temple." " He likes it immensely," Alexander reported to MacLehose. " I hope you will like Miss Mulock's poem about it."

There is another letter of his, written at this time to David Watt, which so describes Alexander in his professional and private life that it is to be quoted. David Watt, a friend of the Macmillans' childhood in Irvine, had been a fellow-student, with David Livingstone, of the London Missionary Society and had gone to India to preach the Gospel as long ago as 1841. He was still there. Alexander, who dropped no one, had corresponded with him for nearly twenty years. Now he had sent home some writings of his own and Alexander had to refuse them : ". . . About the Homilist papers, being business, I did look at them and read several carefully, but I did not feel that they were likely to meet any public that I have access to. They seemed the result of careful thought, as no doubt they were. But I conceive of three classes of readers. 1. A general public to be moved by broad, strong representations of truth. 2. A thoughtful class who demand some striking originality, or 3. a learned class who want the pabulum suited to their special digestion. I did not seem to see that you met the popular — you were too meditative, I fancied, for them ; I did not feel you were, or aimed to be, so original as to attract the thinking fellows, and as for learned pundits, you did not aim at them."

The unrevised awkwardness of the way in which Alexander avoided saying that poor Watt was a fool among scholars, is evidence of how fast he wrote and how spontaneously. Thereafter, the unpleasantness of refusing an old friend's book put behind him, he was on easier ground : " I wish I could see you at Henrietta Street occasionally — or better still, down here [Cambridge]. We are all well, I am thankful to say. My work is sometimes a little heavy, but I get on. The strain on one's mind as to what will answer and what will not is perhaps that which takes most out of one. Reading MSS., not for amusement, but with an eye to results, is heavier work than one would think at first sight. Not one in ten of what anyone reads appears, but one must do one's work wherever placed, and be thankful to have it to do." Then he remembered that David Watt was as much Daniel's friend as his own : " Old life at Irvine and elsewhere is always dear to me. I grow more attached to the past, it is fuller of meanings and interest I hardly dreamed of in earlier years. May it grow more so. Dear Daniel and my mother and Malcolm and William are seldom far from me, and their society is most precious to me. Daniel's wife and children are a great comfort to me, and she is a most valuable help."

The whole man is there : his theory of publishing in its relationship to the public taste ; his practice ; his personal life. " Their society is most precious to me " is a sentence good to write of the dead, in haste or at leisure. Alexander's life, past, present and to come, had an abiding unity, and " society " in that context is the grave, piercing word that Emily Brontë might have used.

Among the subjects often discussed on Thursday evenings was the forthcoming number of *Macmillan's Magazine*. As far back as 1855, Isaac Todhunter had been eager that the Macmillans should start a literary paper, and Alexander had inclined towards it, thinking that it might be called *The World of Letters* or *The Chronicle of Literature* ; but those had been anxious days, the good year of '56 with its release from moneyed partners had not yet come, and Daniel's view had been that, if the firm was to expand, the setting up of quarters in London should precede the risk of a periodical. Not that he objected to a magazine on principle. There are those nowadays who have it as an ideal that a publisher should own and control all the tributaries of his trade — a printing works, a binder's, a paper-mill, even the forests that are pulped for the ninepennies. There is an opposite school of thought, to which the Macmillans have adhered, which holds that a publisher should do what he understands, should avoid the commitment of a printing-press so hungry for material that it may compel him to books beyond his judgement, and, because publishing has a duty to authorship, should not confront writers with the inhumanity of a department store. These or something like them would beyond question have been Daniel's opinions, but they did not exclude a periodical, for a periodical, as then understood, was not a diversion from the proper business of publishing, but an integral part of it, an opening for authors, a response to their work swifter and warmer than the publication of a book, and a field for their experiment.

So Alexander kept the project in his mind, and, when the London branch was established and the times were propitious, revived it. Having chosen David Masson to be editor, he set about collecting contributors. Hughes promised a continuation of *Tom Brown*. Dr. John Brown, author of *Rab and His Friends*, would write occasional articles. On July 18th, in the hot summer of '59, Alexander — " as near as I can get to the centre of draught of four doors and a window " — wrote to his old friend George Wilson ; on July 19th to Kingsley ; on the 25th to Masson, sending to him copies of *The Lion*, a Cambridge magazine with articles by Ainger — " a very varied vein — I think a very fine one — of humour." He sent, and recommended also, a small volume of *Joint Compositions* " by Henry Lushington and Venables, Thackeray's friend." Then, as always when anything important was afoot, James MacLehose was informed. " Don't whisper it to a soul, as it may after all come to nothing, but I am in hopes of a poem from Tennyson." The poet had been in Cambridge for two days and had spent a great part of them with Alexander, saying several times that he wished Macmillan's were his publishers, but was so tied that he could not move as yet. " He is such a noble, kindly man," Alexander wrote. " I could not help thinking how he and dear Daniel would have taken to each other."

In early October, Alexander and Masson spent " three glorious days with Tennyson " in the Isle of Wight. To Alexander there was always something orgiastic in the idea of smoking and he seldom failed to record a bout of it. " He smokes," he said of the Poet Laureate, " like a good

Christian," and again : " We talked and walked and smoked and chatted with the ladies, and altogether were as happy as we could be," and again, though with less emphasis, for Kingsley was not the Laureate : " We took Kingsley on our way home, and had dinner and a pipe at Eversley." They brought back with them a promise from Tennyson of a *Seaside Idyll*, but afterwards Mrs. Tennyson had qualms about it and had to be reassured. Much as Alexander wanted Tennyson, he would not disturb his arrangements. " I think I am honest in saying that so long as the Moxon family have any interest in the publications [as books] I would not move a finger to induce their coming to us ; and I simply wish this *Idyll* for magazine purposes, and will unrepiningly see it go back to its natural publishing channels."

Nevertheless, it was indirectly through the magazine that Tennyson came to Macmillan's. Alexander's own title, *The Round Table*, was abandoned — to be used long afterwards for another periodical issued from St. Martin's-street, and the birth of *Macmillan's Magazine* was celebrated by a dinner at Henrietta-street on November 1st, 1859. It was the first of the shilling monthlies, appearing two months before the *Cornhill*, and was described by the *Athenaeum* as " a review of political affairs, from the philosophical rather than from the partisan point of sight." It was very far from being, in any ordinary sense, political, and nothing is harder than to indicate its range, under the editorships of Masson, George Grove, John Morley, and Mowbray Morris, during its forty-eight years of life. Among its serials were four by William Black, including the *Strange Adventures of a Phaeton* ; *Savrola : a Military and Political Romance*, by Winston Spencer Churchill, and Marion Crawford's *Don Orsino* and *With the Immortals* ; Hardy's *The Woodlanders* ; Henry James's *Portrait of a Lady* ; three by Henry Kingsley, including *Ravenshoe* ; Charles Kingsley's *Water-Babies*, and two by Blackmore, not, alas, including *Lorna Doone*. Pater wrote for it continually in the 'seventies and 'eighties. From *The Bishop and the Philosopher* in January 1863 to *Amiel* in September 1887, Matthew Arnold made it his platform for small things and great. A glance at the long list of his contributions for a quarter of a century is evidence of the freedom that the magazine gave to its giants, and that its readers gave to the magazine. It was possible then to be assured of a steady, educated and attentive audience, who, when a man had given them *Spinoza* and *Thyrsis* in the 'sixties, were well content to follow him without impatience for ten years through minor addresses and lectures even unto *A Last Word on the Burials Bill* in 1876, and were rewarded by *The New Sirens* and a group of essays on Wordsworth, Byron and Amiel, which were to stand in the second series of *Essays in Criticism*. A great periodical lives not by little, buzzing attempts to surprise and titillate, nor by cautious solemnities, but by its power to persuade a reader that, though it is but interesting in June and reasonable in July, it may in August take his breath away.

> Cruel, but composed and bland,
> Dumb, inscrutable and grand,
> So Tiberius might have sat,
> Had Tiberius been a cat.

That, *On the Death of a Favourite Canary*, coming from the same author, must have consoled many a reader who had jibbed a little at the *Burials Bill* — a reader, it may be, who remembered the evening on which, letting the pages of a new issue run through his fingers, he had come upon a new thing, and read, and felt his heart tighten, and had cried : " Listen ! " and read again, and drawn in the silence of those who were with him.

> Runs it not here, the track by Childsworth Farm,
> Up past the wood, to where the elm-tree crowns
> The hill behind whose ridge the sunset flames ?

The Signal-Elm, that looks on Ilsley Downs,
   The Vale, the three lone wears, the youthful Thames ?—
      This winter-eve is warm,
Humid the air ; leafless, yet soft as spring,
   The tender purple spray on copse and briers ;
   And that sweet City with her dreaming spires
She needs not June for beauty's heightening.

Lovely all times she lies, lovely to-night.
   Only, methinks, some loss of habit's power
      Befalls me. . . .

Tennyson did not neglect the magazine. *Lucretius*, the *Carmen Seculare*, the *Heavy Brigade* and other work of his appeared in it. Stevenson contributed *Ordered South*, George Otto Trevelyan the *Letters from a Competition Wallah*, William Barnes several Dorsetshire poems, T. E. Brown *Betsy Lee* and Doyle his *Private of the Buffs*. Bret Harte was there, Longfellow, Hudson, Goldwin Smith, Carlyle, George Eliot ; W. K. Clifford, Huxley, Herbert Spencer, Alfred Russel Wallace ; Mrs. Gaskell, Mrs. Craik, Vernon Lee, Christina Rossetti, Mrs. Humphry Ward, Charlotte M. Yonge ; Gladstone himself. And one day of November 1889 the subscribers to the magazine were to find in it *The Ballad of the King's Mercy*, signed Yussuf, and next month *The Ballad of East and West* still signed Yussuf, forerunners of a series from that pen which ran through *The Courting of Dinah Shadd* and *Without Benefit of Clergy* down to *My Lord the Elephant* in the New Year of '93. And on another day, in October 1878, for all those who had not seen or had forgotten Meredith's *Poems* of 1851, the heavens had opened to a new music :

Lovely are the curves of the white owl sweeping
   Wavy in the dusk lit by one large star.
Lone on the fir-branch his rattle-note unvaried,
   Brooding o'er the gloom, spins the brown eve-jar.

Darker grows the valley, more and more forgetting :
So were it with me if forgetting could be willed.
Tell the grassy hollow that holds the bubbling well-spring,
　Tell it to forget the source that keeps it filled.[1]

After this, since there is earth as well as heaven in publishing, it may be of historical interest to note that Meredith
secured sixteen guineas for *Love in the Valley*. A scrap of
paper in the archives, which appears to be in Mowbray
Morris's handwriting, says that the rate of payment to
contributors was twenty-five shillings a thousand words.
Another note mentions that Kipling, exceptionally fortunate,
was paid eighty pounds for *My Lord the Elephant*.

It is useless to persist in a string of names. Even the
few that have been given are too many ; the eye tires of
them. And yet that the list is not to be organized into
groups and movements, that the great critics — Arnold,
Pater, Symonds, Whibley — are all there with the theologians, the preachers, the men of science, the historians, the
Laureate, the young lions, the great story-tellers and the
good story-tellers, reveals a catholic prospect closed to us
since we allowed Austin Harrison's *English Review* and
Squire's *London Mercury* to perish. A magazine in this
liberal tradition, seeing literature as a wisdom and a delight,
without prejudice of sect or fear to sing songs and to tell
stories, is a civilized asset of which we have strangely
deprived ourselves. *Macmillan's* is gone, *Cornhill* is gone,
Scribner's is gone. We have specialized in this as in all else.

In the year before the launching of the magazine, Charles
Kingsley's younger brother, Henry, showed Alexander part
of a novel he was writing — " a story of Australian life —

---

[1] The versions of Arnold and Meredith here given are those of the
Magazine. They were afterwards revised, chiefly for punctuation, the
only substantial change being " Past the high wood " for " Up past
the wood."

chiefly backwoods — partly in England." Alexander found Henry Kingsley's style " wonderfully quiet and yet powerful — a kind of lazy strength which is very charming." The result was the publication in 1859 of *Geoffry Hamlyn* which was successful enough to justify a re-issue in one volume in 1860, and was followed by the more famous *Ravenshoe* two years later.

Meanwhile the firm struck a new vein which was to extend far into the future. Palgrave's *Golden Treasury of English Songs and Lyrics* was gathered together by the compiler with immense labour and appeared in 1861. Alexander, intuitively aware of its importance, determined to " make a gem of it " but published it cautiously, printing at first only 2000 copies. There was, he acknowledged, a sense in which it was true to say that verse was a drug on the market. Had not David Masson mournfully calculated that there were some twenty-thousand respectable versifiers in the British Isles ? But real poetry, Alexander believed — and he could laugh at himself while stating his belief — " will never cease to command the ear and — pray note the merchant spirit, strong even in high moods in the British shopkeeper — the purse of thousands everywhere." Palgrave's anthology justified him in itself and in its offspring. The compiler's own final revision appeared thirty years later. In the ordinary editions, with Laurence Binyon's supplementary fifth book, it holds its ground more than eighty years after publication, and the editions annotated by J. H. Fowler are steadily used in schools. And yet it was, in its first edition, an extremely odd book. Palgrave, with Tennyson as his adviser, took a strongly moral view of his duty of selection. His principle was that " passion, colour and originality cannot atone for serious imperfections in clearness, unity and truth," with the result that Blake, Donne, Quarles and Emily Brontë were omitted ; Coleridge, denied even *Kubla Khan*, was represented by " All thoughts, all passions, all delights " and " Verse, a breeze 'mid blossoms straying " ; Vaughan was given but 32 lines, Crashaw 63 and Herbert 20 ; while Scott had 345 and Campbell 400.

Palgrave's selective attitude was unquestionably that of his age. His aim was to produce " a true national anthology " and, in a sense, he succeeded. But from the publishers' point of view what followed the book was of even greater importance than the book itself, for it was the origin of the whole *Golden Treasury Series*, which included such enduring volumes as Matthew Arnold's selections from Byron and Wordsworth, Coventry Patmore's *Children's Garland*, Henley's *Lyra Heroica*, Andrew Lang's *Theocritus, Bion and Moschus*, and Sir Roundell Palmer's (Lord Selborne's) *Book of Praise*, for which Thomas Woolner, who had an ear for titles and had suggested that of the Series itself, had chosen the name. Alexander's only disappointment in it was its omission of his favourite : " O God of Bethel by whose hand."

The range of Alexander's interest and enterprise was, perhaps, never wider than during this period before the firm's headquarters were moved to London. Frederick Temple of Rugby, Butler of Harrow, R. H. Hutton and J. B. Lightfoot were added to his list. Among the men of science to come in were Clerk Maxwell, E. J. Routh, Francis Galton, Daniel Wilson and Archibald Geikie, and there were popular writers too — Annie Keary, Mrs. Oliphant, Mrs. Norton, and Mrs. Craik, the author of *John Halifax, Gentleman*. At the same time, Alexander was deeply interested in American affairs and in Anglo-American relations. He was a strong adherent of the North in the war then raging, and in his letters to J. T. Fields, the editor of the *Atlantic Monthly*, did his utmost to show that England was less unsympathetic to the Northern cause than *The Times* and the *Saturday Review* might have led Americans to suppose. He was troubled too by the American refusal to recognize mutual and international copyright. It made easy the way of piratical publishers and was a deterrent to the honest exchange of the literature of the two greatest English-speaking countries. In writing of Oliver Wendell Holmes's *Elsie Venner*, Alexander said : " I feel sure that Mr. Holmes will do something greater than this yet. If we had international copyright we would be able really to do something worth doing for such books." The problem that he faced then remains to-day. The American refusal persists.

He always cared greatly for the detail of book production — for outward appearance, that is to say — and gave precise instructions to the designers who worked for him. The design used on the cover of the Golden Treasury Series was made by an artist employed by Burn's, who still do a great part of the Macmillans' binding. It is carved over the entrance to the present house in St. Martin's-street and may be seen on the outside of this volume. Alexander said exactly what he wanted and why he wanted it. Having described the emblem, he added : " All which being interpreted meaneth : the stars for heavenly glory and light, the acorns for earthly growth and strength, the bee for useful industry, the butterfly for beauty pure and aimless." And he was scarcely less firm in treating with Rossetti himself, to whom he wrote about the possibility of publishing some of Christina's poems. Rossetti had offered to supply two designs. Alexander thought he could run the risk of a small edition and " make an exceedingly pretty volume " if some of the poems were omitted. If Rossetti would be good enough to call in, he would " indicate what seemed needful to be left out." *Goblin Market* would be the attraction of the book and should, he thought, furnish any designs. Moreover — " a quaint wood-cut initial — not elaborate and *not* sprawling down the page, but with a queer goblin, say, grinning at a sweet, patient woman face — or

something else of the kind would make a nice addition."
In the middle of the letter there is a saving sentence : " But
we must, of course, leave that to you," and, indeed,
Alexander writes throughout with modest courtesy. Nevertheless there is no concealing his desire that Rossetti, like
the binders' employee, should not remain in any doubt of
what the firm wanted.

The year 1863 was full of events. Charles Kingsley's
earlier works were gathered in from his former publisher,
John W. Parker, who had gone out of business. The earlier
works of F. D. Maurice, of Archbishop Trench and of
Charlotte M. Yonge came with them from the same source
— Miss Yonge being a new acquaintance of the firm,
destined to become one of its closest friends. Henry
Kingsley's *Austin Elliot* appeared and so did *The Water-
Babies*. Charles Kingsley had sent in some early chapters
of *The Water-Babies* in May of the previous year, and three
weeks later, Alexander, visiting him at Eversley, had written
to James MacLehose of his discovery : " I am staying a
day or two with the dear, noble Rector here. We are to
have *such* a story from him for the *Magazine* — to begin in
August when ' Ravenshoe ' is done. It is to be called ' The
Water-Babies.' I have read a great deal of it, and it is the
most charming piece of grotesquery, with flashes of tenderness and poetry playing over all, that I have ever seen."
Back again in Cambridge, he read the book to his children
as it came to him, piece by piece, and his daughter afterwards described those readings as " the greatest excitement
in the nursery world that I remember."

But the Cambridge days were drawing to an end. Bishop
Colenso distressed Maurice by writing what Alexander
described as " an extremely negative book about the Penta-
teuch," and there sprang up one of those remote Victorian
controversies of which it is now useful to say only that, at
the time, they affected the lives of sincere men. " The

whole matter so weighed on Mr. M's mind that he resolved on giving up his cure in Vere-street, London " and wrote " a very beautiful farewell letter to his Congregation." Alexander saw it in proof. He was convinced that Maurice was noble and unselfish but not that the step he had taken was right. His admiration and affection for Maurice never swerved, but it is evident that they were less uncritical than they had been. He was, too, extremely busy ; the Bishop's complaints against Matthew Arnold's criticism of his book in the *Magazine* were answered with firmness ; and he turned his mind to giving effect to the decision he had reached that he and Macmillan's must move to London. The move cannot have been easy, but he allowed none of his old interests to drop and plunged fearlessly into new ones. He accepted the post of publisher to the University of Oxford ; in a letter of his to George Trevelyan, he noted the growth of business with India and was evidently looking in the direction of the great Macmillan branches that now flourish there ; and he wrote untiringly to America on the war and on Anglo-American relations. He had the rare quality of being able to think on a large and on a small scale at the same time, to imagine in terms of continents and to attend to detail. In brief, he had command of his time ; in the midst of all his tasks, he seems very seldom to have felt that he was being pursued by the clock ; and he had the gift of enjoying himself. The large house he took at Upper Tooting was called The Elms. He re-christened it Knapdale after the home of his clan in Argyllshire, and did not conceal his pleasure in it — its rambling passages, its trees, the gypsies on the neighbouring common, the sight of his children " tumbling about the grass and playing croquet and jumping about all day long."

It became, too, as the years passed, a famous meeting-place of writers and artists, men and women, young and old, who seem to have been endowed there with a special gift of laying aside their pomps and vanities and so of enjoying themselves. Alfred Ainger, who was last described as a young curate lately down from Cambridge, became a great man as time went on, but never lost his delight in Knapdale. " The great A.A.," wrote Malcolm Macmillan of a party given there in May 1874, " was in his most prolific vein. I could hear Mr. Hughes ringing with laughter as they took the lawn together. . . . After tea Sara Carmichael played some less-known nocturnes of Chopin, one solemn one in particular. Mr. Ainger was in raptures. It was a most pleasant piano revel. (A piano revel includes all the gracious suavity of artistic enthusiasm as well as the playing). . . . ' I suppose you can't " taste Wagner in sips ", as Dick Swiveller observed to the Marchioness about beer,' said Mr. Ainger." And Ainger's biographer [1] tells how, in the summer, he would often stay with the Macmillans for several weeks on end and read plays to them into the small hours. " And sometimes when his happy hearers discovered it was late and prepared to go to bed, Ainger, excited by Shakespeare — and himself — would hold them by moon-shine antics, breaking forth, Puck-like, into a shadowy dance, swift, graceful, unreal, which seemed part of the witching hour." When these remarkable performances were over, it was understood that they should not be spoken of ; Ainger " would show an added dignity of bearing which forbade any reference to them " ; but there must have been a magic in the house that thus released the " lissom, clerical, printless toe." It is little wonder that Alexander was delighted by his new home. The move required some adjustment of business arrangements. Robert Bowes returned to Cambridge to continue the retail business, called Macmillan and Bowes, which was to become the Bowes and Bowes of the present day, and the publishing business was moved to 16 Bedford-street, where it remained for the next nine years.

[1] *Life and Letters of Alfred Ainger*, by Edith Sichel.

PART TWO

SCIENCE, " ALICE," AND THOMAS HARDY
(1863–72)

CHAPTER FIVE

Design and Fortune

*Partners and Readers—Religion and Science—Newman and Kingsley—
New Authors—Shakespeare and the " Globe"—Matthew Arnold,
Palgrave's "Arabia," "Ecce Homo," and "Alice"*

THE firm's new association with Oxford took Alexander to the weekly meetings of the Delegates and greatly increased his labours. The sale of the Clarendon Press books had fallen away. The reason, as he saw it, was that, though for a time the leaders of the Oxford Movement had stimulated interest in the older theologians as defenders of stability and order, this influence was no longer effective. New controversies had arisen and books of a different kind were necessary. With Oxford's concurrence, policy was given a fresh direction by his advice, and the arrangement continued happily for seventeen years. Meanwhile the other business of the Clarendon Press so expanded under Henry Frowde that it became in the end desirable for the University to resume control of all its publications. The friendly parting in 1881 was marked by Alexander Macmillan's being made an honorary Master of Arts.

It was the addition of the Oxford work to what he was already doing in London that forced him to recognize that he could not continue alone, and he began to look for a partner. He did not " in the least want anyone to bring grist to the mill in the way of new ideas or new connections " but, on the contrary, one who would consult with him on his projects and " see to the details being carried out." Through Miss Dinah Mulock he had come to know George Lillie Craik whom she was to marry in 1865 and who, after James MacLehose had been consulted, became a partner in the same year. It was a fortunate choice, for Craik, though he had an artificial leg and other physical disabilities, was precisely what Alexander needed as an administrator — a man full of energy and character. He stayed in the firm until his death forty years later and was still a legend among the older members of the staff yet another forty years on. " Is your hearrt in your worrk ? " he would demand of them as he passed their desks.

The middle 'sixties were, in a sense, a crisis in the firm's history — a crisis not the less dangerous because it happened to be caused not by failure but by success. Alexander had the habit of rule and might very easily, in view of the intensely personal history of the firm, have been incapable of delegation. But when the warnings came — " a sense of faintness, fits of distressing, and, as far as I know, causeless anxiety " — he accepted them, and not only took Craik as his partner, but ceased to kill himself by keeping all the literary part of Macmillan's affairs in his own hands. Not to be always his own " taster " must have been even harder for him than the taking in of Craik on the side of administration, but gradually he shifted a part of the burden on to the shoulders of other men. They were of remarkable quality ; John Morley, George Grove and Norman Lockyer were among them — Lockyer becoming his " consulting physician with regard to scientific books and schemes." The result was a liberation of Alexander himself. Being no longer overwhelmed by the material pouring in upon him, he had a chance to imagine and, so far as a publisher may, to create. William Allingham's *Ballad Book* sprang from his suggestion; he outlined the arrangement and treatment of Alexander

Smith's edition of Burns, collating the material himself; and what became Mark Lemon's *Jest Book* had its origin in an idea of his. " What do you think of a real *high-bred* Joe Miller ? It wants doing. Think of the lot of exquisite stories floating about and getting lost." He laughingly suggested an advertisement that homeless jokes would " find shelter and have their faces washed." Not only were his ideas abundant, but they appear always to have suggested the right man or woman to carry them out. He wanted a selection of verses that might be " safely put into children's hands on Sunday," not doctrinal, not necessarily even religious, but — it was an idea not easy to define in general terms ; everything depended upon the right choice of a compiler, and he went to Mrs. C. F. Alexander on the strength of her hymns. A successful *Sunday Book of Poetry* was the result. He had, too, the power of grasping the value of ideas put before him by others. At that time books on self-help were coming from the press in a complacent and nauseating stream — the Victorian counterparts of our books wherein it is explained how by planning any section of the community can help itself. As an answer to the self-helpers, Mrs. Daniel Macmillan suggested a book containing examples of self-sacrifice. Alexander saw the point, and Miss Charlotte M. Yonge, liberally interpreting the original commission, produced her *Book of Golden Deeds*.

These books were, so to speak, the side-lines which gave variety to those years and prevented the firm from settling into a groove or relying too exclusively on the learned men of Oxford and Cambridge with whom it had made such fortunate contact. But meanwhile the solid work continued. The Darwinian controversy was still rumbling. Through it all Alexander held steadily to a conviction that religion and science were allies, not foes, in the interpretation and achievement of human destiny, and the firm's policy reflects his view. He had noticed in particular the influence that the work of J. M. Wilson, afterwards Headmaster of Clifton, was having on the public schools by introducing to them the study of botany, geology and chemistry, and for the elementary books that he published he went deliberately, and in accordance with an expressed principle, " not to the ordinary teacher, but to the recognized masters in each branch " — to Balfour Stewart, Roscoe, Jevons, Lockyer and Huxley himself. Books of a different kind and of great importance were coming out at the same time. Palgrave, it will be remembered, had omitted Blake from the *Golden Treasury*, and a publisher, if he is to share the credit of his anthologists, must be held partly responsible for their faults. Macmillan's made amends when, in 1863, they published a book for which at the time there was no obvious public and of which only five hundred copies were sold in its first year—Alexander Gilchrist's *Life of William Blake*, which had been completed by the author's wife with the counsel of Rossetti and Swinburne. Its effect was to rescue Blake from oblivion and it still has its place near the root of later studies of its subject.

The next year brought the famous battle between Newman and Kingsley, the story of which has been told too often to be repeated here. It was a cause of distress to Alexander, for it had its origin in a passage written by Kingsley in *Macmillan's Magazine*. There was no doubt that Kingsley was intellectually outmatched, and he was an old friend. The ensuing correspondence, published by Newman with crushing effect, contained a letter addressed to " X. Y. Esquire, a gentleman who had interposed between Dr. Newman and Mr. Kingsley." It was Alexander who had been so rash, for he took full responsibility for the *Magazine's* article, and so far persisted in his peacemaking as to bring about a feeling of esteem between Newman and

Kingsley, though they did not meet. To one who looks back on the controversy over a distance of nearly eighty years, it is evident that Kingsley said more than he meant, and afterwards became entangled in the web of Newman's dialectic ; but, in all conscience, Kingsley had written with a violence that deserved what it received : " Truth, for its own sake," he said, " had never been a virtue with the Roman clergy. Father Newman informs us that it need not, and on the whole ought not to be ; that cunning is the weapon which Heaven has given to the saints wherewith to withstand the brute male force of the wicked world which marries and is given in marriage. Whether his notion be doctrinally correct or not, it is at least historically so." In a dispute thus provoked, the warm-hearted, downright author of *Westward Ho !* could not stand against the man who was to produce the *Apologia*. It is of some interest that Alexander, though he read the cause of offence before it was published, had failed to see the danger of it. He had a deep and long-standing respect for Newman and would have gone far to avoid wounding him. " Precious memories of more than twenty years since," he wrote on January 6th, 1864, " when your sermons were a delight and blessing shared (and thereby increased) with a dear brother no longer living . . . would add strong weight to my desire to answer such a letter from you with peculiar care and reverence," and whatever Newman may have thought of the theology of the letter that followed, he cannot have failed to be impressed by its conciliatory spirit and its almost naïve honesty. But, against Alexander's advice, Kingsley wrote also ; Hutton, in the *Spectator*, added fuel to the fire ; and by the end of April poor Kingsley was in so bad a way that Alexander was saying : " I wish I had a yacht and I would go and get Mr. Kingsley and take him to see Garibaldi — that would do him good." Once again, in an emergency, a Macmillan was thinking of taking to the water, as Macmillans always had in times of trouble. But, in the end, the fire burnt itself out. Alexander's summing-up was pleasantly blunt : " The old saying attributed to Talleyrand that the use of words is to conceal thought might be extended in certain cases to intellects which would thus be described as having the power of perplexing the truth. In this art, Newman is a master, and thank God C. K. is not even a learner." The comment is loyal to the old friend at Eversley, but it is not hard to imagine with how persuasive a subtlety Newman, if he had heard it, would have pointed out that others before himself had asked what truth is, and that what Alexander called his " power of perplexing " it consisted in his patience, which Kingsley lacked, to stay for an answer.

While the Kingsley fire was burning, writers new to Macmillan's were being added to their list. Bryce's *The Holy Roman Empire*, which began as a prize-essay and became a classic, appeared in the same year. *A French Eton* was the first of Matthew Arnold's books to carry the imprint, and *Clara Vaughan* was the first novel of R. D. Blackmore, written as though by a woman and published anonymously. Alexander believed in it but it was not a success, and Blackmore, though he made a little money from it, cheerfully refused to allow his ambition as an author to come between him and his market garden at Teddington which, in the season, was producing £120 a week — two tons of " top of the market " two-ounce strawberries. Nevertheless, as there were not always strawberries, he wrote two other novels which appeared as serials in the *Magazine*. How, after all this, *Lorna Doone* went elsewhere, no record shows, though George Macmillan is reported to have said : " The story only missed us by an accident." Seeing how unfortunate the accident was, there is a certain grandeur in having forgotten the way of it, or else a proof, if proof be needed, that, in contradiction of the public view, the substance of a publishing house does not, and ought not to, consist in fashionable novels. While they were debating with the theologians and experimenting with *Clara Vaughan*, the firm were beginning their publication of *The Statesman's Year-Book* and laying the corner-stone of a new series.

In 1860, W. G. Clark, the Public Orator, and other Cambridge scholars had discussed the possibility of an edition of Shakespeare to be edited with the careful scholarship ordinarily reserved for Greek and Latin texts and giving all the various readings that had authority and value. The library of Trinity had a superb collection of the early quartos, and the project greatly appealed to Alexander, who appears to have believed that such an edition would be, in effect, final and settle the text for ever. The result was *The Cambridge Shakespeare*, dedicated to the Duke of Devonshire as Chancellor of the University. It was, and still is, a great edition, rich in learning, uncommonly free from pedantry, a trifle heavy to hold but good to read — which is a fair balance in a book, for do not laps and knees endure longer than eyes? Its first volume, edited by Clark and John Glover, the Librarian of Trinity, appeared with Volumes II and III, edited by Clark and W. Aldis Wright, Glover's successor in the librarianship, in sixty-three, and the nine stately volumes were completed within three years. They were proudly presented — as a faded inscription shows — by the publisher to the Garrick Club, of which, at Thackeray's proposal, he had become a member in 1861.

From the *Cambridge* sprang the *Globe Shakespeare* and so the whole *Globe Library*. Once more, Alexander made MacLehose his confidant, and on May 24th, 1864, wrote to him :

Please consider this confidential in the strictest sense. If my small deed is to be done it must be done silently and swiftly as well as *well*.

Design and Fortune

I enclose a page for a *Shakespeare*, which I fancy doing in one volume, on toned paper for 3s. 6d., very nicely bound in Macmillan's choicest cloth binding. The text to be gone over by our Cambridge editors, but done in this edition with an eye to more popular uses than they felt themselves at liberty to consider in their critical and scholarly edition. Now your judgment is always as you know precious to me, even when I cannot quite follow it. I want you to tell me whether you think I have a reasonable chance of selling 50,000 of such a book in three years. For if so I can do a nice stroke of business. You see it would be immeasurably the cheapest, most beautiful and handy book that has appeared of *any kind*, except the Bible. Clark and Wright, our editors ; Clay, our printer, and Fraser say it is a great idea and a safe one. What say you ? No one else has been asked.

Whatever MacLehose had answered, Alexander would have gone forward. This was an occasion on which his mind was clear and urgent. Clark and Wright strongly opposed the title, " Globe," which he had chosen. They thought it " claptrappy " and pleaded for " Hand Edition," but he stood firm, explaining that he wanted to give the idea that the book was intended for the million without saying it. Work must have advanced at a rare pace when debate ended, for the book, though still under discussion in June, was completed and on sale in December — a feat which, in all the circumstances of that edition, makes modern experts rub their eyes. " Even in peace-time," said one of them in 1943, " we could hardly work to that schedule nowadays — and *they* did it over and over again." Among the technical peculiarities of the *Globe Shakespeare* was that it created a new dimension in books, the Globe octavo. Though the sales were slow in the first weeks, they soon became lively, and twenty thousand were gone in a few months. Editions of Burns, Goldsmith, Pope, Spenser, Cowper, Dryden and many others followed, and the *Globe*

Library entered upon its enduring career. But not without difficulty. To publish books cheaply means working on a small margin of profit, and a small margin is made difficult unless the bookseller's, as well as the publisher's and the author's, share of it is clearly defined. At that time, there was no uniformity in booksellers' terms to their clients. Each gave what discount he pleased, trying to undersell his rivals, and a publisher who set 3s. 6d. as the nominal published price of the *Globe Shakespeare* had no means of knowing how much a member of the public would have to pay for it. From this confusion no advantage came to any section of the trade and certainly none to book-buyers, who are bound to lose by any conditions the uncertainty of which forces up the published price ; but how to straighten the confusion none yet could see. The Net Book Agreement, initiated, fought for and secured by Daniel's son, Frederick, lay in the future. Meanwhile, Alexander himself was on the trail. " I don't see my way to any further move in the underselling matter. . . . I had a plan, but I don't think it would have worked — which was to subscribe it to the London trade in the new edition, offering it at 2s. 7d. to all who would sign a paper agreeing not to sell it for less than 3s. 6d. . . . I think I could almost sell my second 20,000 before Midsummer if the trade would do this." Nothing came of it then, but his plan was an early looking forward to a system which, when it did come, gave new health and order to the book trade.

A reader is fully entitled to say if he will that such matters are the mechanism of the book trade and, therefore, of no interest to him. Indeed they would be very tedious if they stood alone ; but it is one of the peculiarities of publishing that, though it is a trade and looks always a little ridiculous when it is spoken of as an art, it includes in its trading a unique clash : at one moment a publisher is calculating a margin in halfpennies as if he were a pork butcher or a maker of tin cans, at another he is called upon to take action in which the most delicate distinctions of principle are implied, and always, while he exercises his taste or laboriously defends his integrity, manna may fall upon him from heaven. The romance of publishing may appear to an outsider to consist in the miracles, but its character certainly, and perhaps even its romance, may be said more truly to arise from its sharp intermingling of calculation and industry with intuition and mere chance. Thus, as Mr. Fairlight said of something quite different, it resembles marriage in its conditions, though not in its results.

There was now to descend upon Macmillan's in Bedford-street an extraordinary shower of the plain and the coloured. The year 1865 yielded to them a solid work, *The Coal Question*, by W. Stanley Jevons, from which Gladstone appropriated a great part of his argument on the prospective decline of the country's prosperity ; Matthew Arnold's *Essays in Criticism* which gave, at any rate at the booksellers', no evidence of the long career for which they were destined ; a rare book of travel which has some claim to be regarded as a classic of exploration ; a religious book, published anonymously, which drew the firm into the hottest of all its controversies and was discussed, often with ferocity, from one end of England to the other ; and a small volume for children of which 48 copies were sent out and at once withdrawn but which became nevertheless the most famous book to bear the Macmillan imprint. That it came to them was due to no enterprise of theirs nor at the outset were they, in the full sense, its publishers, for the author had taken it not to them but to the Clarendon Press and he carried his own risk and gave his own orders.

The book of travel was William Gifford Palgrave's *Narrative of a Year's Journey through Central and Eastern*

Arabia. Palgrave, a brother of the compiler of *The Golden Treasury*, was both a Jesuit and by race a Jew. His father, Sir Francis, was the son of Meyer Cohen, a Jewish stock-broker, but in 1823 he had, on his marriage, changed his religion and his name. William Gifford had, therefore, been born Christian. After graduating at Oxford and serving in the Bombay Native Infantry, he had become a Jesuit and gone as a missionary to Syria. In his thirty-sixth and thirty-seventh years, he had disguised himself as a physician and made a journey through Arabia of which his *Narrative* was the result. It is worth recalling not only because it broke new ground but for its motto, the choice of which marks the author, and, if his antecedents and training are remembered, the age in which he lived :

> Not in vain the nation-strivings, nor by chance the currents flow ;
> Error-mazed, yet truth-directed, to their certain goal they go.

It was translated from the Arabic, perhaps with convenient freedom.

The religious book, of which its opponents would have given a different description, came to Alexander as an anonymous manuscript. It was a treatment of the life and work of Jesus as the life and work of a man, and was called, therefore, *Ecce Homo*. Alexander was overwhelmed by it at a first reading and never swerved in his defence of it. It aroused so violent a curiosity that he was blamed for preserving its anonymity as though he had concealed a crime. Its authorship, which belonged to Professor J. R. Seeley, a son of Seeley the publisher by whom Daniel and Alexander had been employed, who now held, at the age of thirty-one, the Chair of Latin at University College, and four years later was to become Professor of Modern History at Cambridge. In excluding the supernatural from his

78

account, he had as his object to insist upon the humanity of Jesus' mission rather than to contradict faith, but there were thousands who read him otherwise. The power of the book was so great that, while it remained anonymous, it was attributed to the most brilliant and effective controversialists of the day : by some to Mill, by some to Maine, by some to Goldwin Smith, and, by Lord Shaftesbury, to the Father of Lies. Gladstone fortunately disagreed with Lord Shaftesbury and said so in a letter to Alexander, who, thus encouraged, invited a party of distinguished men to meet the author. He kept his word, for Seeley was present ; but he kept his counsel also, and the guests, having vainly searched one another's faces for the marks of authorship, went out, none the wiser.

The children's book made a very casual and unspectacular first appearance in the Macmillans' history. Its author, the Rev. Charles Lutwidge Dodgson, a mathematical don at Christ Church, made arrangement with the Clarendon Press to produce *Alice* at his expense, and the first references to it in the Macmillan files are on the subject of binding. There was never an author more elaborately careful than Lewis Carroll for the details of production or one that can have more sorely tried the patience of his publisher. The beginning was harmless enough. He wanted *Alice* to be a table-book and thought that red would be most pleasing to childish eyes ; the edges were to be cut smooth but to be ungilded — though he afterwards liked the gilding used on a new impression. He was anxious, he said, to have fifty of the two thousand copies as soon as possible, as his young friends were all growing out of their childhood so fast, and one copy was to be bound in white vellum for Alice Liddell. The edition, an octavo, was peacefully printed by the end of June 1865, but, when forty-eight copies had been given away, a storm broke. The author, dissatisfied with the printing of the text and of the Tenniel illustrations, recalled them, cancelled the whole edition, and shipped off the 1952 unbound sheets to Messrs. Appleton of New York. Some of the presentation copies were not returned and have since made fantastic prices at auction, with the result that a year seldom passes even now in which no one sends to the Macmillans a copy plainly marked " 86th thousand " and an offer to part with it for a few hundred pounds. There have been bibliographers, too, who have maintained as contrary to human nature that a man so sensitive to the appearance of his book should have allowed the defective sheets to go to New York, but it was by no means contrary to Dodgson's nature. The correspondence is full of evidence that supplies which did not come up to his standard were considered by him quite good enough for Americans, of whose taste his opinion was low. This opinion was confirmed in 1888. The coloured pictures in the first printing of the *Nursery Alice* were condemned by him as too gaudy. No copy, he said, was to be sold in England ; all were to be offered to America. They were offered, and declined as not being gaudy enough.

When the 1952 of the first printing were safely out of sight, Richard Clay prepared another edition, dated 1866. The sales were not rapid. Dodgson was nervous of printing another three thousand copies in the same year, and thought it would be some time before he again indulged in paper and print ; nevertheless, he had " a floating idea " for a sequel. Next year, the other half of him produced *An Elementary Treatise on Determinants and their Application to Simultaneous Linear Equations and Algebraical Geometry* — " for the use of beginners." While they were beginning, *Alice* loitered in her tenth thousand, and the author was pleased to find that he had made in two years a profit of £250 on his original outlay of £350, which had included the illustrations. Not that he greatly cared how many copies were sold ; it mattered to him only that each copy should be flawless. He was fully prepared to miss the Christmas market rather than hurry an edition, and yet for all his care mistakes crept in. They became an obsession ; he felt them as an old lady feels draughts. Uneven inking, cropped margins, irregular levels of opposite pages — he missed nothing. Genuinely faulty copies, with pages in the wrong order, found their way to him as they do to all authors, and it struck him as exceedingly odd that these defects had a habit of appearing in his specially bound copies. It was less surprising than he supposed. The binders were called upon to produce at the same time a large ordinary impression and fifty copies in red, twenty in blue, twenty in green, two in vellum, one with edges uncut, one with primrose edges, and one with a piece of mirror on the cover — and the binders' heads span. The publishers' also : " Have you done any more with coloured inks and papers ? " " Have you ever considered the effect of *gold* type ? " and when, in 1869, he produced his book of verses, *Phantasmagoria*, he wanted one edition, containing an Oxford squib, to be sold for 5s. 6d., and another, without it, for sixpence less.

CHAPTER SIX

Long-Term Publishing

Alexander looks to America—Long-term Publishing—" Nature "—
Young Thomas Hardy—Alexander at Home

LEXANDER, as always, was unperturbed by detail. He had a way of riding through it. All was well at home, and the time had come for expansion abroad. He was deeply moved by F. W. H. Myers' *St. Paul* and, it may be added, more eager for it than for Matthew Arnold's *New Poems*. To publish a new edition of *Guesses at Truth*, which had first brought him and Daniel into contact with Archdeacon Hare, gave him pious satisfaction. Kingsley brought him *Hereward the Wake* and Miss Yonge her *Dove in the Eagle's Nest*. F. H. Doyle's *Return of the Guards* contained at least two poems that were for long to be inescapable at penny readings : " The Private of the Buffs " and " The Red Thread of Honour." The double family at Knapdale prospered. Though Alexander lost his youngest son, William, in 1866, and Daniel's wife died in January of the following year, the boys were growing up. Frederick, Daniel's eldest, was by then sixteen and would soon be in the firm. Maurice was fourteen, and his own Malcolm and George fifteen and twelve. It was at this moment that Alexander made one of those half-reasoning, half-intuitive moves which, though uneventful in themselves, often, in the history of growing businesses, are seen, in retrospect, to have been of great importance. He went to the United States, not, it seems, with any clear-cut intention of establishing a branch there, but rather to see what the conditions were and, if possible, to safeguard existing interests which appeared to be threatened. Two things were clear to him : that he wished to obtain " the good-will of gentlemen engaged in educational work " and that the sale of his books in America was handicapped by high tariffs and the absence of international copyright. The only compensating advantage was that the English costs of production were less than the American, but that might change ; if so, he would be shut out of the American market unless he had " manufacturing and distributive power on the spot." He went, therefore, with an open and receptive mind. He visited his elder sister, Margaret Bowes — the only other survivor of old Duncan's twelve children, stayed with the Lippincotts in Philadelphia, called on President Grant, and was the guest of J. T. Fields in Boston, where he met Longfellow, Emerson and Holmes. He was impressed, as so many others have been, " by the utter ignorance in England of the country's power, resources, and the enormous amount of great and good work going on," in particular as a consequence of educational endowments. " A great international publishing house is possible," he wrote, " and would be a grand idea to be realized," but he had learnt long ago the advantage of small beginnings and was content at first with having a direct agent in New York. George Brett, grandfather of the George Brett who is now President of the Macmillan Company, was sent out, not to print and publish, but with a consignment of English books, and orders to take an office and sell them. George Brett was a man whose life was work and who allowed nothing to distract him from it. The American branch was soon and firmly established. Alexander mentioned it to MacLehose as existing in November 1869. The imprint " London and New York " appeared in that year and grew more frequent from 1870 onwards. Soon afterwards Frederick Macmillan went to New York and stayed five years.

About the time of Alexander's American journey, Masson

became Professor of English Literature at Edinburgh, and George Grove succeeded him as editor of *Macmillan's Magazine*. The *Journal of Anatomy and Physiology*, begun in 1866, was followed by *The Practitioner* and by a steady output of general and specialist works on medicine and surgery, including Russell Reynolds's *System of Medicine*. The basis of the firm had greatly broadened. Gladstone's *Juventus Mundi* appeared in the same year, 1869, with a novel, once greatly popular, Samuel Baker's *Cast Up by the Sea*, with Galton's *Hereditary Genius*, and with Alfred Russel Wallace's *Malay Archipelago*, which was followed in 1870 by *Natural Selection*. From the long list of books published during this period, there emerges a principle which has a deceptive appearance of simplicity : books were chosen to last. This is not to say that they were chosen or selflessly published because they were immortal works of art or science ; but long-term publishing which, when capital was scarce, had been a luxury, was now a habit, and brought cumulative rewards. Church and Brodribb's *Tacitus*, for example, was slow but steady ; J. Brook-Smith's *Arithmetic* had a long career ; E. A. Abbott's *Shakespearian Grammar* and Hales's *Longer English Poems* sell to this day, and, with the Education Act of 1870 quickening the general extension of educational publishing to secondary and primary schools, the success of Sonnenschein and Meiklejohn's series, *Teaching to Read*, was a sign of an enduring change. In order to pursue this policy, it was, however, necessary to endure initial losses and to hold on without slackening of confidence. That Alexander Macmillan and Craik had the resources and the nerve for this is very clearly proved, not in their books only, but in their establishment of a scientific journal from which no profit came, or could reasonably have been expected, in its early years.

The idea was put out by Norman Lockyer, the astronomer

and spectroscopist, in 1868. Huxley, Tyndall and nearly all the leading men of science of that day promised their support. Alexander, convinced that science would benefit by the devotion of a journal to it, did not hesitate. As he had helped Masson, so he now helped Lockyer by calling upon his scientific friends, by publishing the paper, as *Nature* itself has lately recorded, " for several decades at a financial loss " and, above all, by giving to the editor an absolute editorial independence. The risk was not small. *The Natural History Review*, in spite of Huxley's labours for it, had failed in 1865. *The Reader*, a weekly less highly specialized than the *Review*, had struggled for a little while and perished. Lockyer had been science editor of *The Reader*. The reasons underlying his persistence and the principles of the new journal have been well expressed by Sir Richard Gregory, as President of the British Association. " The more contacts Lockyer could find between science and the public mind, the better he was pleased. With Huxley and Tyndall, he combined scientific authority with literary power. . . . They were not only skilled in the descriptive exposition of scientific knowledge, but also militant advocates of the aims and claims of scientific inquiry in fields in which it was then regarded as an intruder. . . . It was to assert the rights of science to an honoured place in national service, as well as its responsibilities in the development of natural resources, both intellectual and material, that *Nature* was founded." This linking of science with the community's life was set out as the journal's first intention ; the second was " to aid scientific men themselves by giving early information of all advances made in any branch of material knowledge throughout the world and by affording them an opportunity of discussing the various scientific questions which arise from time to time."

The battle for the recognition of science as a means to truth and against the suspicion and prejudice with which it was then attacked has long ago been won and *Nature* has played an honourable part in winning it. It might even be said that the balance of public favour has swung dangerously far and that one of the duties of such a journal has become that of using its influence to restore equilibrium in the public mind, to prevent charlatanry from masquerading under the cloak of science, and to make clear that to treat men of science as witch-doctors, alone competent to direct policy and morals, is itself unscientific. There is genuine peril, both to the community and to the scientific interest, in the possibility that a vulgarization of science in men's thought may combine with the excessive claims sometimes made for it to provoke against it a reaction comparable with the reaction against religion often produced by the excesses of priestcraft. However that may be and however the relationship of *Nature* to the general public may be affected by changing times, its function as what Sir Richard calls " an intelligence service " among men of science themselves has been continuous. After its foundation, specialization, and so the need for a means of contact between specialists, steadily increased. The first number (November 4th, 1869) contained a free translation by Huxley of Goethe's rhapsody on the wonder and mystery of Nature with comments which compared the permanence of the poet's vision with the necessarily changing theories of the natural philosophers. It contained also accounts of the fertilization of winter-flowering plants, of a recent eclipse of the sun, of scientific teaching in schools, of a meeting of German naturalists and physicians at Innsbruck, and an answer to those who held that the Suez Canal would soon be filled up by silt carried eastward from the Nile. Important papers contributed to scientific societies at home and abroad were summarized in a way that foreshadowed the journal's continuing policy of swift and thorough intercommunication, and won recognition of it as a medium for the announcement of new discoveries.

On September 29th, 1892, Lord Rayleigh described experiments made by him on the densities of nitrogen gas — experiments which, after Sir William Ramsay's association with Lord Rayleigh, led to the extraction of argon from the atmospheric air. Two years later, Sir William Ramsay announced in *Nature* that a gas extracted by him from a mineral had been identified by Sir William Crookes as an element, helium, previously unknown on earth, though Lockyer himself, twenty-seven years earlier, had found it in the sun and named it. So *Nature*, sustained by the publisher who had founded it, justified and at last established itself. In the middle 'nineties, after nearly thirty years of life, it began at last to pay its way. Lockyer edited it for fifty years, and Sir Richard Gregory from 1919 until the year of Munich, when A. J. V. Gale and L. J. F. Brimble jointly succeeded him. In 1943, they were able to write that " financial problems do not exist " and to add that " to-day as much as ever, if *Nature* feels that, in the interests of science, any book, whether published by Macmillan's or not, should receive adverse criticism, then it gets it." The two statements, taken together, are good to read in a naughty world. Alexander, losing money on the new venture, would have smiled if he could have read them in the year of the Franco-Prussian war.

Instead, he was at that time, or soon afterwards, called upon to face a new problem. That he grasped its full significance no one will pretend. It is to the point that he did not, and yet behaved with generosity and discretion.

The story had begun a little earlier. In the summer of 1868, he received from John Morley a report on the manuscript of a novel, *The Poor Man and the Lady*, by Thomas Hardy, an unknown writer twenty-eight years old. Morley said :

A very curious and original performance : the opening

pictures of the Christmas Eve in the tranter's house are really of good quality ; much of the writing is strong and fresh. But there crops up in parts a certain rawness of absurdity that is very displeasing, and makes it read like some clever lad's dream : the thing hangs too loosely together. There is real feeling in the writing, though now and then it is commonplace in form as all feeling turning on the insolence and folly of the rich in face of the poor is apt to sound : (e.g. p. 338). If the man is young, there is stuff and promise in him : but he must study form and composition, in such writers as Balzac and Thackeray, who would I think come as natural masters to him.

For queer cleverness and hard sarcasm — e.g. p. 280 — a little before and after : p. 333-p. 352. For cynical description, half worthy of Balzac, pp. 358-9.

Alexander took time to consider this and read the book himself. On August 10th he wrote to the author a letter which, though a few sentences from it referring to Thackeray have already been quoted, is worth giving at length as an example of his method :

I have read through the novel you were so good as to send me, with care and with much interest and admiration, but feeling at the same time that it has what seem to me fatal drawbacks to its success, and what, I think, judging the writer from the book itself, you would feel even more strongly — its truthfulness and justice.

Your description of country life among working men is admirable, and, though I can only judge of it from the corresponding life in Scotland, which I knew well when young, palpably truthful. Your pictures of character among Londoners, and especially the upper classes, are sharp, clear, incisive, and in many respects true, but they are wholly dark — not a ray of light visible to relieve the darkness, and therefore exaggerated and untrue in their result. Their frivolity, heartlessness, selfishness are great and terrible, but there are other sides, and I can hardly conceive that they would do otherwise than what you seek to avoid, " throw down the volume in disgust." Even the worst of them would hardly, I think, do things that you describe them as doing. For instance, is it conceivable that any man, however base and soul-corrupted, would do as you make the Hon. Guy Allancourt do at the close, accept an estimate for his daughter's tomb — *because it cost him nothing* ? He had already so far broken through the prejudices of his class as to send for Strong in the hope of saving his daughter's life. Then is it at all possible that a public body would *in public* retract their award on the grounds you make them avow in the case of the Palace of Hobbies Company ?

The utter heartlessness of *all* the conversation you give in drawing-rooms and ball-rooms about the working-classes, has *some* ground of truth, I fear, and might justly be scourged, as you aim at doing, but your chastisement would fall harmless from its very excess. Will's speech to the working men is full of wisdom — (though, by the way, would he have told his own story in public, being, as you describe him, a man of substantially good taste ?) — and you there yourself give grounds for condemning very much that is in other parts of the book. Indeed, nothing could justify such a wholesale blackening of a class but large and intimate knowledge of it. Thackeray makes them not greatly better in many respects, but he gave many redeeming traits and characters ; besides, he did it all in a light, chaffy way that gave no offence — and, I fear, did little good — and he soothed them by describing the lower class, which he knew nothing of and did not care to know, as equally bad when he touched them at all. He meant fun, you " *mean mischief.*" " Dukes and duchesses and all the kit are humbugs, society is based on humbug, but it's rather pleasant and amusing, when you can get pleasant dinners and nice wines, and everybody is the same — it's all natural. When we can't pay our tailor and he duns us, and won't give us another coat, or when we have to dine off cold mutton, and perhaps not enough of that, we don't like it, but let us wait our turn." That was his tone ; but then, he added, and with truth, " there are many of us who wouldn't grudge giving a poor fellow a dinner, or even a five pound note, when it did not greatly inconvenience us — and even when it did some of us." I don't think Thackeray's satire did much good ; indeed, I fear it did harm. He was in many respects a really good man, but he wrote in a mocking tone that has culminated in the *Saturday Review* tone, paralysing noble effort and generous emotion. You seem in grim earnest, and, as I said, " mean mischief," and I like your tone infinitely better. But it seems to me that your black wash will not be recognised as anything more than ignorant misrepresentation. Of course, I don't know what opportunities you have had of seeing the class you deal with. My own experience of fashionables is very small, and probably the nature of my business brings me into contact with the best of the class when I do meet them. But it is inconceivable to me that any considerable number of human beings — God's creatures — could be so bad without going to utter wreck in a week.

Of the story itself I hardly know what to say. I should fear it is very improbable, and would be looked on as a sort of Reynolds' Miscellany affair, though your really admirable handling often gives a certain dignity and power that greatly redeems it. Much of the detail struck me as strained and unnatural. The scene in the church at midnight has poetical qualities — but could it happen ? Then is it within the range of likelihood that *any* gentleman would pursue his wife at midnight and *strike* her ? Though you give a good deal about the family life afterwards, there is nothing to justify that very exceptional scene. It is too palpably done to bring about the meeting of the lovers.

Much of the writing seems to me admirable. The scene in Rotten Row — seen as it is and described by an outsider — is full of real power and insight. And the characters, on the whole, seem to me finely conceived and presented. The fault of the book, as it seems to me, is that it lacks the *modesty of nature* of fact. *Romeo and Juliet* and *Hamlet* have many unnatural scenes, but Shakespeare put them in foreign countries, and took the stories from old books. When he was nearer home and his own time you don't find such things in his writing. King Cophetua and the beggar-maid made a pretty tale in an old ballad ; but make a story in which the Duke of Edinburgh takes in lawful wedlock even a private gentleman's daughter ! One sees in the papers accounts of gentlemen's daughters running away with their fathers' grooms, but you are not in that region. Given your characters, could it happen in the present day ? The " modesty of nature " takes into account *all* the conditions.

You see I am writing to you as to a writer who seems to me of, at least potentially, considerable mark, of power and purpose. If this is your first book I think you ought to go on. May I ask if it is, and — you are not a lady, so perhaps you will forgive the question — are you young ?

I have shown your MS. to one friend, whose judgment coincides with my own — I wish to show it to another man of a different stamp of mind, who knows more of the upper class than either, and is yet a very noble fellow, that I may get his view as to whether it would do with modifications. Would you be willing to consider any suggestions ?

P.S.—I have just got my friend to write his opinion in his own words, and I enclose it. I mean the one who has already read the MS.

Hardy waited a month exactly ; then, as the silence continued, wrote :

BOCKHAMPTON, DORCHESTER, *Sept.* 10, 1868

DEAR SIR,

I have become anxious to hear from you again. As the days go on, and you do not write, and my production begins to assume that small and unimportant shape everything one does assumes as the time and mood in which one did it recedes from the present, I almost feel that I don't care what happens to the book, so long as something happens. The earlier fancy, that *Hamlet* without Hamlet would never do turns to a belief that it would be better than closing the house.

I wonder if your friend meant the building up of a story, and not English composition, when he said I must study composition. Since my letter, I have been hunting up matter for another tale, which would consist entirely of rural scenes and humble life, but I have not courage enough to go on with it till something comes of the first.

Faithfully yours

THOMAS HARDY

To this he added a postscript so gentle and, in the light of after-events, so deeply moving, as to make the reader marvel at the bullying arrogance of certain little writers whose letters prove them to be without modesty or patience. " Would you mind suggesting," Hardy added, " the sort of story you think I could do best, or any literary work I should do well to go on upon ? " That was Alexander's reward for having written as he did. Never has a correspondence done greater credit to author and publisher. Unfortunately Alexander's reply is not to be found and two or three of Hardy's letters are missing. All we know is that Hardy took back his manuscript for revision, sent it again to Macmillan's late in November and called for a verdict in December, when the book was refused. Alexander felt that *The Poor Man and the Lady* was unsuited to his own list, but he did not fail, as Morley had not failed, to remark the writer's quality. He gave him an introduction to Frederick Chapman of Chapman and Hall, with whom, after an unpromising interview, the manuscript was left. When in January 1869 Hardy next came to London, it was to Macmillan's he went, though his story had been rejected there. Alexander suggested — perhaps with less than his ordinary discernment — that the young man should try to have articles accepted by the reviews, and Morley offered him an introduction to the editor of the *Saturday*. No doubt Hardy was glad enough ; for many years he was, in his own eyes, above all else a craftsman looking for employment ; never was a great artist less of an intellectual snob ; but he was at heart a poet and a story-teller, not a controversialist, and when Chapman offered to publish the book if he were guaranteed against loss, Hardy accepted, and waited in Dorset for the glory of his first proofs. To his astonishment they did not come. Instead he was invited to London to see the publisher's reader, who he discovered was George Meredith. Chapman's were not attempting to repudiate their agreement ; they were prepared to carry it out ; but Meredith urged that it was not in Hardy's interest to appear before the public with so sweeping and unsparing a satire as his first novel, and, as Mrs. Hardy has told us in her biography, suggested that he might soften it or, better still, drop it altogether and write another without any similar purpose and with a more intricate plot.

Hardy took his manuscript home. What became of it he could not afterwards remember. Sensitive and amenable, overawed perhaps by the high company he had been keeping in London, he took Meredith's advice without a grain of salt and wrote *Desperate Remedies*, a work with a plot of fantastic complexity. He was disappointed by the failure of his first manuscript to please but neither embittered nor deterred. It is no secret that in writing of her husband's early life, Mrs. Hardy was the transcriber of his own opinions, and she says of this incident that the great thing was that " a first and probably very crude manuscript by an unknown young man, who had no connection with the press, or with literary circles, was read by a most experienced publisher, and by two authors among the most eminent in letters of their time." That has the ring of Hardy's own proud modesty.

Accordingly, even before *Desperate Remedies* was finished, he sent it to Alexander with the final chapters still in draft. This was on March 5th, 1870, two days before he went to St. Juliot Rectory where he was to meet his future wife for the first time. A month passed. Then John Morley reported :

Shews decided talent for invention and construction, the plot being complex and absolutely impossible, yet is worked out with elaborate seriousness and consistency. The dialogue is good, and there is a general firmness and closeness of texture about the style.

But the story is ruined by the disgusting and absurd outrage which is the key to its mystery. The violation of a young lady at an evening party, and the subsequent birth of a child, is too abominable to be tolerated as a central incident from which the action of the story is to move. After reflection, I don't see how this could be modified in any way.

There are also some scenes (e.g. between Miss Aldclyffe and her new maid in bed) wh: are highly extravagant.

Yet the book shows *power* — at present of a violent and undisciplined kind.

Don't touch this — but beg the writer to discipline himself to keep away from such incidents as violation — and let us see his next story.

(J. M.)

The book was refused on April 5th. Hardy paid Tinsley £75 to publish *Desperate Remedies*. Of five hundred copies printed, three hundred and seventy were sold, and the author lost a third of his money.

What would he attempt next ? The result of following Meredith's advice had not been fortunate, for it had led him to exaggerate his tendency towards elaborate contrivances of plot, and he had the good sense to fall back upon the natural resources of his own countryside. When the new book was done, he sent it neither to Chapman nor to Tinsley, but, on August 7th, 1871, again to Macmillan's :

GENTLEMEN,

I have sent by railway the manuscript of a tale called " Under the Greenwood Tree."

It is entirely a story of rural life, and the attempt has been to draw the characters humorously, without caricature. General reasons have induced me to try my hand on a story wholly of this tone — one reason being some reviews of a late novel of mine — (in its leading features of a different nature from the present). In that story the rustic characters and scenery had very little part, yet to my surprise they were made very much of by the reviews. The *Athenaeum* said " the characters are often exceedingly good. . . the parish clerk ' a sort of Bowdlerized rake ' who refers to the time ' before he took orders ' is really almost worthy of George Eliot. . . . We see no reason why the author should not write novels but little, if at all inferior to the best of the present generation." The *Spectator* said " there is an *unusual* and *very* happy facility in catching and fixing phases of peasant life — in producing for us, not the manners and language only but the tone of thought . . . and simple humour of consequential village worthies, and gaping village rustics. So that we are irresistibly reminded of the paintings of Wilkie and still more perhaps of those of Teniers, etc. The scenes allotted to these humble actors are few and slight but they indicate powers that might, and ought to be extended largely in this direction." They then animadverted on the plot — though, such is the contradictoriness of reviews — this was the element which received the most unqualified praise in the *Morning Post*.

This, however, has nothing to do with the present tale. The accessories of one scene in it may possibly be recognised by you as appearing originally in a tale submitted a long time ago (which never saw the light). They were introduced advisedly, as giving a good background to the love portion.

I trust that your opinion of the work may be favourable, but in any case I shall be extremely glad to have your remarks on the MS.

Faithfully yours,

THOMAS HARDY.

This time it was Malcolm Macmillan who replied for his father. It seems that Alexander was unaware of Tinsley's ill-fated publication of *Desperate Remedies*, for Malcolm asked for the title of the novel already published to which Hardy's letter had referred. Hardy diligently collected his press-cuttings and a week later (August 17th, 1871) replied from Bockhampton :

SIR,
     I have delayed my reply till I could send you perfect copies of the reviews which appeared — the extracts sent having been taken from notes I made in my pocketbook at the time. The novel was *Desperate Remedies* and the MS. was submitted to you in the first place.

If you have time to read the reviews you will perceive

that each takes for commendation a different element, and that they were therefore useless as guides to me for my second story. It seemed however that upon the whole a pastoral story would be the *safest* venture.

The article in the *Spectator* seemed strange enough to me — my object in the story having been *simply* to construct an intricate puzzle which nobody should guess till the end — and the characters were, to myself, mere puppets or pegs to weave the work upon — without reality or character enough in them to warrant their being denounced for want of moral attributes — the villain being in fact just about as human as the giants slain by Jack, and capable of corrupting to the same degree. This the *Spectator* did not see — or would not, and produced an article which contradicts itself, most noticeably. A novel which was good enough to justify two columns of lauded quotation could not possibly be so bad as to warrant opening remarks that are really little else than personalities. Still, being on the weaker side, I thought it just as well not to dabble in plot again at present, even though both *Athenaeum* and *M. Post* thought the " power " lay there.

Yours faithfully,

Thomas Hardy.

From this point onwards, the history of the MS. is of particular interest because only during the preparation of this centenary volume has it become clear. Mrs. Hardy's biography offered an explanation which, since she offered it, was probably the one accepted by Hardy's own memory in his later years, though the letters themselves invalidate it. Morley was favourable :

The work in this story [he said in his report] is extremely careful, natural and delicate, and the writer deserves more than common credit for the pains which he has taken with his style and with the harmony of his construction and treatment. It is a simple and uneventful sketch of a rural courtship, with a moderate and reserved climax of real delicacy of idea. The writer is wanting in the fine poetic breath wh gives such a charm to George Sand's work in the same kind, but he has evidently a true artistic feeling, if it is somewhat in excess the feeling of a realist.

The opening scenes at the cottage on the Xmas Eve are quite twice as long as they ought to be, because the writer has not sufficient sparkle and humour to pass off such minute and prolonged description of a trifle. — *This part should decidedly be shortened.*

It would only, I suppose, make a one-volume story. I don't prophesy a large market for it, because the work is so delicate as not to hit every taste by any means. But it is good work, and would please people whose taste is not ruined by novels of exaggerated action or forced ingenuity. The writer wd do well —

1. To study George Sand's best work.
2. To shut his ears to the fooleries of critics, as his letter to you proves he does not do.
3. To beware of letting *realism* grow out of proportion to his *fancy*.

On September 11th, Malcolm Macmillan forwarded a copy of this to the author :

Sir,

We send you herewith a criticism of your MS. story by an accomplished critic, to whom we have submitted it. We think from what you said, that you will be glad of this ; but hope that you will not object to waiting a little longer, before we decide finally about taking the story.

Let us assure you again that we shall give careful attention to the question, and that so favourable a judgment from a critic, whom we have found most trustworthy makes us feel strongly inclined to avail ourselves of your offer.

We are, Sir,
Your obedient Ser[ts]
MACMILLAN & CO.
per M. K. M.

This unquestionably is the letter referred to by Mrs. Hardy in her *Early Life*, for she quotes from it. She says :

" The pages of this idyll — at first intended to be called

The Mellstock Quire but altered to *Under the Greenwood Tree* because titles from poetry were in fashion just then — were dispatched to the Messrs. Macmillan some time that same autumn, and in due course Hardy received from them a letter which, events having rendered him sensitive, he read to mean that the firm did not wish to have anything to do with his " Rural Painting of the Dutch School," although they said that " they felt strongly inclined to avail themselves of his offer of it " ; hence he wrote to them to return the MS. This was an unfortunate misunderstanding. It was not till its acceptance and issue by another publishing-house the year after that he discovered they had never declined it, and indeed would have been quite willing to print it a little later on.

They had taken the trouble to enclose when writing about the tale the opinion of the ' accomplished critic ' to whom they had submitted it. . . ."

But it cannot have been true that Hardy misunderstood Malcolm Macmillan's letter of September 11th or that he then asked for the return of his manuscript, for on October 14th, 1871, he wrote from St. Juliot Rectory, Boscastle :

GENTLEMEN,
I am hoping to hear from you again. I was glad to receive the favourable judgments on my story enclosed in your last, and still more to hear that you were disposed to make some arrangement concerning it. The scene alluded to as being too long might of course be shortened as suggested.
Yours obedly.
THOMAS HARDY.

My *Desperate Remedies* was favourably reviewed in the *Saturday* of Sept. 30.
The above is my address till Oct. 30.

Here for a long time there was nothing but mystery, for the index to the book in which the letters for 1871 were copied gave no clue to any further letter to Hardy. It seemed, however, so unlikely that Alexander or Malcolm

would have left the matter there that the faded tissue-paper
leaves of the letter-book itself were carefully examined, and
they disclosed a misty page that had almost failed to take
the ink. The name at the head of the letter dated Oct.
18, 1871, was illegible, and the indexer had ignored it.
Deciphered as accurately as possible, it read as follows :

MY DEAR MR. HARDY,

I read through your story when I was down at
Brighton for a short holiday, carefully. There is really much
charming writing in it, and the characters are clearly defined
and well given. But I think the public will find the tale very
slight and rather unexciting. The first 50 or 60 pages too
are really rather tedious and should at least be shortened by
about one half.

It is difficult to know in what form it would best attract
the public. It is too small for a circulating library and if one
makes it a small price to attract sale to the general public a
large number of copies are needed to pay.

We could not venture on it now, as our hands are full of
Christmas books ; besides it is hardly a good time for
"Under the Greenwood Tree." But if you should not
arrange otherwise before the spring I should like to have the
opportunity of deciding as to whether we could do it for an
early summer or spring book. I return the MS.

Yours very truly,

A. MACMILLAN.

How Hardy came to believe that his book had been definitely
refused or that he had asked for the manuscript's return is
still unexplained. All we know is that the manuscript lay
idle until Tinsley, meeting Hardy, asked for another book
and paid thirty pounds for the copyright — to sell it back
later for £300. To which should be added that Macmillan's
relationship with Hardy was unimpaired. When he and
his first wife lived at Tooting from 1878 to 1881, they were
friends of Alexander and his family, and visited at Knapdale.
The second Mrs. Hardy says that it was at a garden-party
there that a thunderstorm broke which served for a scene

in *The Laodicean*, and that a scene in *Jude* was suggested by Margaret Macmillan's using a looking-glass to let Hardy watch a sunset when he was lying ill. In 1884, while he was writing *The Mayor of Casterbridge*, he arranged to supply a long serial to *Macmillan's Magazine*. This, *The Woodlanders*, appeared two years later and was published by the firm as a book on March 15th, 1887, to be followed a year later by the *Wessex Tales*.

Alexander's wife had died on July 21st, 1871. Their daughter, Margaret, Mrs. Louis Dyer, has recalled that her mother, during her last illness, liked to be kept in touch with current affairs — the Franco-German war, the Tichborne trial — and to have Archibald Forbes's letters in the *Daily News* read to her. " These readings took place in the late afternoon, and my father would come in from town and, having set aside all thoughts of business, sit and chat quietly to my mother as if he had not a care in the world." The success of the firm had never been so great, the American branch was in its infancy, and in May 1872 Macmillan's moved again, this time to larger premises that had been built at 29 and 30 Bedford-street. In the autumn Alexander married Miss Emma Pignatel, a former schoolfellow of his children's governess, and was persuaded by her — and he needed persuasion, for he was no European traveller — to make his first journey to Italy.

PART THREE

THE END OF THE OLD ORDER
1872–90

***

CHAPTER SEVEN

John Morley's Influence

" A Macmillan Book "—Receptions in Bedford-street—Walter Pater —Grove and Green—Lewis Carroll again—Henry James— " English Men of Letters "

HE story which began as the story of two brothers and became that of the survivor now gradually shifts its emphasis. Alexander remains its central figure, but, as his own and his brother's sons come into the firm, he begins, almost imperceptibly at first, to withdraw from it and to broaden the basis of its control. By the end of the 'eighties he has ceased to be active in the business, and the period intervening between his second marriage and his seventieth year is a period of transference.

As Craik, Grove and the younger Macmillans took more and more on their shoulders, it was in the readers' reports, not in Alexander's personal correspondence, that the firm's view of manuscripts was chiefly expressed. But what Alexander handed down — and nothing is more difficult to pass without spilling from one pair of hands to several — was a tradition or, more truly, a marked character which bound the parts of the firm together in such a way that all who had a share in its work were able to feel, though they might not so easily define, what was and what was not " a Macmillan book." There are exotics in the catalogues, particularly in the earlier ones. A book on billiards by a Q.C. ; *Ye Hole in Ye Walle*, a merrie metrical and monastical romaunce ; *A Guide to the Unprotected in Matters of Property and Income*, by a Banker's Daughter ; and, later in date, *A Lyttel Booke of Nonsense*, containing ancient woodcuts interpreted by modern limericks, conform to no evident rule. They were freaks published at a venture without, it may be supposed, much hope of endurance, though the Banker's Daughter was blessed with five editions ; but, in general, the catalogues, year by year, have a consistency of their own — or the kind of related inconsistency that goes to the making of an individual character. Endurance is the aim ; the deliberately topical, unless there is a promise of endurance in it, is little sought after. This being granted as a basic principle, it is interesting to observe the application and, sometimes, the misapplication of it. Macmillan's had more than a hint of Hardy's potentiality, were by no means blind, as Morley's reports and Alexander's correspondence prove, to the as yet ill-disciplined strength of him. Were they therefore wrong to refuse his early work ? Ought they to have taken it, and borne what loss there was, and nursed him ? The hasty answer is that they were wrong, and, if any man reading *Desperate Remedies* will swear that he would have known by this evidence only that the writer was a great artist, then let him cast his stone. It is a duty of a great publisher not to shut the gate against a great artist and to recognize the authentic knock. Nevertheless, even when the knock is recognized, though the gambler's answer would be to secure the newcomer at all costs, the right and patient reply may be : " Though you are our man, this book is not yet our book. In your interest and in ours, wait a little while. If you decide otherwise, we will not complain, but introduce you to another publisher, and take the risk of losing you, and wait." This was, in effect, the reply given to Hardy. His later coming to the Macmillans suggests that he did not condemn it. That a publisher is found to have rejected the early manuscript of genius is not in itself proof of blindness ;

the real, damnable blindness consists in refusing a great book, and a lesser, debatable blindness in failure to recognize the sun through a morning mist.

There were receptions at Bedford-street in those days. Some of the old names appear — Edward Dicey's and Sebastian Evans's for example. Gladstone came, Andrew Lang, A. J. Butler, Wallace, Dilke, Verrall, the Lane-Pooles ; Trollope, Henry James, Oscar Wilde — it is a varied list with evidence in it of the changing times. Hughes is still there, Randall Davidson puts in an appearance, but the general impression is at once less hearty and less theological than in the past. Nevertheless, if John Fiske's experience was typical, these receptions were hearty enough. An American historian and a Positivist, he had been recommended by Herbert Spencer in 1873 to take his *Outlines of Cosmic Philosophy* to Macmillan's. The summer of 1879 found him in London on his second visit to England, and on a June evening he went after dinner to one of Alexander's parties. " It was," he said, " a *stupendous* affair. . . . There were at least 400 people there I should think. What did the bonny old boy do but throw his arms about my neck and hug me like a grizzly bear ! " Alexander pretended to reproach him for not having announced his coming to England and Fiske began to apologize, whereupon " the old fellow hit me an awful thump between the shoulder-blades and said : ' De'il tak it, mon : I shall have ta forgie ye, for ye're sach a gude boy.' " The visitor was introduced to " a lot of celebrities," all of whom were praising *Cosmic Philosophy* when suddenly " Macmillan came up and said : ' Fiske, here's Gladstone a-askin' ta be antradooced ta ye.' . . . Well, we had a high old P.M."[1] The phrase refers to the evening, not to Gladstone, who was not to be Prime Minister for a second time until after the Midlothian

[1] *The Letters of John Fiske*, edited by his daughter Ethel F. Fisk (The Macmillan Company, New York), 1940.

campaign in the following spring. Even so it is a summary of what must have been a very odd scene.

Not only entertainment but publishing also was less theological than it had been. Except for Farrar's perhaps, there was a slackened enthusiasm for volumes of sermons. Laymen and women fell to the making of symposia on aspects of belief, and the professional battles of theology had neither their old grandeur nor, indeed, their old audience. Philosophers and logicians multiplied, the psychologists arrived, and economists, once single spies, gathered in battalions for internecine war. The encyclopaedic Marshall's became a predominant name. Educational books reached out yet further into the elementary field. Fiction, so far as the Macmillans were concerned, though kindly enough to them at the time, seems a trifle bleak to us. William Black, George Fleming, Mrs. Oliphant, Frances Hodgson Burnett, Mrs. Molesworth and Charlotte M. Yonge — the two last have at any rate survived.

And there was Henry James. Like Walter Pater, he proposed himself. " Dear Sir," Pater had written from Brasenose on June 29th, 1872,

I send you by this post the papers of which I spoke when I called on you in London and must apologise for not having sent them before.

The paper in MS. has not been published hitherto, that on Winckelmann appeared in the *Westminster Review* and the other four in the *Fortnightly*. I enclose a table of the proposed series which I hope to complete by the end of the long Vacation, with a short Preface. I think in the form in which I should like the essays to appear they would make a book of about 300 pages. Of the ten essays five only will have appeared before. With many thanks for the kindness with which you have consented to consider my proposal,

I am, dear Sir,

Faithfully yours

W. H. PATER.

This was a modest introduction of *The Renaissance* or, strictly, *Studies in the History of the Renaissance*, which, published in 1873, was to have more influence than any other single book on the Aesthetic Movement in England. Alexander wasted no time. Within two days of receiving Pater's letter, he accepted, proposing an octavo volume of which the publisher should carry the risk and the author share the profit. There was a little trouble ahead, interesting rather for the manner than for the matter of it. Like all good authors, Pater cared for the outward appearance of his book and not only busied himself in the choice of paper and type but suggested that it should be bound " in paste-board with paper back and printed title," thus reverting to an earlier custom which the coming of cloth and gilt-lettering had superseded. It would, he thought, be " economical and very pretty " and " be much approved by many persons of taste, among whom the sale of the book would probably in the first instance be." Covers of greyish blue and a paper back of olive green were what he wanted ; " nothing could be prettier or more simple." Four days afterwards Alexander went to Oxford to attend a funeral, intending to take Brasenose and the binding on his way, but his train was an hour late, he could not visit Pater and the grave. He had to write on his return to London. Paper boards and labels were, he said, unpractical. Booksellers would be reluctant to stock such a book. " Besides I don't like it any way. It is like recurrence to the *fig leaf*. The cloth and gilt is infinitely more useful and surely not less beautiful. Please don't wish for it." But Pater did wish for it. " I was disappointed at the contents of your letter," he wrote. If he were to see Alexander, he could, he was sure, persuade him, and, having already used the word " pretty " as we seldom do, he now used " artistic " with a freedom from our genteel inhibitions that is illuminating in him and gives a keen flavour of the early 'seventies to his correspondence. At the same time, he resisted Alexander's fig-leaf imputation that he was old-fashioned. " For a book on art," he wrote, " to be bound quite in the ordinary way, is, it seems to me, behind the times ; and the difficulty of getting a book bound in cloth so as to be at all artistic, and indeed not quite the other way, is very great." The debate continued. It says much for Pater's moderation that he did not flare up, for there was some asperity in Alexander's answer, in which he reverted to the fig-leaf and put an unmistakable sting even into his seeming concession. " But I will most gladly cede my tastes to yours as far as possible," he wrote, but added : " I send you by this post a book in a style of binding which I devised for the author, and which he liked. His tastes were ' artistic.' He is an intimate friend of Mr. Burne-Jones and others who think in that line. . . . Perhaps we can meditate on the binding a little further." What did Pater think of this ? The book was in proof. Perhaps he thought the struggle not worth pursuing. Certainly he surrendered with grace on the following day :

BRASENOSE, *Nov.* 13*th*, 1872

DEAR MR. MACMILLAN,

The volume you send seems to me a beautiful specimen of printing, and I should much like to have the same sort of paper. I like the black cloth cover, and think, with some modifications, about which I will write shortly, it will do very well for my book.

Believe me

Yours very truly

W. H. PATER.

So it came about that in February 1873 *The Renaissance* was being bound in green cloth.

There is an early hint, in the correspondence of 1873 with E. (Sir Roper) Lethbridge, of the future development of a business in India, and in 1874 Grove began work on his great

Dictionary of Music and Musicians, which was to appear in four volumes between December 1877 and May 1889, and remains, in its latest edition and with its supplementary volume, unchallenged in its own field. In the autumn, while Grove was setting out on his labour, J. R. Green, after five years of ill-health and long absences abroad, reaped the fruits of his. Grove and other advisers had been doubtful of the *Short History of the English People* but Alexander had believed in it and arranged with the author to buy it outright. Consequently Green received £300. When the book was published, *Fraser's Magazine* attacked it for inaccuracies, many of them trivial and already corrected by the time *Fraser's* article appeared, but its success was instantaneous. After 8000 copies had been sold, Alexander decided that he had made too good a bargain, sent for the contract in which Green assigned his copyright, destroyed it, and substituted for it a royalty agreement greatly and continuously to the advantage of the author and his heirs. Thirty-five thousand copies were sold in the first year.

The past was slipping away, the future appearing. F. D. Maurice was dead and now Charles Kingsley died ; seven years later his younger daughter, Mary, under the Macmillan imprint, was to make her mark as Lucas Malet with *Mrs. Lorimer*. Alexander's second son, George Augustin, came into the firm during January 1874, fresh from Eton and in his nineteenth year. In 1876, Daniel's eldest, Frederick, after five years' work in America, returned to London and settled down in Bedford-street. At the same time, there came in from outside the family William Jack, who remained a partner and an adviser on mathematical subjects until he accepted a Chair at Glasgow in 1879.

Lewis Carroll, who never allowed himself to be far absent from the minds of publisher, printer or binder, had reappeared conspicuously with *Through the Looking-Glass* (1871, dated 1872). It came through the press without mishap, but with Dodgson you were never safe, his genius for the discovery of error was infinitely retrospective, and in 1878 he observed, in a copy of the forty-second thousand, that both the Kings had vanished from the chess-diagram. This was present calamity — but how far back did it go ? A slip must at once be inserted, and if the Kings were found to have escaped long ago the fact must be advertised. When they had been caught again he turned his attention, moral and mathematical, to the conditions of the trade. His trouble was, first, that booksellers had the lion's share of what the public paid for a book, and, secondly, that their system of underselling one another was preposterous, as indeed it was. He calculated that, from the sale of a 6s. copy of *Alice*, the author received 1s. 2d., the publisher 10d. and the bookseller 2s. His view was that the author should have 2s. 2d., the publisher still 10d., and the bookseller be content with 1s. The suggestion that booksellers might, in these circumstances, refuse to stock his books did not intimidate him. In that case, he proposed to notify the public that they could obtain his works carriage free from the publisher. As a skirmish in the attack on the old discount system which Frederick Macmillan was to carry through to the Net Book Agreement, this outburst of Lewis Carroll's has its historical place. It has to be remembered that his books were, by his own wish, published " on commission " — that is to say at his own and not the publisher's risk. " A former pupil of mine," he said in one of his letters to the firm, " wants you to publish a book for him. He seems to be suffering from a nervous fear, not uncommon to authors, that publishers are an inscrutable race, who make money vanish as if by magic, and never render up any profit to their victims. What *other* publishers may do I know not : but I gave him full assurance that he was in good hands." What Lewis Carroll understood, though few others do so, is that in persuading a great house to publish for him on commission he was rarely fortunate. In fact, the Macmillans, and all other publishers of repute, avoid this form of contract unless there is exceptional reason for it. It is applicable to works of science or scholarship, sponsored by learned societies, from which honour but not profit is to be expected. In such cases, for the sake of prestige, the Macmillans have consented to publish on a basis of commission, or sometimes, in the public interest, at their own cost, but where there is a normal risk and a normal chance of profit they, and other publishers of standing, have generally preferred to make a half-profits or, nowadays, a royalty agreement with the author, the publisher bearing the production costs. If the book succeeds they make more ; if it fails, the author is exempt from the financial penalties of failure. An established writer who has capital and is prepared to back his own work will unquestionably profit financially if he can persuade a first-rate firm to act for him at his risk, but he will be troubled with a thousand cares — with binding and printing and advertising of which he has seldom a professional knowledge, and so, to save himself trouble, to release himself to write, he ordinarily accepts a royalty. Unless he has a delight in business, he does better to stick to his last. And a beginner is deluded if he supposes that all he has to do is to write a cheque in order to command the name, the services and the distributing organization of a publisher. If the book is good, the publisher will take the risk and the profit ; if it is bad, he will not, unless he is dishonest and a man of straw, accept the cheque. To this day, innocents with money and a manuscript walk in to St. Martin's-street, believing that a publisher who is paid will publish anything. As their books are always about the Great Pyramid or the more esoteric aspects of the prophet Ezekiel, they are naturally suspicious of worldly men, as the children of Light so often are. When their eager cheque is gently refused and it is suggested to them that they should leave their work to be considered on its merits, they imagine that Macmillan's can have no other motive than to steal their secret. Nothing will make them understand how rare, how rich in prestige, how gloriously unprofitable a book must be, or how powerful its author, before a publisher with a reputation to lose and money to invest will accept it " on commission."

Lewis Carroll was not only in good hands ; he was, while his books prospered, the most fortunate of men, for he appears to have delighted in the detail of production from which other writers wish to be exempt. As a boy he had provided earthworms with weapons in order that they might fight the more intelligently, and throughout his life he had, with an intense shyness, a passion for little changes, little inventions, oddities of all kinds. For *The Hunting of the Snark* (1876) he made a suggestion more practical than most of his. Plain white paper wrappers had hitherto been put upon his books. Now he asked that the title used lengthways on the spine of the book itself be repeated on the wrapper in sloping letters which might be easily read when the book stood upright on a shelf. This plan, which may claim a share in the ancestry of the elaborate wrapper now called a " jacket," made up most of the satisfaction that Carroll had out of *The Snark*, for reviewers were hard on it and buyers reluctant. But the author was undeterred. Books, ingenuities and trouble poured from him. When he wished to go to a theatre, Macmillan's were asked to buy the tickets — on the extreme right, if possible, because he was deaf in the right ear, and at all costs not in the centre of the first rows because, from there, his line of sight was interrupted by waving conductors. When he sent his watches to be mended, his publishers were asked to retrieve, and did retrieve them, by what he called " a trusty and resolute messenger." And he knew better than anyone else how to tie up parcels. He supplied a diagram, which long hung in the post-room at Bedford-street, showing how the string on all parcels should be, and how the string on all his parcels must be, knotted. This queer love of telling a lion how to roar and a cat how to lap milk grew upon him. *Doublets*, a word-puzzle of 1879, was to be priced at " Five Groats " and *Euclid and his Modern Rivals* ought, he thought, to have a few words added to its title to indicate that it was not a funny book. Dodgson and Carroll were becoming a little entangled. The binders, perhaps undesignedly, had their own back when, upon his asking for a dummy copy of *Doublets* (for he wished to invent more puzzles on its blank sheets), they filled the binding with pages from assorted works on religion — an incongruity that touched Dodgson-Carroll on the quick. For *Lawn Tennis Tournaments. The True Method of Assigning Prizes, with a proof of the Fallacy of the Present Method* (1883, price sixpence), he used his own name — " my usual course with *mathematical* books " — and mathematical it was indeed.

Having gone so far with this strange man — in many respects so likable and yet, with his itch for interference, so sharp an irritant — it is, perhaps, worth while to break chronological sequence and go with him to the end. *A Tangled Tale*, written at the request of Miss Yonge, was slashed by the reviewers and never accepted by the public as part of the canon. A reproduction of the manuscript book, *Alice's Adventures Under Ground*, upon which the first *Alice* had been based, contained the author's own illustrations, but had little success. Carroll blamed the uneven printing. *The Game of Logic* — a game with cards and counters — led him into corresponding distress : here it was the Oxford production that was at fault, and there had to be a reprint by Clay. Next he undertook a children's book, grimly named *Bumblebee Bogo's Budget*, written by " a Retired Judge " — a friend of his named Synge. He gave as much attention to it as to his own work — writing one morning to say that the author was anxious to have the book out and the next morning to explain that he would not have his trouble brought to nothing by Macmillan's hurrying to save a few days. When Carroll and Dodgson took in a partner and so could speak with three voices simultaneously, life in Bedford-street could not be tranquil. Worse was to come. In thousands of copies of his books he had inserted at the end of his list of works a " Caution " in which he had disavowed authorship of a story, *The Land of Idleness*, published in a magazine over his signature. He had not written it, the " Caution " explained ; he had done no more than forward it to the editor on behalf of a foreign lady, whose name he gave. Now, when it was too late, he found he had given the name of the wrong lady. There was no remedy but to insert thousands of erratum slips. Gradually, as the years pass, one begins to think that to Carroll erratum slips were a form of pleasurable vice.

Two hundred and fifty copies of *Curiosa Mathematica* appear to have come through unscathed, but the *Nursery Alice* was a disaster. The first printing was doomed to America for the reason already mentioned — that the colours were too bright ; America refused them ; nevertheless another ten thousand must be done. Then the covers were wrong : the thickness of the book had not been allowed for and the March Hare was out of centre. When all this had been put right, still the early copies were returned. They cracked when he opened them ; their leaves curled obstinately.

Of all this Carroll, not without protest, bore the cost, but he was not a little perturbed. His books were not selling. Neither *Sylvie and Bruno* nor *Sylvie and Bruno Concluded* fluttered the nurseries, and their author thought that the position might be saved if only a good morning paper could be induced to fold a leaflet about the book inside each copy of a day's issue. By June 1890, he felt that somehow he must have a larger share of the proceeds of his work. The whole problem was complicated by his having kept to his own special terms of sale to booksellers, though by this time the firm were applying the Net System to other publications. There was nothing for it — Dodgson had to amend the terms of sale printed in all his works.

It is pleasant to recall that, though he was never again to enjoy success comparable with that of *Alice*, and though, with the possible exception of his *Euclid*, none of his mathematical works was of much value to mathematicians, his devotion to logic brought him in the end some reward. *Symbolic Logic, Part I*, was a development of the *Game of Logic*. It appealed to people who had what would now be called a cross-word mind, and had much greater success than might have been expected. This was in 1896. Part Two was never published. The last work produced by the firm for Lewis Carroll was " a tale for tiny boys," *The Lost Plum Cake*, by E. G. Wilcox (his cousin, Mrs. Egerton Allen). In January 1898, he died. To study the record of his publishing adventures is to be persuaded that he would have been better — on all grounds except, possibly, those of enjoyment — to have held firm to authorship. He wasted his own and everyone else's time by his detailed wilfulness. He wrote so many letters about printing and binding and prices that he had little time left to write the books themselves. A publisher might have saved it for him. But not even a Scottish publisher could have cared as desperately as he — and desperately is the word — to give the public perfection. This was his theme-song, and his justification.

Nor must it be forgotten that he made, or intended to make, noble amends to his publishers, for Collingwood's *Life* quotes the following passage from a pamphlet explaining his trade terms entitled *The Profits of Authorship* : " The publisher contributes about as much as the bookseller in time and bodily labour, but in mental toil and trouble a great deal more. I speak with some personal knowledge of the matter, having myself, for some twenty years, inflicted on that most patient and painstaking firm, Messrs. Mac-

millan & Co., about as much wear and worry as ever publishers have lived through. The day when they undertake
a book for me is a *dies nefastus* for them. From that day till
the book is out — an interval of some two or three years on
an average — there is no pause in ' the pelting of the pitiless
storm ' of directions and questions on every conceivable
detail. To say that every question gets a courteous and
thoughtful reply — that they are still outside a lunatic
asylum — and that they still regard me with some degree of
charity — is to speak volumes in praise of their good temper
and of their health, bodily and mental."

It is very much in the tradition of the Snark that, although
the *Life* mentions this pamphlet as having been published
by Macmillan's in 1884, the bibliographers who faithfully
include it in their lists are also compelled to add that no copy
of it has ever been found.

While the sequel to *Alice* was winning its way, new stars
were rising. Alexander's youngest son, John Victor, who
was to marry F. D. Maurice's granddaughter and become
Bishop of Guildford, was born in May 1877 ; John Morley
was brewing the *English Men of Letters* Series ; and Henry
James was proposing a volume of critical essays : *French
Poets and Novelists*. Frederick Macmillan invited Henry
James to send the manuscript and to call. The essays, said
a report which seems to be in Morley's hand, were written
with excellent sense and in a thoroughly rational temper.
But " of charm, delicacy, finesse, they have none. They are
prosaic to the last degree, and *as criticism* not at all interesting,
I think, and to test my impression I took down a volume of
Sainte-Beuve. Mr. James, by such a test, must be called
mediocre. On the other hand, though the criticism as such
is not interesting, the subjects *are* particularly so. . . . When
all is said, I feel that the book might have some slight sale,
but it would certainly make no deep literary mark. There
would be no harm in printing it, but neither to literature

would there be any good. . . . It is honest scribble work
and no more." Nevertheless, Frederick Macmillan accepted
the book on August 22nd, 1877. The correspondence is
flat and unprofitable, with little of Henry James's character
in it. He wanted *The American*, already published in
America, to be issued here, but Grove broke down in his
attempt to read it. Henry James next brought *The Europeans*,
and there is a certain pathos in his acknowledgement of
the firm's acceptance of it. Even if the profits were only
moderate, he said, the book " will be a beginning of my
appearance before the British public as *the* novelist of the
future, destined to extract from the B.P. eventually (both for
himself and his publishers) a colossal fortune ! " The letter
is dated " 1878 " without month or day. Through all the
many volumes and the great collected edition, neither
fortune nor even her poor sister came with the honours.

Morley's own plan went on steadily. At the end of June
1877, he had written to Craik about schemes he had in mind.
One was the *English Men of Letters*, not yet spoken of by that
name, and the other, presumably, what became the *Twelve
English Statesmen*, for a little note of Morley's says : " Grove
suggests Gladstone for Pitt." To fit author to subject was
not easy and there is interest in watching Morley feel his
way. *Punch*'s notion of him as a chilly Jacobin has little
confirmation in the Macmillan legend. He came to the office
every Tuesday in the early days of his association with the
firm, and in the intervals would write brief notes to Alexander, Craik or Grove ; there is a warm friendliness, often
a geniality, in them which must have made them good to
receive. Nor while he edited the *Fortnightly* and Grove
Macmillan's was there a sign of rivalry between them ; they
exchanged comments, advice and even material itself with
generous freedom. It is not surprising that authors rallied
to his editorship. Nevertheless there were refusals and

difficulties — above all the difficulty of obtaining, from among those who accepted, what a theatrical manager would call a balanced cast. Among Morley's earliest choices was Arnold, but what would he choose ? " If Arnold chooses Shelley we must have him," but Arnold did not ; he did not appear in the series until, long afterwards, he was himself the subject of a volume by Herbert Paul ; and it was John Addington Symonds whom Morley found for the *Shelley*, which turned out to be a volume after Alexander's own heart. Mark Pattison, the Rector of Lincoln, was regarded as so valuable that Morley thought " we ought to give him *Milton*." Cotter Morison took *Gibbon*, Hutton *Scott*, Goldwin Smith *Wordsworth*, but he did not produce it and the subject went to F. W. H. Myers. Morley's original idea was that he himself should write of Swift, but he offered the task instead to Lord Coleridge who shied at it, wanted *Wordsworth*, accepted *Southey* and ended by doing none at all, leaving *Southey* to Dowden. By August 1877, with Nichol promised for *Byron* and Leslie Stephen for *Johnson*, Morley felt his list " would do for a launch provided we can only get *one* recognized divine, Caird or Dean Church. We need that for respectability's sake." Arnold was approached again without success. Church, hesitating between Dryden, Jeremy Taylor and Spenser, chose the last. There was hope of Froude. His own suggestion for a subject was Giraldus Cambrensis, and Morley inclined towards it, partly because there was " some advantage in having one faraway man of this sort," chiefly for Froude's name — " the highest respectability and the highest capacity — an impossible union, O my dear Macmillan ! " The chief difficulty was to find an author who would accept responsibility for Shakespeare. Morley's first suggestion had been Symonds, but soon he and Alexander were looking for a greater prize. Having paved the way through G. H. Lewes, Alexander went to see George Eliot. His account of his visit is evidence of the esteem in which he held her and of her own modesty. She did not at once say no ; she would think it over and write ; but repeated what Lewes had already suggested — that she had a dread of coming forward in her own person and passing judgement on authors. Lewes came to the door with Alexander, who was " by no means hopeless." He asked and received permission for Morley to send a formal invitation by letter. " But I think," he wrote to Morley, " it would be well that we should have our talk on Monday before you do write. My own feeling is that when you write you should name the sum we are willing to give her. It is clear that our *Prima Donna* must be paid on a different scale from the others — whether 3 or 5 times we must consider and consult." The result was a courteous refusal, but George Eliot spoke so well of the first books in the series when they appeared that the offer was unavailingly renewed. She read Hutton's *Scott* aloud to Lewes — and the *Johnson* and the *Gibbon* as well ; — such was the leisure or the energy of those days. " Although," Lewes reported, " Scott is to her an almost sacred name, she was so delighted with Hutton's largeness of feeling and sympathetic insight that, as she told a lady yesterday, ' she was in a glow all the time she read it.' " This, as well it might, meant much to Morley and to the Macmillans, but it brought them no nearer to a solution of the Shakespearian problem. Seeley was tried, but they would not go out into the highways and hedgerows ; Shakespeare must be done well or not at all, and in fact remained un-represented in the series until, long afterwards, Walter Raleigh's volume appeared. Though Morley himself was disappointed in William Black's *Goldsmith*, the early books were well received. Five were published in 1878, ten more in the following year. There were perils then of a kind not now to be looked for. Thackeray was a touchy subject ; there was to be no full or official life of him — " for good reasons, I daresay," wrote Morley ; Leslie Stephen indicated that he would not undertake so awkward a task, and Morley counted himself fortunate in having persuaded Trollope to accept it. Then, of T. H. Huxley's contribution, he confessed : " I am *a trifle* unhappy about *Hume*. It hath a savour of heresy in every page. However, I suppose the world is less sensitive in these things than it used to be, when it flew at a young author for making his printer use *the wrong case* in certain matters " — this was an allusion to his having himself been attacked for spelling God without a capital letter. He was unduly alarmed about Huxley, but now and then a manuscript, when it came in, distressed him. " I agree with you wholly about ——. It is most disappointing and truly dreary. The man cannot get off the ground. . . . I like him so much, that I'm sorry for this miscarriage. . . . Well, we have some strongish ones to come." Before the second year was out, the series, which amounted to thirty-nine volumes under Morley's editorship, was unquestionably and firmly established. Over twenty years later a second series, with Morley still to advise though not to edit, was begun with Leslie Stephen's *George Eliot* and, in recent years, new volumes have been added upon the advice of Sir John Squire.

CHAPTER EIGHT

Losses and Triumphs

The Shavian Puzzle—" John Inglesant "—Saintsbury and Marion Crawford—The Early 'Eighties—Shaw lost—" Robert Elsmere " lost—Alexander's Last Years

IN January 1880, Macmillan's reader — whether in this instance the report is Morley's is not sure — was set a puzzle by which the world has been a little distressed ever since. His attempt to solve it and his recognition of the strange quality of the mind that propounded it may arouse sympathy even to-day. " A 3 vol. novel," he wrote of *Immaturity* by G. B. Shaw. " I have given more than usual attention to this M.S., for it has a certain quality about it — not exactly of an attractive kind, but still not common. It is the work of a humourist and a realist, crossed, however, by veins of merely literary discussion. There is a piquant oddity about the situations now and then : and the characters are certainly not drawn after the conventional patterns of fiction. It is dry and ironic in flavour. . . . Recognizing all these things," he added, " I ask myself what it is all about : what is the key, the purpose, the meaning of a long work of this kind without plot or issue. . . . It is undoubtedly clever, but most readers would find it dry, unattractive, and too devoid of any sort of emotion. And then it is very long." Not satisfied with this and evidently troubled in his mind, Macmillan's adviser went back to the manuscript. " On reflecting over the MS. of Mr. Shaw," he wrote in a second opinion, " I am very doubtful of the expediency of publication," and the book, evidently with regret and misgiving, was refused. Within a year, G. B. Shaw submitted another, *The Irrational Knot* —

" a novel," the reader said, " of the most disagreeable kind. It is clearly the work of a man with a certain originality and courage of mind. There is nothing conventional either about the structure or the style ; and the characters have a curious flavour and ' sapidity ' about them. But the thought of the book is all wrong ; the whole idea of it is odd, perverse and crude. It is the work of a man writing about life, when he knows nothing of it. . . . So far as your publication is concerned, it is out of the question. There is too much of adultery and the like matters."

The wisdom or unwisdom of this judgement can be estimated only if it be considered in its relation to all the circumstances of the firm at that time. From one point of view they were plainly wrong, and it may be argued that they were the more wrong because what they did they did deliberately, being fully aware of the originality and courage of Shaw's mind. Alexander's decision must have been hard. Probably in the end he asked himself the final question that a publisher must ask when in doubt of policy and duty : " Do I *like* this book ? Is it the kind of risk that it will please me to take ? " His mind was bold and humorous ; it had never been unresponsive to fresh challenges ; but its very merits, though they would have bidden him admire, were of a sort to prevent his enjoying the Shavian attack. At that time, he was writing a preface to F. J. Church's translation of *The Trial and Death of Socrates* and was publishing *John Inglesant* — a novel that deservedly lives, by J. H. Shorthouse. These were his pleasures. Moreover he may well have decided that in this company and in the circumstances of that day, publication of *The Irrational Knot* by him would have been incongruous. It was good, but not so good even in its own kind as to justify a revolution of policy.

Shorthouse, a Birmingham chemical manufacturer of Quaker upbringing, had finished *John Inglesant* five years

earlier. Other publishers had refused it and not until 1880
had he printed a hundred copies for distribution to his
friends. When Smith Elder had said it was not their kind of
book, Shorthouse had let it rest until a Birmingham schoolmaster persuaded him to send a copy to Arthur Johnson at
Oxford, through whom it came into the hands of Mrs.
Humphry Ward. She was well equipped to see it as what it
is — a book which, in its merit of wisdom and its demerit
(which has merit also) of gentle, unforced and sometimes
somnolent narrative, is like none other in English. That it
is a great book no one will claim who is thinking in terms of
Balzac's energy or of Turgenev's perfection, but for those to
whom quietism is not a heresy it stands alone — lovable,
cool, speaking of good things, their own. Mrs. Humphry
Ward brought it to Alexander at Tooting. A report by
George Macmillan was wrong in saying that it " strikes no
chord " but shrewd in all else. " It is the work of a man
who, for one thing, knows how to write : the style is not
quite bright enough nor vivid enough, but it is the style of
literature and not the weak stuff to which one is accustomed
. . . but I doubt whether it would be widely popular . . .
it is interesting and romantic but strikes no chord." Alexander read and accepted it, but he had no more confidence
in its popularity than his son. It was for the printers, Clark
of Edinburgh, to grasp the truth. They printed beyond their
order at their own risk, and, when Macmillan's, surprised
by the public demand, telegraphed for a new impression,
were able instantly to supply the market. On August 16th,
Gladstone called on Alexander, " specially to thank me for
sending him *John Inglesant*, which he wished me to tell you
he thought a work of real genius and of a class which interests
him greatly." Manning, too, approved, smilingly safe-
guarding himself against the author's heresies. " I am
writing as a Literary Critic," he said, " not as a Catholic
Inquisitor. In the latter office, I should of course burn the

book and John Shorthouse. Happily I have no need or duty to do so, and I wish him long life to give us many more books."

Nine thousand copies were sold in the first year. Shorthouse and Mrs. Shorthouse attended a reception at Number Ten and breakfasted with Gladstone next day. Printer, Prime Minister and publisher together made a legend of *John Inglesant* which continual reprinting has confirmed. The book remains a minor classic, a grave enchantment to be surrendered to in Italy or an English garden whenever again there is leisure and sanity in the world.

The year of *Inglesant* brought also George Saintsbury. Though he had previously contributed to Ward's *English Poets*, his *Dryden*, in the *English Men of Letters* Series, was his first book for the firm. Saintsbury is remembered by the world for his scholarship of literature and his legendary knowledge of great wines, but there are members of Macmillan's staff whose most vivid recollection is of his handwriting. Something warm and easy in Frederick Macmillan's character won Saintsbury's affection for him, as it won Morley's, and Saintsbury's letters and postcards were frequent. He had a mis-shaped hand, and, as he grew older, his writing became worse and worse. When he attempted a typewriter, the results persuaded him to revert to a pen. Frederick Macmillan reached a point at which all hope of reading what he wrote had to be abandoned, and Saintsbury's communications were interpreted by an informal committee of the staff. Their first task was to determine in what language, ancient or modern, each sentence was written, and then to decipher it. Even printers were defeated. Even Clark's of Edinburgh, who are the blessing of all authors that love accuracy and speed, when one of his later books had been sent to them and they were reproached for delay, replied that they had but one man who could read the manuscript at all and that he, after a fortnight with it, had broken down.

F. Marion Crawford was another man of character whose work was to be long associated with Macmillan's and who was to be among Frederick's personal friends. Though his works enjoyed great fame in their day and were steadily published by Macmillan's from 1882 onwards, they were not consistently profitable. Marion Crawford lived magnificently and seems to have liked to be paid in bulk. For the copyright of *A Cigarette-Maker's Romance* he received £1250, and Macmillan's presumably reaped a moderate harvest, but, in 1891, they lost £100 out of the £2500 paid for *The Witch of Prague*, and on *Khaled*, bought for £1250 in the same year, they showed no profit until 1918. The books were widely sold ; there is no questioning their public success ; but it appears to have been more often the author than the publisher who made money by them. After a time, the practice of buying the copyrights was abandoned and royalties were paid instead. Even so, in 1895, *The Ralstons* showed no profit and the advance of £900 on *Casa Braccio* was not covered. On the other hand, when £1000 was paid on account of a 20 per cent royalty for *Ave Roma Immortalis*, there was a profit of £1180 in three years. The figures are incomplete, but they are enough to indicate that even the publication of a greatly successful author is not on each occasion profitable if the author succeeds in driving up his price ; the publisher has to face his own problem of what might, perhaps, be called speculative patience. In this instance, the problem was made easier by the Macmillans' liking for Marion Crawford which fortified their confidence in his work. But once more there is evidence that they knew precisely where they stood. They were publishing a good novelist, but not an immortal — above all, a man with a grand swagger. " Crawford was up for a day or two lately," wrote Malcolm from Rome on May 15th, 1889,

" and I am more than ever struck with the fact that he is far more remarkable than his books. He speaks four languages so that the natives cannot detect him for a foreigner. He knows a good deal of Sanskrit, though he hardly ever refers to it. . . . He is a good fencer, a good sailor and can do silver-repoussé work. With no training, he designed the entire reconstruction of his house at Sorrento. Both in mathematics and draughtsmanship, he is more than mediocre. He seems to be able to do almost anything he turns his attention to. The one thing he has almost entirely neglected is modern literature ; and he always says that he is not really a literary man. In this there is some truth, though he has a kind of imagination which he throws into everything. . . ." It is a good, lively portrait, explaining much.

Green's *Making of England* had appeared in 1882 and was followed in the next year by his *Conquest of England* and by Seeley's *Expansion of England*. This was the year of Green's death at Mentone, and so close had the friendship of publisher and author become that Alexander spent five weeks there in order to be near him. In spite of this loss, which was a real loss to the firm as well as to Alexander personally, the year was one of expanding prosperity. *The English Illustrated Magazine*, which was to run in the Macmillans' hands for ten years, was launched in October. Its earliest editor was J. Comyns Carr. After a few years Sir Clement Kinloch-Cooke succeeded him, and Emery Walker, to whom the firm was for many years indebted for counsel of unrivalled authority in such matters, superintended the illustrations. Though it was the first of the illustrated monthlies, it is scarcely to be regarded as a forerunner of the popular magazines that followed it, for its tendency was from the outset a little nostalgic ; it looked to old cities, old and stately houses and the old coaching-days for its subjects ; and its chief surviving interest is in its employment of artists and engravers during the decade immediately preceding the conquest of the illustrated press by photography. Anning Bell, Caldecott, Walter Crane, George du Maurier, H. R. Millar, Joseph Pennell, William Strang, E. J. Sullivan, Herbert Railton, Hugh Thomson — all are remembered, but the engravers, those splendid craftsmen, whose names in those days came before the artist's own, are recalled only by a few — Quick, Lascelles, Taylor, Lacour, Kellenbach. They were proud men. One of them, scornful of his material, sent in his account in these terms : " To engraving and endowing with artistic merit. . . ." For a time the magazine prospered, but one cannot resist an impression that it never clearly made up its mind what its purpose was. The list of contributors is remarkable, but exceedingly mixed. Lord Lytton contributed *The Ring of Amasis*, and William Morris *The Glittering Plain*, as serials. The scholars and the giants are there : Ainger, E. A. Freeman, Gosse, H. D. Traill ; Hardy, Henry James, Meredith, Swinburne, Stevenson, Kipling ; but there is a poem by Clement Scott, and there is George Augustus Sala. Frank Harris provided *The Sheriff and his Partner*, Oscar Wilde *London Models*, Shaw *Wagner at Bayreuth*. And yet Mrs. Molesworth and Miss Yonge were there and Archdeacon Farrar and Archibald Geikie. Evidently there were divisions of policy and perilous compromises. As the circulation fell away attempts seem to have been made to encourage advertisers. There were articles on cocoa-works and piano-factories which, whatever their commercial effect may have been, provoked Canon Ainger to reproof in verse that was in itself a punishment :

> In puffing the Brinsmeads,
> Who've I hope paid the bill,
> Sure the *Illustrated*
> Have trated us ill.

The offender passed away from Macmillan's in 1893, to

survive, in different forms, for another seventeen years.

It is better to look back to the year of its birth and observe what more fortunate enterprises the Macmillans were then undertaking. The list is very strong : Green, Seeley, Henry Sidgwick's *Principles of Political Economy*, Stephen's *Criminal Law of England*, Ziegler's *Textbook of Pathological Anatomy*, and the names of Verrall, Welldon, Sayce and Page among the classical scholars, give one indication of its scope. Meredith's *Poems and Lyrics of the Joy of Earth* went into two editions, and in 1884, after years of longing and patience, during which he steadfastly refused to press his claim against rival publishers, Alexander saw realized one of his greatest ambitions. All Tennyson's works were transferred to the firm.

But they lost another chance of Bernard Shaw. A report dated " 22 January 1884 " thus described *Cashel Byron's Profession* : " A two vol. novel, by no means without flavour or originality ; the writing, too, is brisk and rapid. But the story is too whimsical for anything. A young gentleman runs away from school ; goes to Australia as a stowaway ; becomes a prizefighter ; returns to England ; falls in love with a very original young lady, and she, being original, with him. . . . He is a sound-hearted creature at bottom and the lady takes to him by way of reaction against the unreality of literature and politics. . . . I shld. like to see the writer at work on a happier theme. He has some promise of writing in him if he did not disgust us by his subject." On the strength of this, the book was politely refused — a refusal less reasonable and explicable than those which had preceded it. To be irritated by *Cashel Byron* is possible but to be " disgusted " by its subject is exceedingly odd.

The same year saw the publication of *The Life of F. D. Maurice*, by his son, afterwards General Maurice. Its appearance carried Alexander's mind back to the battles he and his brother had fought long ago in Maurice's cause.

Confidence in him, affection for him, and a dutiful determination, as publishers, to support him though they knew he was not and could never be a profitable author, had been part of the Macmillan religion and this biography was for Alexander an emblem of faith. " What changes in these thirty years since Maurice's *Theological Essays* were published have we seen," he wrote to Professor Daniel Wilson. " People then shuddered at the very look of the book, and Daniel and I were warned by friends, who were attached to us, that we were doing vast harm to religion — and to ourselves ! — in publishing such a book." Now, how different it was ! Cardinal Manning, a Dissenting Minister and Mr. Gladstone himself had all written congratulatory letters. The reviews, " with one base exception," had " all been respectful," and Alexander, without pausing to wonder whether this hush of controversy about Maurice was anything else than a sign that his influence was dead, found a quiet pleasure in deciding that, " in all higher senses," religion had gained by the Prophet's works.

Regular as clockwork, faithful to the month of January, Bernard Shaw submitted another manuscript at the beginning of 1885. This was *An Unsocial Socialist*, and John Morley had no doubt of its quality :

" A curious bit of writing which has appeared in the socialist magazine *Today*. It is a *jeu d'esprit*, or satire, with a good stroke of socialist meaning in it.

The story is designedly paradoxical, absurd and impossible, as if it were one of Peacock's. But whoever he may be, the author knows how to write ; he is pointed, rapid, forcible, sometimes witty, often powerful, and occasionally eloquent. I suppose one must call his book a trifle, but it is a clever trifle. Would it be popular ? I half fear that it is too clever for the general : they would not know whether the writer was serious, or was laughing at them. Nor are pages of socialistic irony upon things as they are, and *a priori* demonstrations of the injustice of private property, very attractive to a large public. The present book is Ruskinian doctrine ; theories with a whimsical and deliberately extravagant story, served up with pungent literary sauce. The result is a dish, which I fancy only the few would relish. On the other hand the subject is much in vogue and likely to be — and the writer has a telling style of presenting current arguments. I would not prophesy a financial success (it is not more than two small vols.) but the writer if he is young, is a man to keep one's eye upon."

To reject a book after receiving such a report on it is a surprising timidity. In writing to Shaw, Macmillan's said they " would be glad to look at anything else he might write of a more substantial kind." The word " substantial " reasonably stirred the Shavian wrath — and yet the reply was gentle :

36 Osnaburgh Street, N.W., 14th January 1885

Gentlemen,
Many thanks for reading *An Unsocial Socialist.* Your demand for " something more substantial " takes my breath away. Your reader, I fear, thought the book not serious — perhaps because it was not dull. If so, he was an Englishman. I have only met one reviewer and one oral critic who really took the book in. They were both Scotchmen. You must admit that when one deals with two large questions in a novel, and throws in an epitome of modern German socialism as set forth by Marx as a makeweight, it is rather startling to be met with an implied accusation of triviality.

Yours faithfully,
George Bernard Shaw

After a week's pause, Macmillan's conducted a defensive retreat. The plain truth was that they did not believe the book would sell.

Jan. 22, 1885

Dear Sir,
We had meant to send you the enclosed copy of our reader's opinion to shew you that the character of your story

" An Unsocial Socialist " had been by no means unappreci-
ated. Our reader is not responsible for the epithet " unsub-
stantial " which was perhaps not quite fortunate though we
could not think of any other that would better express our
meaning. What we really doubt is whether the book would
find enough readers. But as we said before we should be
glad to see anything else you may write on a larger scale.

We are,

Yours faithfully,

MACMILLAN & CO.

G. B. Shaw, Esq.
 36 Osnaburgh Street, N.W.

It seems not to be altogether wisdom after the event to say
that a belief that this particular book would be unprofitable
was not a good reason for a long-term publisher's refusal of
it ; but Shaw replied with excellent humour :

36 OSNABURGH STREET, N.W., *22nd January* 1885

GENTLEMEN,

Many thanks for your letter. I forgive your critic,
although the book is perfectly serious — which is precisely
why people take it as a joke. Its impossibilities are the
commonplace occurrences of life. All my readers, as far as
I know them, like the book ; but they tell me that although
they relish it they don't think the general public would.
Which is the more ·discouraging, as this tendency of each
man to consider himself unique is one of the main themes
of the novel. Surely out of thirty millions of copyright
persons (so to speak) there must be a few thousand who would
keep me in bread and cheese for the sake of my story-telling,
if you would only let me get at them.

However, I hope to attack you again with something
more or less tremendous, if I can afford to write it.

I am very sensible of your kindness in sending me your
reader's opinion, and am,

Yours faithfully,

GEORGE BERNARD SHAW

In replying to a request from Daniel Macmillan for

permission to reprint the above correspondence, Shaw made it clear, in a letter of 11th September 1943, that he felt the firm had treated his early work with unusual consideration :

DEAR MR. MACMILLAN,

I have read the galley slips you sent me concerning myself in Mr. Morgan's history of Macmillans with interest and a very agreeable measure of astonishment.

I had no idea that the reports on novels I submitted were so appreciative. I consider them highly creditable to the firm's readers ; for they make it clear that what was wrong was not, as I thought, any failure to spot me as a literary discovery, but the strangeness at that time of my valuations. In fact they thought more of my jejune prentice work than I did myself ; for I really hated those five novels, having drudged through them like any other industrious apprentice because there was nothing else I could or would do. That in spite of their disagreeableness they somehow induced readers rash enough to begin them to go on to the end and resent that experience seems to me now a proof that I was a born master of the pen. But the novel was not my proper medium. I wrote novels because everybody did so then ; and the theatre, my rightful kingdom, was outside literature. The coterie theatres in which I first reached the public as a playwright did not then exist.

But of course I did not understand all this at the time. My recollection, until your letter arrived, was far less encouraging. I began, not very wisely, by calling on all the publishers in person to see what they were like ; and they did not like me. I did not like myself enough to blame them. I was young (23), raw, Irish from Dublin, and Bohemian without being in the least convivial or self-indulgent, deeply diffident inside and consequently brazen outside, and so utterly devoid of reverence that a phrenologist whom I asked what my bump of veneration was like replied " Why, it's a hole ! " Altogether a discordant personality in the eyes of the elderly great publishers of those days, a now extinct species. As I had a considerable aesthetic culture, and the English governing classes, of whom I knew only what I had picked up from Thackeray and Trollope, had none, they were barbarians to me ; and I was to them a complete outsider. I was in fact outside the political world until I had written the first three of my novels ; and when I came in I came in as a Marxist, a phenomenon then inconceivable even to Mill, Morley, Dilke, Auberon Herbert, the Fortnightly Reviewers, the Positivists, the Darwinians, and the rest of the Agnostic Republicans who represented the extreme left of the most advanced pioneers in the eighties of the last century. The Transvaluation of Values in which I was an obscure pioneer can hardly be imagined nowadays by people under 70. I was a Nietzschean and an Ibsenist before I had ever heard of Nietzsche or Ibsen.

In view of all this you will see that Macmillans were very much ahead of the older publishers (I tried them all) in recognising my talent. They corresponded with me a little ; and George Macmillan tried to soften my rejection by Alexander, who didn't like me personally, by sending me a long report by Morley, who turned me down as a victim of undigested Ruskin, of whom I had read little or nothing. Meredith turned me down for Chatto without extenuating circumstances. Blackwood accepted my first novel ; but afterwards renaged, to the distress of his oldest reader. Smith Elder were polite and asked to see future efforts. None of the rest would have anything to say to me ; and even those who gave some attention to my first attempt found its successors more and more impossible. When William Archer made Stevenson read *Cashel Byron's Profession*, and he and Henley applauded it, Bentley, who had refused it, sent for it urgently, and was furious because it was no longer at his disposal ; but that was after I had given up novel writing, having designed a mighty work which I found myself too ignorant to finish ; so I let its opening section go as *An Unsocial Socialist*. The novels, printed as padding in Socialist magazines, got pirated in America ; and when I, being ashamed of them, tried to suppress them, they broke out in spite of me as persistently as they had suppressed themselves before.

Macmillan's attention and George's kindly civility certainly made a difference to me. There are so many amateurs sending in crude MSS to publishers and managers that no beginner can be sure that he is not one of the hopeless failures until his work is accepted, or he has had at least some response indicating that he is not quite out of the question. If Macmillan had simply declined with thanks like nearly all the rest, I should have had to set my teeth still closer.

I am now one of the few who personally remember the Grand Old Men of the publishing world of that day : Alexander Macmillan, Longman, and Bentley. They were so powerful that they held the booksellers in abject subjection, and were denounced by Walter Besant and his newly organised Society of Authors as remorseless sharks. When they died and were succeeded by their sons, the hereditary system did not always work as well as it did in Bedford Street ; and the booksellers got the upper hand. John Murray's Byronic prestige was so select that I did not dream of trying him until years later, when I was an author of some note and had already helped to bankrupt three publishers. I offered him *Man & Superman*. He refused in a letter which really touched me. He said he was old-fashioned and perhaps a bit behind the times ; but he could not see any intention in my book but to wound, irritate, and upset all established constitutional opinion, and therefore could not take the responsibility of publishing it. By that time I could command sufficient capital to finance my books and enter into direct friendly relations with the printers (this began my very pleasant relations with Clarks of Edinburgh). I took matters into my own hands and, like Herbert Spencer and Ruskin, manufactured my books myself, and induced Constables to take me " on commission."

Walter Besant never understood that publishing, like Insurance and turf bookmaking, is a gamble, with the important difference that whereas an insurer can employ an actuary who will tell him the odds at which chance becomes mathematical certainty, and a bookmaker who bets against every horse can lose on one only and is being supplanted by the tote, the publisher has to take chances which are incalculable, and must therefore play with all the advantages he can get, leaving the author to take care of himself. Besant assumed that a successful book ought to pay for itself only, not knowing that it has to pay for several others which, though they keep the shop open, barely repay the overhead and the cost of their manufacture and sometimes lose even that. A loss of 100% on the swings makes a large hole in a profit of 300% on the roundabouts. If both authors and publishers understood this there would be much less friction in their dealings. But the publisher often knows everything about publishing practice and nothing about its economic theory, whilst the author as a rule knows nothing about either, and is constitutionally unfit to conduct his own business. I served for ten years on the Society's Committee, and know the ropes pretty well.

Faithfully,

G. BERNARD SHAW

Later in 1885 the firm lost from one of their own authors what was to be a novel as famous as any of its period. They have been accused of having rejected *Robert Elsmere*. In fact, they did nothing of the kind. To explain fully the circumstances in which it came to them and yet was not published by them would be to go into detail that lies outside the business of publishing. It is enough to say that there were good reasons for their unwillingness to accept the terms that Mrs. Humphry Ward had suggested and to quote the letter sent to her after she had taken her new book to Smith, Elder. There is to-day a tendency among certain publishers to think that, though they are free to reject an author's work, they are entitled to be morally indignant if an author leaves them. Macmillan's letter to Mrs. Humphry Ward makes pleasant reading :

3rd March, 1885

MY DEAR MRS. WARD,

It is a disappointment that we have failed to satisfy you in our terms for the new book and that you have left us. It is a disappointment, for we are personally interested in you and all you do in an unusual way. But I am glad you have been able to get better terms than we could give — just because you say it is important you should have money. That we are not to be the pilots does not in the least take away from my interest in the book and my sincere wish that it may be a success.

Yours most truly

GEO: LILLIE CRAIK

There was nothing in the incident discreditable to either publisher or author. Mrs. Ward had at the time no alternative to the driving of a hard bargain, and it happened to be one which, though Smith was free to make it, would have been for the Macmillans a rashness inconsistent with their policy.

Shaw was lost, Mrs. Ward was gone, and before spring was out J. M. Barrie, who came to Alexander with an introduction, had been allowed to pass by. On May 6th, 1885, Alexander wrote to Barrie : " I have submitted your papers on the *Auld Licht* to an English literary friend, who has wide sympathy with, and knowledge of, Scotland and its literature and thought. He sees no likelihood of even a small book proving attractive enough to an English audience to give any hope of an adequate sale. . . ." In face of this, 1885 might be supposed to have been a year of triple misfortune, and so it would have been for a firm that lived by novels alone. Even Hugh Conway's *A Family Affair*, though popular, made no approach to the fabulous success of *Called Back*. But the structure of the firm was by this time very wide ; their prospects of fortune were distributed ; and the twelve months that lost Shaw and Barrie and *Robert Elsmere* had many compensations. Hall and Knight's *Elementary Algebra for Schools* began a series that has produced rewards which few school books can ever have equalled. Alfred Russel Wallace made an excursion into politics with *Bad Times*. F. O. Bower and Sidney H. Vines published, with help from George Macmillan so active that it amounted almost to collaboration, their *Course of Practical Instruction in Botany*.

Losses and Triumphs

Mark Pattison's *Memoirs* appeared, and Arnold's *Discourses in America*, Pater's *Marius* and Tennyson's *Tiresias* all did honour to the imprint within the course of a few months.

Alexander, though still in his late 'sixties, was now becoming an old man. The establishment of the Colonial Library, which included standard works and popular fiction for circulation in India and the Colonies only, though important to the firm did not greatly concern him, nor did the beginning of the *English Classics* series in 1887. But he had his personal prides and pleasures — Tennyson's *Locksley Hall Sixty Years After*, Frederic Harrison's *The Choice of Books*, and, for personal reasons, a short historical novel *Dagonet the Jester*, published anonymously in 1886. This was the work of his son, Malcolm Kingsley Macmillan, now thirty-four years old, whom he had described when he came of age as " a queer wayward boy." The book had abundant individuality and promise, but Alexander, who must have wished to boast of it a little, was so firmly bound by his publisher's conscience that he guarded the author's anonymity as he had guarded Seeley's long ago. Many who read it ascribed it to Shorthouse. Shorthouse himself and Jowett and Professor Ward wrote to praise it without having an idea of its authorship. Even from Gladstone, Alexander resolutely concealed the truth.

Thomas Hardy's *The Woodlanders* appeared in 1887 together with a new Meredith, *Ballads and Poems of Tragic Life*, a new Pater, *Imaginary Portraits*, and Saintsbury's *History of Elizabethan Literature*. The firm was now making successful experiments with cheap editions of fiction and *belles lettres*. The old " three-decker " at thirty-one shillings and sixpence was not to vanish for several years, but the reprints at six shillings were well established and there were two-shilling editions of William Black, Hugh Conway, Mrs. Oliphant, Annie Keary, and even Henry

James. The new editions of Kingsley and Miss Yonge issued at three shillings and sixpence proved remarkably popular, and other authors — F. D. Maurice, Hughes, Shorthouse, Mrs. Craik, Marion Crawford — were to find new audiences at this price. These were the forerunners of some well-known three-and-sixpenny uniform editions of a later date : of an edition of Dickens with the original illustrations and with special prefaces by Charles Dickens the Younger, of Lewis Melville's edition of Thackeray, of the illustrated Border Edition of Scott, and of the works of Hardy. One of the most popular of the earlier volumes was Rolf Boldrewood's *Robbery under Arms* (1889). In that year, Macmillan's went yet further and began a great extension of their sixpenny editions with monthly volumes of the works of Kingsley. A million were printed of the first issue and there was a reprint of another million. Half a million were of *Westward Ho !*

Alexander meanwhile was withdrawing more and more. In 1888, he celebrated his seventieth birthday at Bramshott Chase, his country home, and, having presented his house at Tooting to the diocese of Rochester, took 21 Portland Place as his town house. Next year Herkomer painted him and Lowes Dickinson drew him in his library at Bramshott. Perhaps he might have lived long in his retirement, but he now received a blow from which he never recovered. Malcolm, the author of *Dagonet the Jester*, disappeared.

Malcolm was a remarkable character, and his father, though he had never been able accurately to " place " him and was a little nervous of men whom he could not place, knew it. In 1870, when he was working with his cousin, Robert Bowes, in the Cambridge shop, he had written to his father suggesting that he should aim at a scholarship there and work for the Moral Science Tripos, and Alexander, perhaps unwisely and with too modest or too conservative a desire that his son should follow in his own footsteps, had inclined to his being trained in business. But in the end the boy had his way. On Green's advice, he went up late to Oxford, but there and elsewhere ill-health interrupted his study, and in 1887 he went abroad, visiting Greece, Cyprus and Egypt and spending a long time in Italy. He read widely, noting, analysing and criticizing what he read, and it is evident from his letters that whether his concern was with history, music, anthropology or pure literature, he brought to it an alert and critical imagination. He had had in his youth neither liking nor aptitude for the routine of a publisher's office, but it is not improbable that, if he had lived, his influence, direct or indirect, would have been exercised upon the firm. During the 'nineties and the early part of the twentieth century, they were, for a firm of their range and enterprise, surprisingly weak in their connexion with modern European writers, yielding to the brilliant enterprise of William Heinemann the territory from which, as much as from his taste in English novels, he won distinction for his new imprint ; and this defect Malcolm, whose taste and knowledge were complementary to the qualities of Frederick, Maurice and George, might have remedied. But he died before this was possible. In 1889, he went to Constantinople to stay with Arthur Hardinge, and, just before he was due to sail for England, made an expedition with Hardinge to Mount Olympus. Approaching the summit, the two climbers took different routes. As he was about to pass out of sight, Malcolm turned and waved. No more was seen of him. In spite of prolonged search, no trace was found. " A modern mystic and macaronic " was his description of himself, and there seems to have been marvellously combined in him the depth, the intuition and the grand freakishness of a connoisseur.

Alexander suffered from the long uncertainty, and, though he was to live until January 26th, 1896, he passed at this point out of the history of the firm. Already in 1890

John Morley was writing to him as to a man whose work was done : " Tomorrow, my dear Macmillan, is your birthday, and I wish you all good things with all my heart. It is pleasant to think of you after your brave voyage as resting in your comfortable haven. Think kindly of storm-tost mariners still out in the open sea. . . ."

PART FOUR

THE SECOND GENERATION
1890–1914

CHAPTER NINE

Fiction

Younger Partners—Travellers and Staff—Frederick Macmillan and Fiction—" The Forest Lovers "—Kipling—Hardy Returns.

NOT the least of Alexander's qualities was his grasp of the strategy of business and his power to subordinate his personal inclination to it. He neither seized control too soon nor relinquished it too late ; he made transitions easy by foreseeing and preparing for them. While Daniel lived, though his sickness and long absences had greatly added to the younger brother's burden, Alexander, recognizing his powers as well as loving him, had carefully held the second place ; when Daniel was gone, he was ready to succeed to the first, and infuse into the firm that boldness and imaginative extension which Daniel's over-anxious nature might have withheld from it. It seems probable that Daniel had gone as far as his nature would have allowed him to go from his small beginnings ; he had made his spring ; and Alexander's fresher mind was necessary to grasp the truth that the firm might grow to international dimensions without becoming what to-day would be called a department store or losing its individuality. Towards the end of his career, and indeed long before the end, he had shown, in altogether different circumstances, an equal and even rarer power of delegation and transference. He had taken in Craik, and had the wit to trust him. He had taken in the younger Macmillans and bred them to responsibility.

By the time he was, in effect, out of the firm, his successors were experienced in the management of it.

Craik remained. He lived until 1905, but his part was less than that of the three Macmillans. They made a good team. In 1890, the eldest, Frederick, was thirty-nine ; George Augustin, Alexander's second son, was four years younger ; and Maurice Crawford, the second son of the first Daniel and Frederick's younger brother, was thirty-seven. Of Frederick something has already been told. There was little in the whole range of the book-trade that he had not learned by hard work and personal experience. He had learned retail bookselling under his cousin, Robert Bowes of Cambridge, and had acquired a general knowledge of printing at the University Press. He had worked through the departments of the Bedford-street office and for a time had been town traveller, " subscribing " — that is to say, offering in advance, describing and recommending — new books to the London trade ; and it is worth while to remark how difficult and responsible the work of a publisher's traveller is.

Much more than the patter of salesmanship is required of him. Booksellers still retain many of the qualities of Daniel and Alexander themselves ; they are tradesmen, but they are also responsible judges and often deep lovers of books ; a slick young salesman to whom books are as tubes of toothpaste is an offence to them and damaging to the publisher who employs him. Books are not sold " on sale or return." A bookseller buys them from the publisher outright. Those that he fails to re-sell to the public are left on his hands and he loses by them. It follows that if many books bearing one imprint are among his losers, he takes warning for the future. A good traveller's purpose is, therefore, not to over-persuade a bookseller into buying what he is unlikely to sell, but, with his knowledge of each book's quality and of all the conditions that will accompany its issue, to take care that the bookseller is well-stocked but not over-stocked. He is a salesman but also an adviser. He and the booksellers he visits are partners in a common enterprise, and it is a long-term enterprise. It sometimes happens that trust between the two partners becomes so well-established that booksellers invite a traveller to write his own order. When this point is reached, the traveller has proved himself and, at the same time, increased his personal responsibility. He has won the power, in the case of some unusual book in which the publishers have well-founded confidence but about which booksellers might be reasonably timid, to give it the chance it needs. He thus becomes, not a salesman merely, but a man whose patience and discrimination enable him to be of great service to literature and to the authors whom indirectly he represents. But if he should abuse his power, or even make mistakes in the exercise of it, he will lose it. For this reason — if we look a little further up the scale — a sales-manager who drives his travellers into " pushing " a particular book beyond their own belief in it is serving his firm ill. What matters is a cumulative confidence among booksellers in the firm's imprint, and only a traveller can win it who has studied the local requirements of each shop, who balances them with the qualities of each book, who feels himself to be in a position of trust, and speaks — or writes in the bookseller's order — the discriminating truth that is in him.

Such a traveller Frederick Macmillan was, for he himself had been a bookseller, and such an understanding of the travellers' need of backing and respect Frederick Macmillan had when he controlled the firm, for he himself had been a traveller. The whole movement of books from the author's pen to the reader's lap is continuous ; no part of it is separable from another part ; and this is too little acknowledged — too little sometimes by authors themselves. Hence, in part, this volume. For authors learn slowly, discovering first that a rigidly divided, impersonal department store is death and that a publisher's steady confidence is worth all the advances in the world ; then that a printer is a father whose value is increased by an author's own care for his manuscript, his typescript, his second typescript, his third typescript, his galleys — so that there is little misery " in page " ; then that the choice of fount, the shape of page, the binding — all that there is in " production " — is, in a great publisher's hands, amenable to an author's taste but ought not to be nibbled at by his inexpert fads ; and, finally, that throughout the office — in packing-room and post-room, at the ledgers and at wise men's anonymous desks — are his allies, some of whom go out and are called travellers and extend the alliance.

In the 'nineties these allies, collectively " the staff," appear to have been blessed by a remarkable absence of regimentation. It was, the elders say, a laborious but none the less a golden age. Where there were no typewriters, there was great labour of penmanship and copying, but, as long as your work was done, there was a permitted elasticity in the doing of it. Even in a boy, truancy was scarcely a crime — as long as his work was done. Neither employer nor employee counted the minutes. Overtime and time-off were, within limits, gloriously interchangeable — as long as the work was done. Vans and posts must be caught ; they, not the clock, were your conscience. If you were willing to put in a long spell of work on Wednesday night, you might well elect to play billiards on Thursday afternoon. If you thought the journey home too long or too late, you made yourself comfortable for the night and played a game of cards before turning in. Somewhere on the premises there was always, with or without official recognition, a barrel of beer. And if you came as a boy, you did not find yourself adrift among strangers, for it happened that the mother of the present Chairman, Mrs. Maurice Macmillan, who was a school visitor under the old London School Board, often at the turn of the century visited the Walton-street and Marlborough Road Boys' Schools in Chelsea, and there she would recruit for the firm, giving boys their first chance, and afterwards mothering her recruits a little ; so that they knew each other, and grew up together, and were, several of them, heads of departments in the year of the centenary. All of this may explain a little why it is that, to this day, an author who goes into St. Martin's-street feels that from the board-room to the lower stock-rooms he is in a company of friends. Many of those who work there have known one another since boyhood.

During his five years in America, Frederick had in 1874 married an American lady, Georgiana Warrin, who lived until 1943 and so is well remembered even by junior authors of the 'thirties who, as guests in her house, discovered that she knew more about cooking than most women on earth, and saw to it, by daily and personal supervision, that her cook put this knowledge into faultless practice. For the same good reason that prevents the French from travelling, she always entertained in her own home, but there was one legendary occasion when, guests having been invited and her cook having fallen sick, she had to choose between three lines of action — to employ another cook, not trained by her and therefore inferior ; to cook the dinner herself — which she would have enjoyed if it had been possible for a lady of eighty-five to be in two places at once ; or to go into the highways and hedgerows. She chose the highways and hedgerows. " And really, my dear, I had been unnecessarily alarmed. We went to a place called Claridge's, and it was really quite good."

In the 'nineties, she and her husband had a London house in St. John's Wood, but spent half the year at Temple Dinsley in Hertfordshire, where he became a magistrate and afterwards Deputy-Lieutenant. When the firm became a limited company in 1896, he was its first chairman. In the division of responsibility between himself, his cousin and his younger brother, it was natural that the American business should fall to him, and, though the division itself was never water-tight and a director would often continue in charge of a book outside his special province if he happened to know or to have been the first to interview the author, Frederick, in general, left India, education, the classics, archaeology and high scholarship alone, and devoted himself to general literature, poetry, fiction and what by publishers is called " art." What he lacked, as a selector from among new manuscripts, was a nose for a particular kind of truffle, and the intuition which might have enabled him to know when a Reader had run into a groove of prejudice. There are in existence opinions by Mowbray Morris written with a violence that men do not use except subconsciously in defence of a closed mind, and Frederick Macmillan might have been warned by them. His blind spot seems to have been that of one over-suspicious of extremes whether of emotion or of manner. He was by no means cold ; he was a man of genuine taste within the extremes and was sensitive to all kinds of polite or disciplined merit ; for example, he backed Henry James steadily, enthusiastically and to his own loss, and had, in the field of popular writing, a sense of humour which, when Mowbray Morris reported with cautious and patronising favour on *Elizabeth and her German Garden*, decided him to accept that fortunate risk. Henry James, for all his genius, was unquestionably polite ; " Elizabeth," whatever her limitations, was not an extremist " Perhaps her humour sometimes comes rather near to that of Mr. Jerome," Mowbray Morris had written, " but she is neither vulgar nor provincial. The serious reader would possibly call her trivial or flippant, but all readers are not serious, and I should not be surprised if the little book were found to please." But Mowbray Morris and other Readers of the 'nineties and of the following years had an anti-realistic bias which was expressed with a perilous emphasis, and led to the exclusion of some of the young lions — Bennett, Maugham, Sheila Kaye-Smith — who might have brought in others of their generation and added to the list of fiction a vitality different in kind from that which it possessed. With one outstanding exception it was poor in new men in the early 'nineties, depending overmuch on its inheritance — Henry James, Marion Crawford, Shorthouse, Mrs. Molesworth, Mrs. Oliphant, Lewis Carroll ; but, as the years passed, it became steadily livelier, sometimes by the discovery of new writers — Maurice Hewlett, for example, and " Elizabeth " ; sometimes by the acquisition of established novelists ; often by inflow from America. Wells's *Twelve Stories and a Dream* came from Macmillan's in 1903, and in the following year, when *The Food of the Gods* appeared, seven earlier novels were transferred to them. By this time A. E. W. Mason had come in and Maurice Hewlett's *The Forest Lovers* had been the most celebrated novel of 1898. Winston Churchill and Gertrude Atherton were sending a series of books from America, and Owen Wister's *The Virginian* had appeared in 1902. 1905 saw Edith Wharton's *The House of Mirth* and Wells's *Kipps* ; 1907, the strange concatenation of the first collected edition of Henry James and Ouida's *Helianthus* ; 1909, *Tono-Bungay*, Algernon Blackwood's *The Education of Uncle Paul* and *Jimbo*, and a series of sevenpenny reprints ; 1911, the centenary edition of Thackeray with Harry Furniss's illustrations and Edith Wharton's *Ethan Frome* ; 1912, the Wessex Edition of Hardy ; 1913, *A Small Boy and Others*, almost the last of Henry James ; and 1914, two more novels by Wells.

The firm's relationship with Wells, though nearly always friendly, was seldom altogether at ease, for Macmillan's were less adventurous than the author wished them to be.

Ann Veronica and *The New Machiavelli* were rejected for reasons which no publisher would now consider valid, and Wells felt not only that the firm was too narrow in its moral judgements but that it was too restrained in its methods of sale. During the year ending July 1907, only 180 copies of *Kipps* had been sold, and Wells wanted to see what Nelson's could do with a sevenpenny edition. In the summer of 1908 Frederick consented and by October Nelson's had sold 43,000 copies, which, as Wells reasonably remarked, " isn't bad for a book left for dead." In that same autumn, while *Tono-Bungay* was still awaiting publication, came the mournful episode of *Ann Veronica*. Frederick refused it. " I could give you the reasons," he said at first, " but as I know you resent literary criticism from a publisher, I refrain from doing so." When pressed, he explained that, in his opinion, the plot developed " on lines that would be exceedingly distasteful to the public which buys books published by our firm." *Ann Veronica* went to Fisher Unwin. Why Macmillan's refused it but nevertheless published *Tono-Bungay*, which contains at least one lady as uninhibited as Ann, no one now can tell. Even more regrettable was their rejection of *The New Machiavelli*, and it is of no comfort to say that their prejudice was shared by other publishers before John Lane issued the book. Subject to his determination not to issue it under his own imprint, Frederick did what he could. He undertook that the author should not suffer financial loss by Macmillan's refusal to publish, and himself negotiated the transfer. Wells, though he must have been distressed by the episode, wrote sturdily about the future : " The next book I'm planning won't cause any of this trouble — I'm passing out of a necessary phase in handling my medium. Sex *must* be handled and few writers escape the gawky phase," and, in an earlier letter arising from the proposal to issue a cheap edition through Nelson's and from Frederick's having expressed his willingness to relinquish Wells's books, the author had said : " I like your firm in many ways. I don't think you advertise well, and I think you're out of touch with the contemporary movement in literature. I don't think you have any idea of what could be done for me (but that you will of course ascribe to the vanity of Authors). But on the other hand you are solid and sound and sane." It is fair and friendly criticism of the firm's attitude towards fiction at that time. In spite of the rejection of *Ann Veronica* and *The New Machiavelli*, Wells retained enough regard for Macmillan's to bring later books to St. Martin's-street. *Marriage* (1912), *The Passionate Friends* (1913), *The Wife of Sir Isaac Harman* and *The World Set Free* (1914) and *The Research Magnificent* (1915) all came from Macmillan's, and the break did not come until the firm, though *Mr. Britling Sees It Through* was offered to them and they wished to publish it, decided that they would not pay what the author asked. A dozen books of his nevertheless remain in the American Macmillan's current list, the *Outline of History* in particular having commanded a large public in the United States.

In spite of such mistakes as the refusal of *The New Machiavelli*, the list of fiction during the period 1890–1914 is — to adopt Wells's phrase — " solid and sound," but it lacked new blood at the end and would have lacked it at the beginning but for one gigantic infusion not yet mentioned. Through all the years that have just been glanced at, Kipling's stories were capturing the world.

In 1889, three of his best-known works, *The Ballad of East and West*, *The Incarnation of Krishna Mulvaney* and *The Ballad of the King's Mercy*, had appeared in the *Magazine*, and in 1890 Macmillan's published the first English edition of *Plain Tales from the Hills*, previously available only in the edition produced in Calcutta with which " a boy's eccentric blunder " had indeed brought " success to pass."

There is good reason to believe, though no documents confirm it, that what brought him to the firm was the benign and invaluable influence of Mrs. W. K. Clifford. Herself a good writer, the author of *Mrs. Keith's Crime* (1885), of *Aunt Anne* (1892), and of plays that deservedly held the stage, she was by virtue of her own quality and that of her great husband, William Kingdon Clifford, mathematician and philosopher, who died at the age of thirty-four in 1879, a lady of influence wherever in London high intelligence was to be found. She had an intuition for literature, and an incapacity to lie about it whether in flattery or in spite. Even near the end of her days in the late 'twenties, when she was by no means rich, the company in her little drawing-room in Chilworth-street was among the best, though not the smartest, in London. There young men might encounter, as perhaps nowhere else so intimately, those great survivors of the Victorian age who had not forgotten her and would make the journey to Paddington on a Sunday afternoon. Sir Frederick Macmillan, by then nearly eighty, made the journey, and had for her opinion an affectionate, a reasoned, and, one was tempted to believe, an almost superstitious regard. She had brought him *The Forest Lovers*, she had brought him Kipling, and when, in 1928, she brought him the manuscript of another new writer her prestige made easy the way of that young man to St. Martin's-street.

The Forest Lovers Macmillan had sent first to Mowbray Morris, who was lukewarm. Hewlett's intentions, he confessed, were a puzzle to him. " They would, I suspect, puzzle most of his readers, and readers as a rule do not like being puzzled. Some would taste him, I think ; despite my perplexities I have found some entertainment in him, and his much vexed little heroine is a pretty creature. But with the majority I am afraid that irritation might be a more general feeling than entertainment." Frederick Macmillan did not accept this as final. Mrs. Clifford had said with moderate emphasis that it was a good book and with extreme emphasis that it would be greatly popular. It was sent, therefore, to the court of appeal — John Morley. " A romance," he replied, " not without quality but marked by intense *artificiality* in every way. The style is clearly fashioned on Meredith, but not everybody can bend the bow of Ulysses ; it has not the depth, richness or flash of G. M. ; in other words it has the affectation without the thought. The story is of the fantastic kind ; *i.e.* it has no connection with real or possible life either in our own or any other age. There is a faint flavour of *Lorna Doone* in it, only here the actors are not real flesh and blood in any sense. At the same time, I find it readable enough in a *very* lazy moment ; I mean, if I were in a lazy mood, I think the book would hold me in an easy way. But I cannot believe that it will go very far with the public. There is imagination in it, and a feeling for scenery, and occasional pretty bits. Of anything like true excellence either of invention or writing I confess that I find but moderate supply." This was so careful and reasoned a judgement, it contained so good a side-light — " depth, richness and flash " — on Meredith, and was written by a man of such quality and credit that, even though Morley's special genius might not be for fiction, no publisher could fail to be impressed by it. If Mowbray Morris thought that " the majority " would be irritated, if Morley said it would not " go far with the public," if neither they nor Mrs. Clifford herself suggested that it was a novel worth going to the stake for, a publisher's course was plain. But Frederick happened to meet Mrs. Clifford at an evening party. She asked about young Hewlett's novel. Well, he said, it had been submitted to more than one reader and they did not recommend it ; he proposed to return it to-morrow. She asked him to sit down beside her and spoke her mind — as, indeed, she always did. The way she put it was that he was throwing away a small fortune ; she had never felt more certain of the popularity of any book, but she was aware that others must have said as much to him before and she asked only one thing : that he would not return the manuscript until he had read it himself — but *himself*. He hesitated. After all, he couldn't read every manuscript himself. No, she said, but would he please promise, for old friendship's sake, to read this one ? In courtesy, he gave his promise ; in honesty, fulfilled it, and decided to publish. Even then, he did not believe the book would be popular. " The net result is," he said in his letter of acceptance to the author, after telling him that the manuscript had been read by four people (including himself), " that we are disposed to undertake the risk of publishing the book although we shall be more sorry than surprised if the circulating library public finds it too fantastic for its taste." The result is well-known.[1]

Kipling's letters to the firm are even fewer and less illuminating than Henry James's, and that for a particular reason. Three of the earliest settle a small point of bibliography. One speaks of the *Plain Tales'* successor by what was at that time its title : *The Book of the Forty-Five Mornings* ; the others prove that this was not, as has been authoritatively supposed, the first name of *From Sea to Sea* but of *Life's Handicap*. Soon afterwards, when Craik made an inquiry of Kipling about continental rights, the reply came from A. P. Watt, the agent, and thenceforward everything from Kipling was at third hand — through Mrs. Kipling, through Watt. Kipling was more suspicious of publishers than Byron himself, but had not the grand manner which enabled

[1] There is no mention of Mrs. Clifford in the letter-books which touch upon *The Forest Lovers*. This account is her own. One strange circumstance appears to confuse it. Frederick Macmillan's letter of acceptance is dated " 5th March 1898 " and Mowbray Morris's report two days *later*. But as the letter refers to four opinions and as Frederick Macmillan cannot have asked for more opinions after accepting the book, one of the dates must be wrong.

Byron's affability towards Murray. Byron thought of them as tradesmen and knew how to treat tradesmen ; Kipling had a different point of view and would never have been at ease, even in Albemarle-street. Part of his prejudice may have dated back to his experience with *Departmental Ditties*, turned out on the office plant of *The Civil and Military Gazette* and sold by the sending out of reply-postcards. Thus all middlemen and sinners had been eliminated. " There was," as Kipling said, " no trade discount, no reckoning of twelves as thirteens, no commission, and no credit of any kind whatsoever. The money . . . was transferred from the publisher, the left-hand pocket, direct to the author, the right-hand pocket." The effect upon his mind of this profitable if primitive experience was reinforced by less fortunate experiences in America, where his earliest work was ruthlessly pirated before it could receive the benefit of the 1891 Act. Not only did he receive no payment, but, much worse, material he had wished to suppress was re-printed, and he was driven in self-defence to publish it in *Abaft the Funnel*, which was not allowed to appear in England until released for the Sussex Edition.

Therefore Kipling, as author, fenced himself in, though Kipling, as man, was on the best of terms with his publishers when he met them privately. Macmillan's kept his prose and Methuen's his verse, except *Songs from Books*. It became, as the years passed, almost a game to invent new dresses for his work — uniform editions, pocket editions, the Edition de Luxe in red and gold, the Bombay Edition, the Service Edition intended for the pack or pocket of soldiers in the 1914 war. There were, also, school editions, and gigantic volumes in which all the dog stories or all the Mowgli stories or all the humorous stories were assembled, and year by year the wise men held their breath and wondered whether by now the public demand for old wine in new bottles was exhausted. The cautious feared it might be, but they were always wrong. It may be hoped that Kipling gave his publishers credit for an inventiveness in the use of a selling machine more elaborate than his reply-postcards. Certainly he knew his own value, and Macmillan's, even if they had wished to do so, had not the power to reduce the price of his books. But the luck was bound to turn, and it turned with the most costly, complete and ill-fated of all his " limiteds " — the red-leather Sussex Edition. Of this there were thirty-five volumes in five-hundred sets. Special hand-made paper was used, great care was given in St. Martin's-street to every detail of production, and Kipling, playing his part with unfailing courage, wrestled with ill-health so that he might add to it material excluded from other editions and revise his whole work. Before it had begun to appear, he died. The edition proceeded, but the demand was less than had been looked for, and fate decreed that the Sussex Edition should not be allowed to wait for a new generation of collectors. The unsold sets and unbound sheets were stored with the binders in Kirby-street, E.C. An air-raid buried them, and before many could be disinterred the building was struck again, and all but a few odd volumes were destroyed. When visitors in St. Martin's-street are given a chair newly up-holstered in red leather, it is upon what would have been the binding of the Sussex Kipling that they sit.

The firm's connexion with Hardy was altogether different and more personal. Hardy wrote his own business letters and had a keen eye for a percentage as he had for all else, but there is character — a mingling of firmness and gentleness and dignity — even in his negotiation of a contract, which proves him once more to have been what all men found him to be in other courses of life : the most lovable and the least pretentious of great artists. How, after serialization in the *Magazine*, *The Woodlanders* was published by Macmillan's in 1887 has already been told. Other work of his was by this time in the hands of Smith Elder, Sampson Low and other publishers, and his relationship with Macmillan's developed slowly. A collection of his stories, *Wessex Tales*, followed *The Woodlanders*; then, in 1889, says Mrs. Hardy, *Tess* was offered as a serial to *Murray's Magazine*, refused on account of its "improper explicitness," sent to *Macmillan's Magazine* and refused for the same reason. There are no records for the *Magazine*. Mrs. Hardy's statement must be accepted, but was even Mowbray Morris so shocked that, having the manuscript of *Tess* in his hands and regarding it as unsuitable for his magazine, he said nothing of it to the firm ? For there are records of manuscripts offered for publication as books, and neither in them nor in the letter-books is there any mention of *Tess*. It is safe to say that it was not offered to the firm for publication as a book. All the circumstances are a trifle odd, for Hardy's special modesty enabled him to mutilate the story for *The Graphic* and restore the text later, and this he might as easily have done for *Macmillan's Magazine*.

However that may be, there was a breeze — the only one — between him and Macmillan's in 1893. With the idea of a collected edition to be published elsewhere, he wished to withdraw *The Woodlanders* and *Wessex Tales*, but, when Frederick Macmillan had objected to the transfer and pointed out that Hardy was wrong in supposing that he was legally entitled to insist upon it, agreement was reached and the books remained. The agreement was evidently satisfactory to Hardy, for in the following year, the rights in the Sampson Low novels having reverted to him, he began to discuss the inclusion of his works in Macmillan's Colonial Library, and an arrangement was made with Osgood McIlvaine, who were to publish a uniform edition in England, for the manufacture or exchange of plates.

The next valuable group of letters belong to 1902 and

explain how Macmillan's came at long last to be Hardy's publishers, though not even then quite his sole publishers, for *Under the Greenwood Tree* was Chatto's and appeared with their licence under other imprints, and it was not for some time that this early novel came home to him. Meanwhile, the correspondence of 1902 is worth giving not because it contains the ordinary material of anecdote but for the opposite reason — that it illustrates a plain relationship between an author who knows his mind and a publisher who knows his business.

MAX GATE, DORCHESTER, *March* 18, 1902

DEAR MR. MACMILLAN :

The term of years for which I entrusted the publication of my books to Messrs. Osgood McIlvaine & Co. — now the Messrs. Harper — expires on April 4 next — (except as to one novel and the poems, which have a little longer to run).

The unexpected vicissitudes of the firm, owing to which it befalls that my publisher here has become only a subordinate member of a New York house, make it necessary — from obvious considerations of convenience — that I transfer the English edition of the books to a publisher whose headquarters are London.

As you already publish the Colonial edn., and in view of my long personal acquaintance with the members of your firm, I write to you first on the matter, to inquire if you would be willing to take up the books, when they fall into my hands.

The Messrs. Harper, I ought to say, have dealt quite fairly with me since I have been with them, and though they complain of " loss of prestige " by my withdrawal, (which is an error, theirs being the American view, and London differing from New York in that respect) they perceive my natural reasons for the step, and we part amicably enough. Out of consideration for them I have allowed them six months for selling off the stock on hand, which brings the actual end of the term to October 4 next.

I have stipulated that the plates shall be on offer at that date at half cost.

You may perhaps like to know that there have been no systematic cheap editions of the novels (the cheapest uniform edn. having been 6/-) so that the course is open for such ; and that I have had some offers for the publication of a large limited edn. ; but this too has been left in abeyance. The curious accident of a topographical interest having arisen in " Wessex " also helps the vitality of the volumes.

However, I will not go into details now ; and indeed, I did not intend to open communications with new publishers just yet, till it occurred to me that it might be for their convenience to do so. I should add that Mr. McIlvaine asks me not to let it be publicly known that I am leaving his firm.

Yours very truly

THOMAS HARDY

March 19th, 1902

DEAR MR. HARDY,

I write to acknowledge your letter of yesterday's date, and to say at once that we are all delighted at the idea of having your books on our list, and will guarantee that if the transfer is carried out you shall have no cause to regret it.

As to terms we will of course give you whatever royalties you have been in the habit of receiving from Messrs. Harpers on the six shilling editions, and I have no doubt we can make satisfactory arrangements for a systematic cheap edition if it is thought advisable to issue one. I should not however like to give a decided opinion as to this without first having some information as to how the sale of the six shilling books has been keeping up lately.

A so called " edition de luxe " very handsomely printed and limited in number is well worth considering. We have had great success with Tennyson, Kipling, Charles Lamb and Pater in that form.

Perhaps you could let me know about the royalties and the recent sales and I will then prepare a draft agreement for your consideration. There is no reason why the agreement should not be made now although it cannot come into force until October.

We will of course respect your wish that no public announcement of your contemplated change of publishers should be made.

Believe me
Yours very truly
FREDERICK MACMILLAN

Mar. 25, 1902

DEAR MR. HARDY,

I should think, to judge from the statement of sales that you give me, that the time has come when a complete three & sixpenny edition of your novels might with advantage be published. [*A detailed offer of terms follows.*] The royalty which we can pay on the six shilling books is impossible in the case of cheaper ones, as the cost of production can be lessened very little, and there is therefore a much narrower margin between what the books cost us and what we can get for them.

In accordance with your suggestion I am sending you a draft agreement made to cover the fifteen books which you propose to transfer to us in October, and any others that you may transfer later on. I have, as you suggested, made it for seven years certain, and thereafter until the expiration of the copyrights, but terminable by either side at six months' notice. I find that we have proper agreements for the Colonial editions but for the sake of uniformity I have included them.

I suppose that if any arrangement is possible for the sale of *Under the Greenwood Tree* it will have to be made between Messrs. Chatto & Windus and ourselves, as I gather from your letter that you have no financial interest in that book. Is this so?

I should think that Harper & Brothers are not likely to have any very large stock of the existing edition on hand in October next, as you have given them plenty of notice, but if there should be any, I have no doubt that we can arrange to take it off their hands on reasonable terms. They would of course not be at liberty to sell any after the agreement with you has come to an end.

Perhaps you will kindly read through the draft agreement and let me have it back again with any suggestions that occur to you.

I am,
　　　Yours very truly,
　　　　　FREDERICK MACMILLAN

March 31, 1902

DEAR MR. MACMILLAN :

I have examined the draft, and have marked on it all that occurs to me as requisite, which are mainly a few words I find in old agreements.

I transferred the phrase about the new novel to a clause by itself merely because, as it stood, it seemed to say that if, for any reason, you did not wish to publish any such new book, I could not get it published anywhere.

As you surmise, I have no financial interest in *Under the Greenwood Tree*, and I suppose that any arrangement for including it in the series would have to be made between Messrs. Chatto and yourselves, as was done by Osgood. I believe Chatto likes to keep the copyright because he thinks the book helps his list ; but he may part with it.

I find that in my agreement with the New York firm of Harpers for the American edns., they have " control of the Canadian market " for the three or four novels which are copyright in the United States. What this means I do not know, but if it has any importance I presume we shd. except Canada from our agreement.

The clause pencilled at the end of the draft is a sort of memorandum which I thought it would be well to put on record. So many books seem to be coming out concerning " the Wessex of the novels and poems " (the fourth, I see is just announced) that I fancy I shall be compelled, in self-defence as it were, to publish an annotated edn. giving a really trustworthy account of real places, scenery, etc. (somewhat as Scott did) : since it does not seem to be quite fair that capital shd. be made out of my materials to such an extent as promises to be done. These matters wd. then be embodied in my own books. An " annotated edition " wd. perhaps be in demand, as I cd. make the notes very interesting. If you think so I can begin to collect matter. Please consider this idea as a private one.

Yours very truly,

THOMAS HARDY

April 1st, 1902

DEAR MR. HARDY,

I enclose a fair copy of the agreement in which you will find that the suggestions you made on the draft have all been embodied. If you will kindly sign and return it to me, I will send you a duplicate signed by ourselves.

I shall be very much interested to know whether in speaking of " the new novel " you merely refer to a possibility of the future or whether there is anything actually on the stocks. It would be very gratifying to us to look forward not only to taking over your old books in October, but to bringing out an entirely new work of fiction from your pen. Of course we should consider anything that you told us as to this as confidential.

Believe me

Yours sincerely

FREDERICK MACMILLAN

July 8, 1902

DEAR MR. HARDY,

I write to ask whether there is any reason why we should not at once begin printing the 3/6 Edition of your novels which it was suggested we might begin to publish when we take over the books in October. We have plates of them all that we purchased from Harpers for the Colonial Editions. I suppose you are not under any obligation to buy the unsold copies of the old Editions and as Harpers have had plenty of warning of the impending change it is improbable that they have any large stock.

If you are agreeable we should propose to begin the issue of the 3/6 Edition as soon as we have command of the books and to publish a volume every month until the series is complete.

I am,

Yours sincerely

FREDERICK MACMILLAN

Fiction

DEAR MR. HARDY,

I am much obliged to you for returning the proofs of the corrections to your novels. The reason for the variation in type is that the plates were not made by Messrs. Clark but by Ballantyne, and we found Clarks had not quite the same type in stock. I do not think that the variation is sufficient to attract the notice of the majority of people. You must have a very keen eye for such things.

I am,
Yours very truly,
FREDERICK MACMILLAN

Sept. 24th, 1902

DEAR MR. HARDY,

I am sending you by this post a specimen of the cover which we propose to use for the new edition of your novels. I shall be much obliged if you will let me know whether you like it or whether you have any suggestions to make.

We propose to begin the publication of the three & sixpenny edition next month and to bring out a fortnightly volume until the set is complete. We have arranged with Harpers to take over a certain number of sets of their six shilling edition which we shall keep on sale for such people as ask for it.

I am,
Yours very truly,
FREDERICK MACMILLAN

Oct. 11, 1902

DEAR MR. MACMILLAN :

Many thanks for the copies of *Tess*, which in view of the decreased price look very well. But I think you are wise in keeping the 6/– edition in print. Some people tell me they like it. I hope, by the way, you have acquired the plates of the illustrations.

One small feature of the new edition I should like you to reconsider — the omission from the half-title of the words " The Wessex Novels." For commercial reasons, not to speak of literary ones, I fancy the words should be retained. Many people have heard of the Wessex Novels who do not know their individual titles. This inclusive title is, moreover, copyright, and as several writers have used " Wessex " in their productions since I began it they may annex " Wessex Novels " if we let the name drop. I mention this in the belief that, the page being nearly a blank one, the amendment could easily be made in unbound and unprinted copies.

> Believe me,
> Yours truly,
> THOMAS HARDY

P.S.   I enclose herewith a word omitted from list of Errata.

Oct. 14th, 1902

DEAR MR. HARDY,

I do not know how we came to omit the words " The Wessex Novels " from the half title of *Tess*. It was not done intentionally and I will have the half title reprinted at once.

The new edition has started very well. We have already disposed of nearly 500 copies of *Tess*.

I have received the further correction for Wessex Poems and will have it attended to.

> I am,
> Yours very truly,
> FREDERICK MACMILLAN

Thus, after so many vicissitudes, Hardy and Macmillan's found common ground. On September 28th, 1903, the first part of *The Dynasts* was despatched, accompanied by a letter of which the modesty consisted in its having its feet so firmly planted on earth. Never did poet more quietly announce a masterpiece that had been with him for seven years :

DEAR MR. MACMILLAN :

I send to-day the MS I spoke to you about in the early summer. It is not as yet typewritten, but this could be done.

I hope you will be inclined to print it, and if so, will ask you to propose to me as good terms as you can.

It would, I suppose, be advisable to publish it at 3/6, to match the other books ? That however you will consider.

As you will see, it is Part I of a Trilogy. But it is, at the same time, complete in itself, and though I hope to finish the two remaining parts at an early date it is not indispensable that I should do so. I am inclined to wait and see how this part goes off before proceeding further.

A practical question that would depend largely upon your estimate of its sale would be in relation to America. Ought it to be printed there, or can we send over copies and risk the copyright ?

I can run up to town if you would like to talk over the matter.

Believe me
Sincerely Yours

THOMAS HARDY

P.S. I have only a rough copy of the MS.

The first edition (variously dated 1903 and 1904 to the delight of collectors and bibliographers) was formally published on January 13th, 1904, and consisted of a thousand copies. The English reviews were more than respectful and Max Beerbohm wrote, in the *Saturday Review*, of " a noble achievement . . . a really great book." 750 copies were sold in 1903–4, but only 42 in 1905. In 1906, when there was a reprint of a thousand, 234 were sold, in 1907 but 44, and in 1908, on a rising but not rapid tide, 208. Hardy, in arranging his contract, had providently suggested that, if the sale should rise above " say 8000 or 10,000 " copies, the scale of royalty should rise with it, and had ended his letter : " Having mentioned this I shall leave it to you, and say no more about it whichever way you decide." Frederick Macmillan had at once amended the contract, and Hardy acknowledging this said : " I am much obliged by your embodying my suggestion on advanced numbers — but I fear the sales will never get up to such a figure ! " They were, indeed, slow, but there is such a thing as long-term authorship as well as long-term publishing, and Hardy was right and knew what he was doing. The long, peaceful story of his association with the firm until his death in 1928 does not need to be retold. It includes the Wessex and Mellstock Editions, *A Changed Man*, the appearance of his *Chosen Poems* in the *Golden Treasury Series* and a long list of volumes of poetry. His last visit to London was made for the wedding of Harold Macmillan to Lady Dorothy Cavendish on April 21st, 1920. Steadily his reputation as man and writer increased, and when, in the same year, he came from Dorchester to Oxford to see an undergraduate performance of *The Dynasts*, he saw in the occasion not what others might have seen, — a condescension on his part, but rather a reason to be glad that the young men who fought the war then lately ended recognized and welcomed him.

CHAPTER TEN

New Worlds

The American Business—Canada and Australia—George Macmillan and High Scholarship—" The Golden Bough"—Tennyson and Copyright—The Net Book Agreement—New Premises—The Bentley Purchase—Maurice Macmillan : India and Education —Large-scale Enterprises—Morley's " Gladstone"

HE name of Frederick Macmillan led to the subject of fiction, and fiction, by way of Hardy and Kipling, has drawn the narrative far into the future ; from which it is now necessary to return to the general life of Bedford and St. Martin's-streets during the quarter of a century before the war of 1914.

It has been said that it was among Frederick's special tasks to look after the firm's interests in America. They were to expand fast. When the health of the Macmillans' first agent there, George Edward Brett, began to fail, his son George Platt Brett assumed his responsibilities, and in 1890, on his father's death, formally took over the management. At the same time, the American Macmillans were established as an independent partnership consisting of members of the London firm with George Platt Brett as resident partner. In 1896 the English firm became a limited company and, as a part of the reorganization which followed the death of Alexander, the American group was incorporated and became, as the Macmillan Company of New York, a separate entity under the presidency of G. P. Brett. It ceased to be merely an agency for the sale of English Macmillan's books and became a publishing house. Brett's policy was so to build up the business that each department, regarded almost as an independent kingdom, should rival and if possible outstrip firms that specialized in its particular field. Under his direction and afterwards under that of his son, George Platt Brett, Junior, who joined the firm in 1913 and succeeded his father in the presidency of it in 1936, this policy has been so far successful that the volume of business, which was about fifty thousand dollars annually in 1896, has since been multiplied some two hundred times and now approaches ten million dollars. The firm has branches in Chicago, Dallas, Boston, Atlanta and San Francisco. Before the war of 1939 it maintained its own agencies in Cuba, the Philippines, Hawaii, South America, China and Japan, and acted as agents in the United States for many English publishers as well as for the parent house.

Though the two firms, in London and New York, are independent of each other not only in their organizations but in their choice of books, the link between them has always been close. A book from the London house, likely to find a market in America, will normally go to the American house unless there are reasons to the contrary, and London will usually produce its own edition or import copies of a New York book likely to interest English readers ; but there is no rule in this matter, each firm judges independently its own interest, and both frequently issue books from across the Atlantic produced by houses other than their counterpart. Evidently the educational requirements of the two countries are so different that an interchange of educational books is unusual, but in other departments the exchanges have always been many, and the London lists from 1890 onwards show a steady enrichment from American sources — some American authors attaining so firm a popularity here that they were, so to speak, granted double nationality by admission to the English section of the alphabetical catalogue. Among these was Winston Churchill, of whose *Richard Carvel* a quarter of a million copies were sold in America during its first year, and whose *The Crisis* illustrated the general principle that the author of a novel about the War between the States or Civil War will seldom lack readers if he can write — a principle that Margaret Mitchell has lately put into renewed practice in both countries.

Another stronghold in North America, the Macmillan Company of Canada, dates from 1905, when an opportunity occurred of acquiring the stock of the Moran Publishing Company, and with this as a nucleus and the powerful lists of the London and New York firms at its command, the Canadian Company began business in Toronto. A fortunate purchase of land gave what is now St. Martin's House a site in the business centre of the city. In thirty-eight years the population of Canada has almost doubled ; it has a high standard of education and a keen appetite for books ; but it is still too small to absorb large editions produced for that market alone. The usual practice is therefore for Canadian publishers to represent a group of leading English and American publishers and to import their books for sale in Canada according to demand. Thus the Macmillan Company of Canada handles not only the products of its kindred houses in London and New York, but also those of several other firms for which it acts as agent.

Here again, however, the Macmillans have kept in view a long-term policy, looking to the future of their enterprise and not being unduly discouraged by the immediate financial aspect. They have steadily developed their list of books for the special interests and educational purposes of Canada, given encouragement to Canadian writers, introduced their works to this country, and made a gradual progress towards building on a solid foundation a native Canadian publishing house. No small part of this progress was due to the zeal and the devotion to Canada and Canadian letters of the late Hugh Eayrs, an Englishman who emigrated as a youth and became President of the Canadian company at the age of twenty-six. Conspicuous among the Canadian writers whose work he first published were Louis Hémon, author of the French-Canadian classic, *Maria Chapdelaine*, and Mazo de la Roche, creator of the Whiteoaks of Jalna.

The Australian branch of Macmillan's, in Melbourne, which began its operations in 1904, resembles the Canadian house in that it acts as agent for a number of other publishers, is active in the production of educational books for the special requirements of the Commonwealth, and has struck firm and vigorous root in a country of high literary achievement and unbounded promise for the future.

The English firm, however much it grew, always remained less departmental than the American, division of responsibility being allowed to arise from the tasks and interests of the directors. George Augustin, Alexander's second son, thus attached himself by natural inclination to the firm's music and scholarship. When, having been a King's Scholar at Eton, he joined the business in 1874, he shared a room with George Grove, who was then planning his *Dictionary of Music*, and became his friend. Grove took the young man to the Crystal Palace concerts, trained him in a lexicographer's habits of zeal and thoroughness, instructed his natural taste for music and, said George in reminiscence, for three-cornered jam-tarts. It is possible that George was a little overwhelmed at first by Grove's exuberance, for he was — or at any rate gave an impression of being — of an austerer nature than Frederick. The Sargent portrait shows him with a twinkle in his eye and a good saying ready on his lips, but to his subordinates in the office — and indeed to young authors — his commanding figure, his pale, scholarly face, his stately walk and precise speech, his habit of sitting in a high-backed chair with his fingers pressed together and his gaze aloofly directed at the opposite wall, made him a little intimidating. Not for him, Frederick's delighted fondling of a book that pleased his taste, or Frederick's springy step or eager, impatient tantrums now and then, or his rewarding generosities of praise ; for Frederick had in him much that Edwardians inherited from the Regency and beyond, while, upon George, Victorianism sat earnestly. Such was the probably unfair impression of those who knew him on duty. He was just according to his severity, he was profoundly conscientious, but with a magisterial justice and conscience. At the firm's annual dinner he would unbend and make a cordial and witty speech in the spirit of the Sargent portrait ; but young clerks remembered Sinai as men did who saw Lord Curzon descend, and on Monday morning, if summoned to the presence, went up with souls unfortified.

If this austerity on duty was a defect, it appears to have been George Macmillan's only one. What is more, it was clearly localized. He gave little impression of it to the Society of Dilettanti, or to his friends in Yorkshire where he grew flowers and raised pedigree stock, or when in pursuit of those musical and scholarly interests which gave variety and colour to his personal life and were of enduring value to the firm. His knowledge and love of music led to his becoming Honorary Secretary of the Royal College of Music and Chairman of Stainer and Bell, many important books on music being as a consequence published under the joint imprint. When he was twenty-two, travels in Greece with Mahaffy had confirmed him in Philhellenism, and the year 1879, in which he married and became a partner in the business, had seen the foundation of the Society for Hellenic Studies, of which he was the Honorary Secretary for forty years. From those origins sprang the firm's extraordinary development in the fields of archaeology and classical art, history and literature. The *Antiquities of Ionia*, the *Annual of the British School at Athens*, the *Papers of the British School at Rome*, the *Journal of Hellenic Studies* and other works issued for the Hellenic Society, Frazer's *Pausanias* and *Ovid's Fasti* — all these were part of a long succession of scholarly publications, with perhaps its culmination during George Macmillan's lifetime in Arthur Evans's *The Palace of Minos*. Never was a man better fitted by temperament and inclination to be publisher to Mahaffy, Bury, Dicey, Bryce or Frazer, to the classics, the jurists, the philosophers, the theologians. He devoted himself to them and to the special problems of their books with rare patience and skill, for he loved what he was doing. In doing it, he held a steady balance between his personal passion for good scholarship and his knowledge that it was a passion that could not be indulged at indefinite loss. In the end, publishing must pay, but he took a very long view of profit, was prepared to count it in prestige as well as in sterling, and would wait many years. He was seldom wrong at long last, even financially, and, perhaps, never wrong if we may accept as just his valuation of the good of scholarship. Whatever the limitations of his geniality as he sat in his hard chair, there is none whose life and work have yielded his firm a more lasting or selfless credit.

Late in year 1889 there had come to him this letter, the beginning of many things :

TRINITY COLLEGE, CAMBRIDGE, 8 *November* 89
DEAR SIR,
I shall soon have completed a study in the history of primitive religion which I propose to offer to you for publication. The book is an explanation of the legend of the Golden Bough, as that legend is given by Servius in his commentary on Virgil. According to Servius the Golden Bough grew on a certain tree in the sacred grove of Diana at Aricia, and the priesthood of the grove was held by the man who succeeded in breaking off the Golden Bough and then slaying the priest in single combat. By an application of the comparative method I believe I can make it probable that the priest represented in his person the god of the grove —

Virbius, and that his slaughter was regarded as the death of the god. This raises the question of the meaning of a widespread custom of killing men and animals regarded as divine. I have collected many examples of this custom and proposed a new explanation of it. The Golden Bough, I believe I can show, was the mistletoe, and the whole legend can, I think, be brought into connexion, on the one hand, with the Druidical reverence for the mistletoe and the human sacrifices which accompanied their worship, and, on the other hand, with the Norse legend of the death of Balder. Of the exact way in which I connect the Golden Bough with the priest of Aricia I shall only say that in explaining it I am led to propose a new explanation of the meaning of totemism. This is a bare outline of the book which, whatever may be thought of its theories, will be found, I believe, to contain a large store of very curious customs, many of which may be new even to professed anthropologists. The resemblance of many of the savage customs and ideas to the fundamental doctrines of Christianity is striking. But I make no reference to this parallelism, leaving my readers to draw their own conclusions, one way or the other.

The MS at present amounts to between 500 and 600 foolscap pages, and when completed will probably contain 700 pages, or a little over. I hope to finish it either by the end of this month or early in December.

In offering you the book there are two conditions which I would propose for your consideration and, I should hope, acceptance. They relate to the " get up " of the book. One is that there should be a frontispiece consisting of an engraving or mechanical reproduction of Turner's picture of the Golden Bough. The other is that a drawing of the mistletoe or Golden Bough should be stamped in gold on the cover. A drawing of the mistletoe has been kindly made for this purpose by my friend Prof. J. H. Middleton.

The title of the book will be " The Golden Bough ; a study in the history of religion," or perhaps instead of this " The Legend of the Golden Bough."

With regard to terms, I have special reasons which make it convenient and desirable to receive a fixed sum in payment of the first edition, rather than accept a royalty or half profits, and I am advised by my friends that I should not accept, for the first edition, less than £100. The copy-right I should certainly retain.

I should be glad to hear whether you would be willing to accept the book on these terms.

I may here add that as soon as the book is off my hands, I intend to go out to Greece and there finish the archaeological commentary on Pausanias, residing chiefly at the British School in Athens.

I remain, dear Sir,
Yours faithfully,
JAMES G. FRAZER

George A. Macmillan, Esq.

The manuscript was sent to Morley, who, though not himself a specialist in comparative anthropology, had insight and wisdom enough to leave George Macmillan in no doubt.

Frazer (James G.).   The Golden Bough.
A Study in Comparative Religion.

I have no claim to be an expert in the later works of the comparative anthropologists, but I feel sure that the present MS is an important contribution.   In the first place it is clear that the author has both the scientific and the philosophic spirit.   That is, he knows how to make great inductions of fact, and he is able to suggest probable and connected explanations.   Second, the industry shown by the wide scope and range of his reading, is most remarkable : no German could be more thorough, precise, or definite in his research.   Third, the book shows true ingenuity of mind, which rescues the enormous collection of primitive customs and notions from chaos.   I am as confident as a man can be who is not an expert, that this is a work of the first rank in its own field, and that it extends that field. . . . [Morley then summarized the work and continued :] The style is lucid, unpretentious, and proper to the nature of the subject. No reader would have any trouble in following its pages. The author hopes that he has written a book which may interest, and may be read by " all intelligent persons, and not merely professed students of anthropology and mythology." There is certainly no reason why it should not, except the indolence of even intelligent persons. To the ordinary reader the appearance of so immense a mass of detail, will undoubtedly be repellent. Maine, Spencer, and others, have rather taught a taste for full-grown generalisations in these subjects, without a sight of the materials from which they have sprung. On the other hand, the immense mass of savage customs which the author has gathered together from every age and society contains much that is lively and entertaining. In one sense the field is narrower than that covered by Tylor's *Primitive Culture*. Mr. Frazer deals with one special group of primitive customs, and the theory of them. But undoubtedly it is a very important group — perhaps the most important — in the history of human religion.

I suppose something will depend on the reception given to the book by one or two critics. Questions of primitive myths rouse as hot emotions as irregular Greek verbs or the nature of the Trinity — and it may be that the Sun-men will be down upon our author who is not a Sun-man.

The Golden Bough was at once accepted. As Frazer was about to make the journeys in Greece necessary to his work on Pausanias, he wished to have the business of *The Golden Bough* cleared up before he started. This he made easy by agreeing readily to the terms offered him. He was, he wrote, " highly gratified by the readiness with which you accepted my book and entirely satisfied with the liberal terms " — which were half-profits and an advance of the hundred pounds for which he had asked. He helped also by setting out clearly his own ideas about type and arrangement. Charles Whibley once said of him that he was very rare " in this closely partitioned world," being " at once a scholar and a man of letters " with " an equal devotion to science and to art," and Frazer himself knew well that his book had far outrun a purely scholarly interest and, as a store-house of human fears and aspirations, struck to the heart of the world.

Therefore he cared greatly that it should reach the world. " I wish," he said, " to attract not only students but the general reader, and for this reason I have aimed at giving the book a certain dramatic effect, especially at the opening and the close." It must, then, be published in a form that was not dry, cumbersome and uninviting, but must be easily readable — and he was precise and wise enough to choose even his own printer. He would like his book, he said, to be printed by R. &. R. Clark of Edinburgh, " as I understand that their work is not surpassed by that of any other printer of the day." He was fully justified, and, on this point, as on others he mentioned, Macmillan's, whose connexion with Clark was close and of long standing, needed no persuasion.

The Golden Bough was nevertheless long in reaching the wide public that Frazer had always had in his mind. It appeared in two volumes in May 1890, and, though it at once placed him in the front rank, the sales were very slow. A second edition in three volumes was not called for until ten years later, from which time it grew to seven and ultimately to thirteen volumes. The publishers and the author had no great reward until in 1922 an abridged edition in a single volume suddenly brought a great part of the educated public to it. But long before that, he and the Macmillans had, as it were, grown together. Modest, retiring and kindly, going steadily and unswervingly on with his life's work and bringing in great books, one after another, with a quiet hopefulness, he was a man whom it was good to shelter a little and to tide through difficulties. George and, after him, Harold Macmillan helped the great scholar in many of the chores of life, housing and transporting his books and papers, lifting from him the burden of foreign rights, and giving him that thing which an author supremely needs — confidence, a sense of not being bothered and beset, peace in which to work. The firm was rewarded not only in its association with him but in the power his masterpiece had to draw to the imprint a long list of works on folk-lore, comparative religion, anthropology and kindred subjects — such books as Westermarck's *History of Human Marriage* (1891) and *Marriage Ceremonies in Morocco* (1914), Arthur Evans's *The Mycenaean Tree and Pillar Cult* (1901), Skeat and Blagden's *Pagan Races of the Malay Peninsula* (1906), and Spencer and Gillen's works on Australia). Long - term publishing does not mean only that a book which does not pay to-day may pay to-morrow, but that there are certain books which have power to magnetize an imprint — and many, many others which, though perhaps immediately profitable, demagnetize it. *The Golden Bough*, for over fifty years, has been a magnetizer. Macmillan's list, which had begun in theology and grown through the religious and scientific controversy of Darwinism, received from it a double infusion of new life.

While George Macmillan was concerned in these high things, Frederick had been launched upon his battle for the Net Book Agreement, and Maurice, his younger brother, of whom more will be said when the subject of India is reached, had carried the unspectacular but important responsibility of the firm's educational department. In October 1892, the year of *The Foresters* and *The Death of Oenone*, Tennyson died, and in 1896 old Alexander followed him. To look back upon Tennyson's association with the firm is to wonder a little why he was so long a-coming. He had repeatedly told Alexander that he wished to come when he was free of Moxon, whom someone once called " not a publisher but a secreter of books," and, though it was against Alexander's principles to induce authors to leave other houses for his own, there is no doubt that the acquisition of Tennyson was among the dearest wishes of his heart. Yet Tennyson did not arrive until 1884, after a series of five-year contracts with H. S. King, Strahan, and Kegan Paul. The explanation of such mysteries is often simple and that advanced by

W. E. Cushon, a retired and very senior member of the staff, though it would have distressed the poet's admirers in the 'sixties and 'seventies, seems to-day neither discreditable to him nor unlikely. It is, simply, that he wanted too much money, and, indeed, when he came at last, the terms, though probably less than those he had at first suggested, made the privilege of publishing him dangerous. He accepted a guarantee of four thousand pounds a year, to which were to be added any royalties earned in excess of that amount. Fortunately he was then on the crest of the wave ; the advance payment of four thousand pounds was always comfortably exceeded ; but, in later days, as his work gradually lost copyright and his popularity declined, the fixed payment had to be reduced until the last was only two hundred pounds. Now that his works are being widely read again, the laws of copyright, discriminating against literary property in what is supposed to be the public interest, exclude his representatives from benefit.

That the public interest is, in fact, served by throwing a great writer's work to the wolves and depriving his representatives of control of it is a delusion, and the argument implied in the question " Do you think that the works of Shakespeare ought still to be the property of Shakespeare's heirs ? " will not hold water. Our modern system of registering title is as well able to keep track of title in literary, as in any other kind of, property, and it does not pass the wit of man to devise means of over-ruling an heir to copyright who should prove a curmudgeon and abuse his powers. The only plausible argument for the present system rests upon the notion that, if an author's heirs are deprived of copyright, his books will be more easily and cheaply available to the public, and this notion is false. Alexander Macmillan himself demolished it in a letter to Sir John (Lord) Coleridge, written on July 30th, 1873. He was referring to the old Copyright Act of 1842. The new Act of 1911, in the framing of which Frederick Macmillan had a share, is an improvement on its predecessor in matters of detail, but under it a book goes out of copyright fifty years after its author's death, and Alexander's strictures are still applicable to it.

" There is one thing that your article brings before me so strongly that I cannot help putting it before your practical legal mind, and that is the in-equity of our Law of Copyright as exhibited in the case of Wordsworth. Theoretically I have no absolute belief in property at all, and have a sneaking kindness for Communism of the old Platonic or Christian kind. But if we have Property with a big or a small p, do, please, let it be on an *equitable* basis. Why the Duke of Bedford should compel me to pay him certain sums of money annually because I have built a nice house on a bit of land which he says is his, and Wordsworth's poems should be open to be made money of or mincemeat of, by me or any publisher who chooses to be reckless in what he does, provided only he does business, I cannot understand. I think there is no better instance of the bold shameless injustice of the law — so-called — of copyright than the story you tell in your paper. At the present moment, if Wordsworth's property had been in his family's hands and reasonably well managed, it would well be worth at least three times what it was in 1844 when I saw him, and he then told me he was making £350 a year. Now — if his books had not been pillaged, distorted, misprinted, and imperfectly printed by dozens of publishers of various shades and degrees of conscience — they would be worth an honest £1000 a year. I read some years ago every word that I could find written presenting the semblance of a reason for this state of things, and the more I read the more I became convinced that if we are to have property at all, property in literature is that which stands on the soundest of public as well as private benefit.

All which means that I think you gentlemen who make the laws of the land and maintain them ought to put property in books at least on the same basis as property in land or in the funds. You don't benefit the public : that is demonstrable. All you do is to let anyone send out so-called cheap, often imperfect, editions of our great writers. That anyone may do what he likes in reprinting a great author's work prevents and does not further the production at a cheap rate of really good editions. That the Wordsworth family are £1000 a year poorer than they would have been with a different law, is not a sufficient reason for different legislation, but to you who know them it is at least a reason why this whole question should be considered. The public might with reasonable management have better and as cheap editions as they now have."

If this argument is not enough, Tolstoy's experiment may be considered. Tolstoy renounced copyright in his lifetime, thinking that he was thus unselfishly giving his work to mankind. His generosity had the opposite effect. It at once became perilous for any publisher to undertake the risk of translation in the face of so many potential rivals, and those who did risk a volume now and then were free to put on the market a version as accurate or inaccurate, as faithful or as debased, as they pleased. In consequence, for many years the publication of Tolstoy, unless it was endowed, was a hasty gamble and not what copyright would have made it — a steady, long-term and consistent enterprise.

A corresponding effect is produced by depriving an author's work of copyright within a few decades of his death. Abroad, the risks of a translation are multiplied. At home, though as long as the author remains easily popular his work will come from the press, there is nothing to prevent its being garbled or bowdlerized, nothing to induce any publisher with a long view to nurse a work of art or scholarship during the periods when it is out of fashion, and, since reduction of the price of a book depends much more upon one publisher's assurance of a steady market than upon a sacrifice of the author's royalty, there is a tendency to raise prices against the public rather than to lower them. The law of copyright has been revised again and again ; it will remain unjust, damaging to literature, and contrary to the public interest, as long as it denies to literary property the same rights that are accorded to property of a different kind. To say that nothing ought to be passed down from generation to generation is at any rate comprehensible ; to say that property in a picture or a savings-certificate may be, but property in a book may not, is a proposition which, on the face of it, is unjust and which, for reasons already given, the customary argument for the public interest fails to justify. Apart from any financial consideration, it is to the public advantage that works of literature should be protected from those whose habit is to mutilate or misapply them, and that the author's representative and one publisher should have power and interest to do so.

Alexander had always been interested in this problem of copyright and in many other problems which affected the whole world of books and not his firm alone. Among these was the custom, referred to in an earlier chapter, of selling books to the public not at the price fixed by the publisher but at an irregular discount dependent on each bookseller's discretion or, rather, upon the conditions which a cut-throat competition forced upon him. Alexander's letters on the subject are dated in the 'sixties, but at that time no remedy could be found and it was left to his nephew, Frederick, to fight and win a difficult battle which resulted in the Net Book Agreement.

The trouble dated from 1852. At that time there existed a Booksellers' Association whose members were pledged not to sell books below their published prices ; the publishers, on their side, having agreed to allow trade terms to none but a member of the Association. A few booksellers began to undersell and their supplies were accordingly cut off ; but some publishers, believing that they were defending the interests of free trade, supported the undersellers, and in this were backed by many of the leading writers of that day, including Dickens. The dispute was submitted to the arbitration of Lord Campbell, Dean Milman and George Grote, whose ruling was, in effect, that the Association was an illegal conspiracy and that a publisher had no right to dictate the retail price at which his books should be sold. The Association was dissolved ; competitive underselling became universal ; and, since a customer would always go where prices were lowest, discounts steadily increased. " Whereas in former days," Alexander wrote to Gladstone on April 10th, 1868, " there used to be many booksellers who kept good stocks of solid standard books . . . and lived by selling books, the case is now that in country towns few live by bookselling : the trade has become so profitless that it is generally the appendage to a toyshop, or a Berlin wool warehouse and a few trashy novels, selling for a shilling, with flaring covers suiting the flashy contents, and the bookseller who studies what books are good and worth recommending to his customer has ceased to exist. Intelligence and sympathy with literature has gone out of the trade almost wholly. I believe the general intelligence of the country has suffered by it. My conviction, based on an experience of some thirty years, is that an intelligent bookseller in every town of any importance in the kingdom would be almost as valuable as an intelligent schoolmaster or parson. How can you get that if you don't pay him for his work and thought ? "

This was the problem that Frederick Macmillan had to face more than twenty years later. He knew that to produce a scheme of reform that would command universal consent was impossible ; the trade must be led gently towards its own salvation. Therefore, on March 6th, 1890, he published in *The Bookseller* a letter headed " A Remedy for Underselling " in which he put forward a permissive compromise. He suggested that new books should be divided into two classes — Net Books, to be sold at the published price without discount, and Subject Books, to be sold subject to discount at each bookseller's discretion. A publisher who preferred the old system would be under no compulsion to publish net books, and an author could make, with regard to his own work, what stipulation he pleased. The project was widely discussed inside and outside the trade. The result was not encouraging ; the hard-heads decided that Mr. Macmillan was a well-meaning but unpractical idealist. Fortunately Mr. Macmillan was not discouraged. He liked his scheme, he knew that it was right, and decided at personal risk to press it. If no one would come with him, he would go on alone. The Macmillans took counsel together and resolved to publish a few books at net prices, to offer them to booksellers on the terms set out in Frederick's letter and to await events. If they were boycotted, they would stand their ground. They knew that they commanded a powerful good-will ; there were many booksellers throughout the country who hated the old system, who had been withheld from the new only by fear or inertia, and would welcome a lead. An even more important consideration, based upon Frederick's own experience as a retailer, was that, if a book is good enough, a bookseller cannot afford to be without it. " It was important," Frederick wrote afterwards in his privately printed volume on the Net Book Agreement, "that the book chosen should be a good one, because, if the first net book did not sell, its failure would certainly be attributed to its *netness* and not to its quality."

Nowadays, a publisher called upon to choose a book for such a purpose might incline towards a novel or a biography by a popular writer for which there would almost certainly be an instant demand. The Macmillans' choice, Professor Alfred Marshall's *Principles of Economics*, was characteristic of them. They saw that what they needed was not necessarily a book of which many thousands would be sold in a few weeks, but one so important in its own field that it would be to a bookseller's discredit not to stock it, and so steadily enduring that the pressure it exercised would be continuous year after year. Marshall's great work, in their judgement, fulfilled these conditions ; it would, they were assured, become a classic in its own kind ; and the author was willing, and even eager, that an economic experiment should be made with it. When it was published in July 1890, advertisements and a notice in every copy explained that the terms on which it was sold to booksellers did not allow of its being re-sold by them at less than the published price.

The book was at once recognized, *The Times* describing it as a contribution of capital importance to the higher literature of economic science. The first edition of 2000 copies at 12s. 6d. net was soon exhausted, and there was a second, with additions to the text, of 3000 copies in 1891. The sequel may be worth recording in parenthesis : the book was for years described as " Vol. I ", but there was never a Vol. II, as the author continually tried new ways of treating his subject and would never allow himself to be satisfied ; there have been eight editions — that is, eight substantial revisions and resettings of the text, apart from innumerable re-printings or " impressions " ; the eighth edition of 1920 has, for example, been reprinted six times ; and it may be added as evidence of the book's endurance that up to July 1942 forty thousand had been sold in England, that its highest sales were in its fourth decade and that they are to-day higher than at any time during its first thirty years of life. Frederick had chosen wisely, but the opposition to net books was stubborn among many booksellers, and Macmillan's had to make a rule that they would allow trade terms to those dealers only who would undertake not to cut prices. They published sixteen net books in 1890, and the number rose yearly until by 1897 it reached 136. Other publishers had followed suit meanwhile, but still the proportion of net books was small. Nevertheless the way in which the wind was blowing could not be mistaken. When

the society of the Associated Booksellers of Great Britain and
Ireland was formed in 1895, it passed resolutions approving
of the net book system and exhorted publishers to enforce
it more vigorously. In October of the same year, the
Publishers' Association was formed as a counterpart of the
booksellers' organization, and the possibility of agreement
throughout the trade became less remote. The Associated
Booksellers, in 1897, put forward a proposal for the limiting
of discount, but the Society of Authors would not accept it.
The booksellers suggested a new but too complex plan ; the
Publishers' Association passed resolutions in favour of the
net system for new books ; but there was no definite step
forward until, in January 1899, the Publishers' Association
sent to the Associated Booksellers a draft scheme for their
consideration. This was examined clause by clause during
February and unanimously accepted. Booksellers throughout the country signed the resulting Net Book Agreement,
and even the most obstinate of resisters, a large City firm
whose account with Macmillan's had long been closed because
they had insisted upon cutting prices, chose to conform at
last.rather than go out of business. Ever since that time the
net system has grown steadily. Even fiction, once considered
to be outside the scope of the agreement, is now, with little
exception, included in it, and net prices apply to almost all
copyright books other than school-books. Many a bookseller
in a small town is still unable to live by books alone, but he is
at any rate free of the fear that he may be undersold by a
larger rival in the next street. Instances of price-cutting are
rare ; penalties are unhesitatingly enforced ; and the whole
trade is more stable and prosperous than it was.

While the battle for the Net Book Agreement was being
fought, new premises had been designed for the firm by John
Cash and built under his supervision. In 1897 they moved
in. Hitherto, in Henrietta-street and Bedford-street, they
had had to adapt themselves ; now, for the first time, they

had elbow-room and a building fully constructed for their requirements. It stood, and stands, in St. Martin's-street, which runs down the hill from the bottom of Leicester-square towards the back of the National Gallery. It was in St. Martin's-street, on the east side, between Long Court and the Huguenot Chapel, that Sir Isaac Newton lived from 1710 until 1725 and passed the proofs of the third edition of his *Principia*, and to the same house, forty-five years later, Dr. Burney came, and lived there from 1770 to 1789, during which time his daughter, Fanny, wrote *Evelina*. Macaulay, thus encouraged to prophecy, declared that Newton's house would for ever be an object of veneration, but fate denied him. In 1913 the house was pulled down and a public library reigns in its stead. Nevertheless with Hogarth's ghost in Cranbourn-street near by and Joshua Reynolds's in Leicester-square, Macmillan's new premises were respectably endowed by the past.

They were, in fact, a block enclosed by narrow streets and had the inestimable advantage, for those whose merchandise goes out in carts, of having three frontages. That in Blue Cross-street was but twenty-four feet long, but there were thirty-three yards in St. Martin's-street in front and thirty-five in Whitcomb-street behind, so that a covered way could pierce the building and allow the vans to come in, load from hydraulic lifts, and go out in a continuous stream. Opening on to the covered way were the packing-rooms, behind and beneath the packing-rooms were stock-rooms with shelves for a million and a quarter books, and, in the front of the house, on the ground floor and first floor, were a hall, waiting-rooms and a series of directors' rooms, looking over the area behind the National Gallery which, having long ago been a mews, was in 1897 occupied by barracks. Not many years afterwards, the barracks were demolished, and the directors have since found themselves looking out over an open space. Odd things have happened there. During the war of 1914 it was a drill-ground for recruits ; during the war of 1939, shouts, splashes and explosions arising from it signified that Civil Defence workers were undergoing their ordeal of fire and water ; and across this space the treasures of the National Gallery were borne to their refuge from bombs.

At about the time of the Macmillans' move, Richard Bentley grew weary of presiding over Richard Bentley & Son at 8 New Burlington-street. The business was not bankrupt ; on the contrary it was flourishing ; and Richard Bentley was neither sick nor old — he was but forty-four in 1898 and had, though he cannot have been sure of it, thirty-eight years to live. He retired from business for the rarest and best of all reasons — that he wished to retire, and this made easy what is known in Macmillan's history as the Bentley Purchase. There can never have been less discussion and bargaining over a complex transaction than is to be found in the correspondence between Richard Bentley and Maurice Macmillan. The problems of stock, authors and staff — each full of trouble for a doubtful buyer or an unwilling seller — were solved without difficulty. A price of £8000 was paid and the transfer completed in August.

Bentley's list, though rich in variety, was not of great size, but his stock was disproportionately large. He had had the optimistic custom of printing ten thousand copies of a novel where Macmillan's might have printed two thousand, and his stock of bound copies and unbound sheets was consequently swollen. He had, too, a great store of steel and copper plates by Cruikshank, Tenniel, Du Maurier and others, and of portraits belonging to such works as Horace Walpole's *Letters*, Bourrienne's *Napoleon Bonaparte* or Thiers' *French Revolution*. Many of these books and plates, being of no interest to Macmillan's, were sold, and fetched so good a price that the success of the Bentley Purchase was put beyond all future question. Maurice Macmillan was able to consider what remained with satisfaction unmixed with anxiety.

What remained was no small matter. Many of the books, valuable in those days, are now forgotten, but a few are memorable : Mommsen's *Rome*, for example, FitzGerald's *Letters to Fanny Kemble*, Barham's *Theodore Hook* and the only complete editions of the *Ingoldsby Legends*. Still in the catalogue are Selous's *Hunter's Wanderings in Africa*, H. Fielding Hall's classic of Burma, *The Soul of a People*, and an acquisition particularly prized, Lord Roberts's *Forty-One Years in India*. Mrs. W. K. Clifford's *Aunt Anne* was among a list of fiction strong in women. There were " Mrs. Alexander," whose inverted commas are to be respectfully preserved, and the lady who, with the economy habitual in some American newspapers, may be called Mrs. Annie (*Ought We to Visit Her ?*) Edwardes. Rhoda Broughton was there, Helen Mathers, Mary Cholmondeley with *Diana Tempest*, Jessie Fothergill with *The First Violin* and Florence Montgomery with *Misunderstood*. These three books were until quite recently in print, as were a dozen of Rosa N. Carey's, though Bentley had said that her popularity was slow in coming. Among the men were Anthony Trollope, represented unfortunately by *The Three Clerks*, J. S. Le Fanu with *Uncle Silas* and *In a Glass Darkly*, and Marcus Clarke whose *For the Term of his Natural Life* is in the list to-day. But the chief prize was Mrs. Henry Wood. Her thirty-one volumes were published on commission and have remained the property of her heirs. Changed fashions and the conditions of war are driving even her work out of print, and yet it is true that until the war of 1914 great cases of her sixpenny editions were sent out every week to satisfy the Australian demand alone. She brought with her, as well as her books, a magazine, *The Argosy*, which had been her own property and which Macmillan's ran for a time, and there was another magazine, *Temple Bar*, included in the Bentley Purchase. Bentley did not sever his connexion with it until 1900, but Maurice Macmillan was in charge and ran it as his personal venture under the editorship of Mrs. Gertrude Townshend Mayer, for a long time one of the firm's Readers. Taken for all in all it was a formidable acquisition, with a few works of genuine quality and many books which were then, and long remained, extremely alive, not because they were challenges to opinion (Bentley's were cautious in that matter) but because they had the virtue of story-telling. With them came members of Bentley's staff whom the Macmillans learned to value. They arrived in the top-hats and formal dress which were the custom of Bentley's employees. Some discarded this uniform on arrival ; others of the old guard, who at first persisted in it, allowed it to fade away ; but one held firmly on through the years. He was, as chance would have it, a packer, and he packed decorously to the last. When all others of his calling were lost to grace, his top-hat remained the memorial and the crown of the Bentley Purchase.

In the old days such negotiations as led to the Bentley Purchase would presumably have fallen to Craik, the firm's " Chancellor of the Exchequer." That they became the special care of Maurice Macmillan is an instance of the flexibility of the understanding between him and his partners, for though it was a foible of his to pretend that his hard-headedness had been given to the world as a check upon his elder brother's enthusiasms, his interests were far from being dully commercial, and the best work of his life was given to the firm's educational publications and to the control of their policy in India. A scholar of Uppingham and of Christ's College, Cambridge, he had taken a First in the Classical Tripos in 1875. For six years, from 1877, he was classical master at St. Paul's School, and in

1883 became a partner in the firm. Having then married an American lady, Helen Artie Belles, he made a tour of India and Australasia in 1884 and 1885.

More than twenty years earlier, Alexander, writing to G. O. Trevelyan about the articles in *Macmillan's Magazine*, which were afterwards to be published as *The Competition Wallah*, had mentioned the growth of the firm's business with India. He saw clearly that it might become much more than a market for certain books exported from London, but at the time he had no other guide to Indian requirements than the demand for those books. In 1873, the first forward step was taken. Lethbridge, afterwards Sir Roper Lethbridge, of the Bengal Education Service and Principal of Krishnagar College, put forward a scheme for the publication of school-books specially adapted for Indian use. As a result, four readers of his own on history and geography, and six Books of Reading by P. C. Sircar of Presidency College, Calcutta, were issued in 1875 as Macmillan's Series of Text-Books for Indian Schools. How great the need for these was is shown by the fact that over five million copies of the Sircar books alone have been sold since they came to the firm.

No one can investigate the history of educational publication in India without being impressed by the special difficulties of the task and by the rare devotion and skill of the Englishmen engaged in it. The English educationists in India evidently combined the virtue of not playing down with an exceptional breadth of view, for, though they were writing for an audience with special needs, many of the books they wrote or edited for use in India have had an enduring success at home when included in the *English Classics* series. Alexander had been eager to carry on this Indian development and studied it with the utmost care. His " great aim," he wrote to Lethbridge, was " to get the very best men in each kind of knowledge to write the most elementary books,"

and so successful was his policy that when Maurice Macmillan made his long journey in '84 the time was drawing
near for another step forward. He visited the chief educational centres and the principal booksellers' of India and
Australasia and returned home to give effect to the experience
he had gained. Nothing revolutionary was attempted at
once, but in 1893, in view of the increasing range and
complexity of the Indian market, the firm appointed an
educational agent in India, whose duty was to travel and
study — in short, to do regularly and consistently what
Maurice himself had done during his tour. At the same time
the previous system of supplying the Indian market from a
base in London was found to be inadequate, and an advance-
base was established in India itself, arrangements being
made with John Dickinson & Co., paper manufacturers, to
accommodate stocks of Macmillan publications. This was
a prelude to the opening, in 1901, of a branch in Bombay,
which two years later was housed in a new Macmillan
Building designed by John Cash, the architect of the London
premises. Other branches soon had their own quarters in
Calcutta (1907) and in Madras (1913), while agencies were
established in Mangalore, Colombo and Rangoon. Travellers
made regular visits to Malaya and beyond, and gradually
there arose a steady demand in China for Chinese books on
English grammar, composition and science.

Thus Maurice Macmillan, when the time was ripe, put
into practice the ideas that had been stirring forty years
earlier in Alexander's mind. The three steps forward are
clear : first, books designed for use in England were, when
they appeared to be suitable, sent out ; second, books were
specially planned for Indian requirements but still published
in London and exported ; and finally Macmillan's began to
publish in India and to produce books in most of the chief
vernaculars of the East. The resulting business has been very
large and may reasonably claim, together with the work of

other publishers, to have done much for the advancement of education in India.

Maurice Macmillan was not a talkative idealist. If he had been asked why he gave unsparing labour to every detail of the Indian publications, his answer would probably have been the plain one : that they were his business and that it paid to do business well ; but he would not have done the business as well as he did if his eagerness for precision had not been fortified by a knowledge that, whatever other criticisms might be directed against British administration in India, there was reason for pride in the devotion of the educational authorities there and in the progress they were making.

Not India only but all the detailed labour arising from the firm's great educational catalogue fell upon him. The established series were continually revised and extended. Dr. W. G. Rutherford's Greek Course was followed by A. M. Cook and W. E. P. Pantin's Latin Course. First Eugene Fasnacht, then Otto Siepmann, produced an elaborate set of books for students of French and German. The series established under the title of *English Literature for Secondary Schools* grew to remarkable scope and success under the editorship of J. H. Fowler, who for many years advised the firm on English books. The names of such authors and editors as Sir Richard Gregory, A. T. Simmons, H. E. Hadley, E. Edser, and J. Duncan were associated with an ever longer array of scientific text-books. As the years passed, elementary education was given increasing attention. There were History and Geography Readers for all seven Standards, Literary Readers from the Primary stage upwards, and a mass of apparatus. As well as special editions for Indian schools, there were Readers in Afrikaans for South Africa, in Swahili for East Africa, in Arabic for Egypt, Anglo-Chinese Readers and Australasian Readers — which may explain the order of the American general to his troops in 1942 : that, when they went to Australia, they were to make themselves familiar with the customs and language of the inhabitants. All these matters, together with the firm's paper supplies, their binding, their travellers' reports and the business of their depots, fell upon Maurice. No man could have borne it who was not an educational enthusiast. As it was, Maurice Macmillan built up what is, perhaps, the firm's most solid asset — an educational series which to-day, under the control of his son, Daniel, continuously renews its youth. The benefit of his work to Macmillan's must certainly extend far into the future.

The structure of a publisher's educational list is built up with many small bricks, but the twenty-four years that followed 1890 were a prosperous and lavish period in which ordinary publishing could afford to make large ventures that may never again be possible. The Furniss Thackeray and the collected Henry James were failures, but little else was. Costly editions of Lamb, Kingsley, Pater, Arnold, Tennyson, FitzGerald and Kipling were bought eagerly. Austin Dobson edited Madame D'Arblay in six volumes and Evelyn in three. There were five volumes of Sir Henry Craik's *English Prose Selections* and six of W. J. Courthope's *History of English Poetry*. Grove's *Dictionary of Music* went into a second edition (1906–08), and in 1899 the firm published the first two of John Fortescue's thirteen volumes on *The History of the British Army* and began an eight-volume *History of the English Church* by W. R. W. Stephens, Dean of Winchester, and the Rev. Dr. William Hunt.

What were called Colour Books poured out from Macmillan's as they did from every publisher at that time. The *Illustrated Standard Novels* and the *Cranford Series* are of more lasting interest because they were rich in the now vanishing art of pen draughtsmanship. The *Highways and Byways Series*, begun with *Devon and Cornwall* in 1897, gave opportunity to such men as Hugh Thomson, Joseph Pennell, F. L. Griggs and Edmund H. New, and, still with John Morley to choose the writers, a new series of *English Men of Letters* was begun in 1902. Frederic Harrison's *Ruskin* and Leslie Stephen's *George Eliot* were exceptionally popular and a bold choice of Chesterton for *Browning* was rewarded by a sale of eleven thousand copies in a year. The *Twelve English Statesmen* should have had its counterpart in *Twelve Foreign Statesmen*, but, as Professor J. B. Bury, the editor, did not produce his own projected *Catherine the Great*, the dozen was never made up. *English Men of Action* was more extensive, ranging from Warwick the King-Maker to General Gordon. The *Golden Treasury Series* continued to prosper, and the *Eversley Series*, which had begun like so much else in Macmillan's history with an edition of Kingsley, had Herford's *Eversley Shakespeare* added to it in 1899. It grew in the end to almost two hundred volumes.

Among the large-scale enterprises of the period were many medical and other scientific works. The *Cambridge Natural History*, particularly dear to George Macmillan's heart, was an undertaking of great cost. Macmillan's carried the whole burden, paying the editors and authors for their copyright, and expecting no profit except in prestige. But once again George Macmillan's ship came home ; never was there a better combination of shrewdness and patience than in that man. This time the voyage was a long one. The first of the ten volumes was published in 1895, and not until thirty-five years later was the *Cambridge Natural History* found by another generation of book-keepers to have paid its expenses. Allbutt's *System of Medicine* (1896–9), issued on the same basis, gave a swifter reward, as did a later edition in nine volumes. Allbutt and Playfair's *System of Gynaecology* (1896 : 2nd ed., 1906), Allchin's *Manual of Medicine* (5 vols., 1900–1903), Stonham's *Manual of Surgery* (3 vols., 1899) and Luigi Luciani's *Human Physiology* (5 vols., 1911–21) were

members of this formidable group. Several of the chief
scientific books were translations : Strasburger's *Textbook of
Botany*, Zittel's *Textbook of Palaeontology*, Gattermann's
Organic Chemistry and Ratzel's *History of Mankind*, which
was issued in thirty-five monthly parts from 1895. Parker
and Haswell's *Textbook of Zoology*, which began in 1898, has
recently gone into its sixth edition. Old Daniel and Alexander's lesson of long-term publishing, which, when they
lacked capital in the early days, they had found so much
difficulty in putting into effect, had been well learned.

Unfortunately for them and, we may well believe, through
no fault of theirs, none of their capital, except their imprint,
was risked in the book which was the outstanding success of
the period. John Morley's *Life of Gladstone* belonged to
Gladstone's family. Morley wrote, and Macmillan's published, it to their commission. It appeared in three volumes
on October 9th, 1903. To those of us who are too young to
remember Gladstone's emotional impact on the people of
England, the excitement caused by the publication of his
biography must seem one of the curiosities of the past, but it
is a fact that historians would do well to take into account.
Seen from the publisher's point of view the *Life of Gladstone*
is fabulous. " When I first came to the office ten years later,"
an observer has recalled, " it seemed to me that the staff was
still mopping its brow after the ordeal. Whatever later crisis
arose, someone would inevitably say : ' You should have
seen us when we published Morley's *Gladstone*.' " There
are stories of the volumes stacked everywhere in lofty piles,
of men running up ladders to hurl down the topmost
packages to collectors fighting for them at the trade counter,
of vast labours without food or sleep ; and, even though we
discount a little the romance of old campaigners, it is plain
truth that such scenes were enacted then as never before or
since. The public was clamorous and insatiable. 25,041
copies were sold in the first year. On May 6th, 1904, within

less than seven months of publication, Macmillan's sent the Gladstones a cheque for £23,872 : 5 : 7. Soon afterwards the family received £4000 and then £2000 from New York. Three years later, in 1906, the *Life* was issued in fifteen sixpenny parts and in two volumes at 5s. In 1908–9, the *Daily Chronicle* arranged to publish a 5s. Lloyd's Edition of 50,000 copies, and in 1911-12 the book had a new and large sale as three volumes of Macmillan's Shilling Library. People wrote letters of almost tearful gratitude to the firm for having made available in cheap editions the *Life* of so noble and revered a man, and partisans observed with grim satisfaction that no equal prodigy of fortune attended the birth of Monypenny's *Disraeli*. What Morley, who was an ironist, may have thought in 1903 we can only guess. He himself had not always been prostrate at Gladstone's shrine. In September 1877, Alexander had invited Gladstone, J. R. Green and the Dean of St. Paul's to dine with him at the Garrick, and asked Morley to join them. The reply was this :

4 CHESHAM PLACE, BRIGHTON

MY DEAR MACMILLAN,

I will dine with you on Monday at the Garrick at 7.0 with much pleasure.

N.B. Gladstone has nothing to say to men like you and me — but it is interesting to see the kind of men whom the world thinks great. Foolish world !

Ever yours affectionately,

J. M.

Sept. 20, 77.

CHAPTER ELEVEN

The Book War

*" The Times " Book Club—Difficulties—Open War—Increasing
Bitterness—Peace*

HE year 1906, when the *Life of Gladstone* was appearing in sixpenny parts, is considered by many to mark the end of a political and social epoch even more accurately than the year 1914. After it, Victorianism was dead ; Liberalism, in spite of such Gladstonian survivals as Morley himself, was electorally at its height but nevertheless on its way to eclipse ; Conservatism was shifting the basis of its power ; a new form of collective materialism was henceforth to be infused into national and international thought. One of the consequences of this change was that battles, large and small, began to be fought with the gloves off. Midlothian, considered fierce in its time, gave place to Limehouse, and even the battles of publishing were fought with a new ferocity. Frederick Macmillan's establishment of the Net Book System had been the reward of a vigorous struggle, but his maintenance of it against assault by *The Times* deserved the name, The Book War, by which it is remembered.

The Times Book Club, Frederick wrote in his account of this bitter contest,[1] was founded in 1905 " for the purpose of improving the fortunes of *The Times* newspaper, and I am sure that there was no deliberate intention on the part of its originator — Horace E. Hooper — to injure a system which he probably knew little about. It so happened that the lines

[1] *The Net Book Agreement 1899 and the Book War 1906-1908*, by Sir Frederick Macmillan. Printed for the Author by Robert MacLehose & Co. Ltd., Glasgow, 1924.

on which Hooper proposed to carry on his Book Club would, had he succeeded, have proved fatal to the publication of net books." The controversy, though once very fierce, is over. *The Times* Book Club as it now exists runs its circulating library and its bookselling business in conformity with the Net Book Agreement. The days are gone in which *The Times* newspaper engaged all its forces in a general attack on publishers. There is no need to revert to them in detail, but Macmillan's part in the affair cannot be passed over in any account of the firm's life.

In 1898, an American speculator, H. E. Hooper, had obtained from Messrs. Black, who owned the *Encyclopaedia Britannica*, the right to use the stereotype plates, and *The Times* had startled the world by participating in the sale of the consequent reprint and launching a gigantic advertising campaign in support of it. What was sold was the Ninth Edition, which had already been offered by Black's to the trade at a much reduced price, but the discontent of many purchasers was countered by the publication of supplementary volumes. Thus, said Edward Bell, " *The Times* and the speculators who worked in their name made a secondary and very handsome profit." Other enterprises followed. " Various large literary works were projected, advertised and sold," and it became clear that *The Times* was bent upon supplementing the ordinary revenues of a newspaper. In 1904 it offered itself to subscribers for £3 instead of £3 : 18s. a year. In 1905, the old price was restored and it was announced that every annual subscriber would enjoy membership of a Book Club or lending library which would lend books as soon as they were asked for. Used copies would be sold at reduced prices.

To make sure of supplies *The Times* approached several publishers individually but made no general treaty with the trade. Hooper had come to St. Martin's-street early in 1905. His argument was that more books could be sold by the employment of new methods. The Book Club would be a buyer on a large scale, would therefore expect the best trade terms, and would like to enter into a contract for a number of years. Similar inducements were offered to other publishers. Some entered into a contract for one year, some for longer. Frederick was more cautious. He says that he " listened respectfully to Mr. Hooper's remarks. When, however, he said incidentally, ' Of course we shall be at liberty to do what we like with the books we have bought and paid for,' I pricked up my ears and asked whether there might not be a danger of his finding himself in difficulties about the sale of net books. All I could get from Hooper was that net books would have to look after themselves, and I told him, therefore, that my firm, although we should be glad to sell him all the books he could buy, could not enter into any contract that would oblige us to continue our supplies to *The Times* Book Club if we found it advisable to stop them. It thus came about that when the Book Club began its operations Macmillan & Co. were almost the only publishers who had no contract of any sort or kind with it. . . . When difficulties arose, most of them appeared to be under contracts — varying as to terms and period, but all obliging them to continue their supplies for a time whether they liked it or not."

Difficulties arose swiftly. The arrangement suggested to the trade by the Club after its formation was that the Club should buy at the lowest trade terms while the publishers should undertake to spend on advertising in *The Times* one-fifth (later reduced to 15 per cent) of the value of the books bought by the Club. Booksellers pointed out that this was only another way of giving a special discount. Although the Manager of *The Times* had signed the Net Book Agreement on behalf of the Club, the booksellers distrusted the whole scheme, and the condition insisting upon advertising in the newspaper was withdrawn. Nevertheless the campaign that followed the Club's opening in September 1905 was in itself enough to make any normal bookseller fear for his livelihood. Books which had been in circulation for about a month, about three months, or for more than three months, some of them described as " clean and uninjured copies " and " virtually as good as new," were offered to the public at discounts (in the case of net books) of 10, 33⅓ and 50 per cent respectively. The argument of *The Times* was that these books were " second-hand " and so not subject to the provisions of the Net Book Agreement. The booksellers said that they were not, in any genuine and reasonable sense, second-hand at all. They protested to the Publishers' Association, which obtained from Moberly Bell assurances that seemed satisfactory. The Club also appeared to take a step forward by defining a second-hand book as one that had been used by more than two subscribers and returned in such a condition that it could not be sold as new. But the booksellers were dissatisfied with the interpretation of this principle and in May 1906 the publishers tried to persuade *The Times* to fix a time limit of six months within which surplus copies of new books should not be sold. The Club would not commit itself so far, but an approach was made to an agreement that surplus books should in the first place be offered to the publishers or the booksellers. The publishers went away from Printing House Square feeling that progress had been made, and were surprised when *The Times* afterwards asserted that they had broken off promising negotiations. Here there seems to have been honest misunderstanding, for it is true that the booksellers, when asked, refused to help the Club to dispose of its surplus stock ; but the course of events suggests that the Club had the bit between its teeth and intended to go on without regard for publishers or booksellers. Within a few days of the meeting *The Times* advertised a sale of " sample bargains." *Lord Randolph*

Churchill, recently published at thirty-six shillings, was offered to the public for seven, and six-shilling novels for ninepence or elevenpence each.

About novels and other non-net books the publishers had not greatly protested, but the sale of recent net books, many of them unused, at low prices, and the treatment of surplus copies of a new book as " remainders," threatened the whole system of the trade. Therefore in July 1906 the Publishers' Association held a meeting. They resolved that a net book should not be sold as second-hand within six months, and referred to the Council another resolution to the effect that, within the same period, a non-net book should not be sold for less than 75 per cent of its published price. Frederick Macmillan proposed and carried a resolution governing the treatment of net books as remainders, and John Murray wound up the proceedings by urging publishers to abstain from advertising in *The Times*.

The outcome of this meeting was a revised Net Book Agreement tightening the provisions of the old. It was signed by almost every publisher and bookseller of standing and was to come into force on October 1st. Publishing firms which had contracts with *The Times* would have to continue, for the period of their contract, to supply the Club under the terms of the old agreement if the paper would not accept the new, and Moberly Bell stood out. He said he had to keep his contract with his subscribers, which had been made under the old terms, and could not accept the new without a year's notice. Seeing the justice of this and desiring settlement, the publishers offered to limit the new terms to new or renewed subscriptions — an offer that Moberly Bell might have done well to accept. At this stage of the contest, it appears to an impartial and distant observer that there was a chance of negotiated peace. *The Times* might have recognized that, whether it was right or wrong in its interpretation of the agreements it had made, its practice was ruinous to a great industry, not because, in its capacity of bookseller, it was a normally successful competitor with other booksellers, but because, by using a newspaper organization extraneous to bookselling and by hitching its bookselling trade on to its struggle for circulation, it was making impossible the life of independent traders. The original project of linking a circulating library to a newspaper was not illegitimate ; the publishers had not opposed it ; but *The Times*, perhaps unwittingly, had committed itself to the granting of privileges to its subscribers so costly that it was driven to desperate courses. The truth seems to be that the Book Club could not be run without disastrous loss unless the outgoings were drastically reduced. They could be reduced by two means : either by revising the terms offered to subscribers to the newspaper — the means ultimately adopted ; or by forcing down the cost of books in such a way as might put all publishers and all booksellers out of business. Moberly Bell chose to fight.

When he had refused the publishers' suggestion for limiting the new agreement, there issued from Printing House Square a pamphlet, *The History of the Book War*, which described the publishers' action as " an insolent repudiation of the agreement " and spoke of " the studious withholding of any alternative agreement." Beginning on September 25th, a series of large advertisements then appeared in *The Times*. The first, called " An Attempt at a Monopoly," accused the publishers of trying to prevent the Club " from giving readers the earliest possible opportunity of purchasing at reduced prices books which have been for some time in circulation at the library, and which are therefore second-hand." This, the publishers may reasonably have felt, was to beg the question, but it was adroit controversy. Next day, another manifesto, " The Real Evil," took a different and less discreet line. It maintained that publishers' prices were out of all proportion to the cost of production. It set out the cost, at low rates, of paper, composition, printing and binding, and estimated that a book published at 36s. cost 4s. to produce. The author's royalty, the cost of advertising, the overhead expenses of a publisher's office and all allowances to retailers were omitted from this calculation, and the publishers were accused of making a profit of 800 per cent. *The Times* was over-stating its case, and over-stating it in a way which in the end was the cause of the publishers' victory, for the figures came up for verification in a court of law, but for the moment a gullible public eagerly believed that they were being cheated. The remaining advertisements were addressed to the booksellers' problem. " A False Plea " suggested that the publishers were defending the booksellers with no more honourable motive than to keep up high prices, while " A Glaring Injustice to the Bookseller " denounced the restrictions of the Net Book Agreement which almost every retailer had gladly accepted. The booksellers finding themselves thus represented as Andromeda may have been a little astonished to see Mr. H. E. Hooper cast for the part of Perseus.

The course set by these four advertisements was strenuously pursued for months. Dr. Arthur Shadwell, an economist, in the course of seven articles in *The Times*, irritated the publishers by his ignorance of their business and of the real issue of the net price and can scarcely have delighted the newspaper by his censure of its blunders in " The Real Evil." Meanwhile the Publishers' Association put the Club on the black list reserved for booksellers who would not conform to the new Net Book Agreement. Until it signed, books would be supplied to it at full price only. A pamphlet was issued setting out the publishers' case, a committee and a fund were created to carry on the warfare, and answers, which the paper conscientiously inserted, were written to *The Times*. Late in October, the publishers, nearly all of whom had withdrawn their advertisements, decided that no books whatever should be supplied to the Club except under existing contracts. The Club was hard-pressed. It could still obtain books from the wholesalers Simpkin's, but only at a price higher than it had been accustomed to pay when buying directly from publishers themselves.

The controversy had by this time become much more than a trade dispute. The prestige of *The Times* itself, and not only the success or failure of the Club and the independent booksellers, was involved in it. Discussion was hot through the length and breadth of England, and, as often happens when Englishmen become angry, the word freedom was freely abused. Many honest people, including Shaw, sided with *The Times*, but the daily and weekly press and the monthly reviews generally opposed it. Most authors, as individuals, hedged, but the Society of Authors formally recorded its disapproval of the Club's methods. Kipling, who, as has been said, was no lover of publishers, on this issue firmly supported them, but Mrs. Humphry Ward, who disliked anything that interrupted the sale of books and had good reasons for being well-disposed towards *The Times* and towards Macmillan's and Smith, Elder, cultivated an olive-branch, attempting to mediate through a committee of authors that had Lord Goschen as its chairman. Nothing came of it, and nothing substantial came of a Livery Dinner of the Fishmongers' Company at which Edward Bell, president of the Publishers' Association, was seated next to Arthur Walter, chief proprietor of *The Times*, and the two Bells, Edward and Moberly, were both invited to respond to the toast of " The Diffusion of Literature." Courtesy prevailed but enmity continued. The Association had black-listed the Book Club, and on October 20th, Arthur Walter had written to his subscribers a letter containing the following passage and the following italics :

The Book War

You can greatly assist us in defending your interests if you will, for the present, *neither put upon your library lists nor buy* the following :

The publications of :

Macmillan & Co. Ltd.	A. Constable & Co.
Alston Rivers Ltd.	Edward Arnold
Geo. Bell & Son	

The ' net ' books issued by Smith, Elder & Co.

This, clearly, was a war that must be fought to a finish.

The publishers next called upon Simpkin to stop supplying the Club, contract or no contract, and Simpkin, having to choose between being blacklisted by the Association and the risk of an action by *The Times*, chose the latter. An action was entered but not brought to court. Hostilities nevertheless continued. Henniker Heaton organized a public memorial in defence of the Book Club, collecting some ten thousand signatures which *The Times* published in batches. *The Times Literary Supplement*, conforming with the practice which Printing House Square steadily observed of not allowing editorial integrity to be tarnished by a commercial squabble, published reviews which Edward Bell described as of " conspicuous ability and fairness," but nevertheless, when the book reviewed came from a publisher who had refused supplies, attached to the review a note asking subscribers to " refrain from ordering the book so far as possible until it is included in The Times Monthly Catalogue." Early in 1907, *The Times* published a series of articles entitled " Publishers' Practice " so adroitly written that they provoked a temporary split in the Society of Authors and enabled Shaw and Sidney Lee to carry one meeting with them in opposing the support that the Society had hitherto given to publishers. One or two small firms outside the Association tried to make profit of this ; a few idealists clamoured for a new co-operative publishing company ; and *The Times*, having decided to become a general publisher itself, approached certain booksellers to that end and even announced a list of books it proposed to publish. But nothing came of it. The booksellers stood firm by the Net Book Agreement. Andromeda would not recognize Perseus, and, while the Club ransacked the world for copies of books it could not buy through normal channels, hostilities continued sporadically until the autumn of 1907 when they reached a climax.

The outstanding book of that season was *The Letters of Queen Victoria* which John Murray issued in three volumes at a price of three guineas net. If ever there was a book that the Book Club subscribers would wish to borrow it was this, and Moberly Bell asked Murray to make an exception in its case. Murray insisted upon an undertaking that the book should not be re-sold for less than its published price within six months of publication ; the undertaking was refused and supplies were withheld. The Club did its utmost to obtain copies through agents acting secretly on its behalf. As these agents were discovered, supplies were refused to them also and the blockade tightened. A long review of the Queen's *Letters* in *The Times Literary Supplement* contained a sentence commenting adversely on the high price of the book. This was a legitimate expression of opinion, but it was followed by letters in *The Times* itself, signed " Artifex," which, pursuing the unfortunate theme of " The Real Evil," argued that the book might have been sold with profit for one pound, attacked John Murray personally and accused him of " simple extortion." When he demanded an apology, the charges were repeated by " Artifex " and others. Murray brought an action for libel which was heard by Mr. Justice Darling early in May 1908. The evidence on costs of production was destructive of *The Times*'s case against Murray and against publishers in general. It was shown that the sentence in the *Literary Supplement*'s review commenting on the book's price had been inserted by Moberly Bell himself and that the " Artifex " letters had been written under instructions from Hooper. Murray was awarded £7500.

By this time it was no secret that there was internal trouble at Printing House Square and that *The Times* might change hands. On May 7th, Heinemann telephoned to Frederick Macmillan to say that Lord Northcliffe was on his way to see him at St. Martin's-street. When Northcliffe arrived, he first asked Frederick for a pledge of secrecy, then told him that he had bought a controlling interest in *The Times*. He had come to ask assistance in putting an end to the Book War. The Book Club must be carried on because it had 27,000 members, but it was costing £40,000 a year. This was too costly an advertisement. He was prepared to lose something by the Book Club — say £20,000 a year — but he wished to reduce the loss and thought that the best way to do so was to work on friendly terms with the publishers. Northcliffe was exceedingly frank. " He said that Moberly Bell and his circle," Frederick wrote in his notebook on the following Sunday, May 10, " were absurdly but firmly convinced that publishers were a wicked race, who made outrageous profits and committed all sorts of crimes against the reading public, and he said that the staff of *The Times* were also so fully imbued with the same idea that he was afraid if he gave in to the publishers too openly they would all resign their positions, as indeed they had threatened to do when it was supposed that C. Arthur Pearson was going to control the paper." Frederick was equally frank. He said that the publishers would be glad to see the end of the Book War. Minor and unimportant concessions might be made to " save the face " of the paper, but unless the Net Book Agreement was accepted negotiation was meaningless. Northcliffe replied that his secretary was working at the Book

Club under the assumed name of " Mr. Bates " and asked whether Frederick would see him if he called. This was agreed and the interview ended.

The discussions that followed were conducted with elaborate care. Frederick, after a conversation with Heinemann, told Bell and Longman (President and Vice-President of the Publishers' Association) what was afoot without revealing Northcliffe's identity, and, after a long talk with " Mr. Bates " on May 10th, drew up in outline a basis of settlement which, he thought, the publishers might reasonably be expected to adopt. As its effect was to put the Club under the restrictions which had been demanded throughout, they had no difficulty in doing so. Preliminary negotiations were left in his hands. He saw " Mr. Bates " on May 15th and lunched with Lord Northcliffe at Sutton Place on Sunday, May 24th. Northcliffe said he was still " struggling with Moberly Bell " who was unwilling to make terms, and, as Frederick already knew that his host was bound to Moberly Bell for five years, he saw clearly why settlement was delayed. He said that if Northcliffe chose to run the Book Club on normal lines, it might be extremely profitable as a bookshop. " He agreed with me," is the cautious entry in the note-book, " but one must always remember in these negotiations that Northcliffe is looking out for himself."

For more than three months nothing further happened. The publishers had stated their terms ; they had no intention of receding from them ; they knew that the Book Club was losing £800 a week and that it was to Northcliffe's interest to settle. They could afford to wait indefinitely and *The Times* could not. At last Northcliffe wrote from Paris asking Frederick to see his partner, Kennedy Jones, who had authority to make a settlement. These two and Heinemann lunched at the National Club on Wednesday, September 2nd. " Kennedy Jones," says the note-book, " was evidently under the impression that it would be possible to bluff us into some kind of concession." Frederick and Heinemann stood firmly for the Net Book Agreement and after four hours Kennedy Jones went away, leaving an impression that he intended to yield. On the 16th there was another meeting. "At one time a settlement seemed impossible but in the end we concocted a scheme which we thought reasonable and which we thought we could carry." The Book Club was to accept the Net Book Agreement without modification. Net books were not to be sold at a reduced price until six months, or non-net books until three months, after publication, though it might take orders before the end of the "close time." Before selling surplus books — that is, new books — at a reduction, the Book Club was to offer them to the publisher at cost. The Council of the Publishers' Association would recommend their members to supply the Book Club on the best terms they allowed to other booksellers or librarians. The victory was so complete and the Book Club's capitulation so nearly unconditional that it was agreed not to rub salt into the wound. No public announcement was to be made and the controversy was to be allowed to die quietly. These terms were a little criticized by publishers who felt that they were not severe enough, but were carried. Kennedy Jones was at once informed and Frederick went off into the country on Friday, 18th. Next morning he received a letter from Heinemann saying that the agreement had been signed by Moberly Bell. Soon afterwards Northcliffe gave a dinner at which his guests were Moberly Bell, Kennedy Jones, Heinemann and Frederick Macmillan. "During the feast, Moberly Bell confided to me [Frederick] that if he had been able to have his own way the war would have gone on. Fortunately the Proprietor of *The Times* did not consult Moberly Bell."

It is, as we look back upon it, a strange controversy. Hooper's part in it is clear. It is more interesting to observe that, not Moberly Bell only, but, on Northcliffe's evidence, a great part of *The Times* staff believed in their hearts that they were fighting a battle of principle and that the publishers were guilty of wrong. How did so bitter an opposition arise between reasonable and honest men ? What led *The Times* into believing that its case was so good that it might win in the action of *Murray* v. *Walter* ? The core of the answer seems to be that the nature and purpose of the Net Book Agreement were misunderstood. That Hooper had blundered and miscalculated, that the Book Club had assumed obligations which proved ruinous in the event, that the original Agreement of 1899 was afterwards revised and forced upon *The Times* when it was in difficulties, no doubt warped judgement and ruffled tempers ; but underlying all this there must have been a misconception of the Net Book Agreement itself. It seems to have been regarded as a kind of conspiracy in restraint of trade, designed to keep up the price of books and produce extravagant profits. The case of *Murray* v. *Walter* proved conclusively that the charge of extortion by publishers was unfounded, and a study of the history of the Net Book Agreement shows that, far from being designed to keep up the published price of a book, it was an act of collective self-control by booksellers. It was not directed towards the public ; it was an agreement among booksellers to abstain from cutting one another's throats by competitive underselling ; its purpose was not to raise prices but to prevent them from being forced down to a point at which a bookseller could no longer live by the selling of books but must run a side-line in stationery, collar-studs and, as Alexander had said long ago, " Berlin wool." Nor was the publishers' part in it acquisitive — so little so that many of them, and many booksellers, could see nothing but disadvantage in it as long as they took a short and selfish view of their business. It had been Frederick Macmillan's power to see, and to persuade others, that the interests of all sections of the book trade and the interests of book-buyers are interrelated which had produced the Net Book Agreement. When it was challenged by *The Times* Book Club, he resisted the challenge in the same spirit and, when the challenge was overcome, abstained from crowing over victory. If from the outset he had been able to explain the issue to *The Times* itself, the misunderstanding might never have arisen, but Horace E. Hooper " probably knew little about the system," on his initiative the Book Club was launched, vast expense was undertaken which had to be justified, and *The Times* was committed. It is, nevertheless, proper to emphasize that disputes of this bitterness do not arise, or at any rate are not persisted in, unless both parties believe that they have justice on their side. Moberly Bell and those who thought with him clearly believed, even after the finding in *Murray* v. *Walter*, that the price of books was extortionate and that, apart from the Book Club's commercial interest, *The Times*'s attempt to force them down was a battle fought in the public interest. With this recognition of honest disagreement, the history of the Book War may conveniently end.

PART FIVE

CONTINUITY THROUGH TWO WARS
1914–43

CHAPTER TWELVE

Growing Younger

*Whibley's Influence—Ralph Hodgson—Hugh Walpole—Yeats
Lost and Found*

HE beginning of the war of 1914 seems now long ago, but it is near enough to be a check upon a historian. From that date onwards many of those who came and went through the house of Macmillan were his contemporaries, and letters of theirs, which will some day become the legitimate material of history, must remain a little longer in the private file. Readers' reports also are to be guarded, except, perhaps, where a reputation as firm as Yeats's may be considered as putting the writer above the battle. The narrative becomes inevitably less personal. Old Alexander is no longer here to be smiled at or admired, and his grandsons are best to be appraised, not now in this book bearing their imprint, but a hundred years hence — or by those who meet them one morning in St. Martin's-street or Whitehall.

Harold Macmillan was still an undergraduate in August 1914. He served in the King's Royal Rifles and the Grenadier Guards, was in the early fighting and was three times wounded. His elder brother, Daniel, was already a director of the firm, together with George's son, Will. Daniel served in the King's Royal Rifles until he was invalided out ; then worked for the Red Cross and at the Admiralty. Will served in the London Scottish, the Cameronians and the

Growing Younger

Intelligence. All the older directors combined public services with their control of the firm.

Continuity, which is the life-blood of publishing, was unbroken by that war or the next. There were, indeed, " war books " and a valuable series of pamphlets. Two speeches by Winston S. Churchill, *The Fighting Line*, were published for a penny. Bryce's *Essays and Addresses in Wartime*, Mabel Dearmer's *Letters from a Field Hospital*, Edith Wharton's *The Marne*, Owen Wister's *Pentecost of Calamity*, and F. S. Oliver's *Ordeal by Battle* mark the period — the last a book of rare force and lucidity which, as a plea for compulsory military service that was much more than a polemic, had great influence on opinion. Oliver was a man of business as well as a student of history and politics. His style, direct and pure, had an ease that made his work acceptable by the many, and at the same time a delicate precision, a vehemence never erratic, which recommended it to the few. His *Alexander Hamilton* ; his *Endless Adventure*, an unfinished work on the art of government as exemplified in the career and period of Walpole ; and the letters, edited with a memoir by Stephen Gwynn as *The Anvil of War*, exhibited, each one, a new aspect of his talent which, combining moderation of statement with a genuine intellectual boldness, made his books, in their own category, peculiarly at home in St. Martin's-street. If an attempt were made to define " a Macmillan book," they might well be called upon to supply a part of the definition.

Kipling produced three little volumes, *France at War*, *The New Army in Training* and *The Fringes of the Fleet* — this last to be included in *Sea Warfare* (1916) ; and two others — *The Eyes of Asia* about the Indians, and *The War in the Mountains* about the Italian front, which, though published in America, have not appeared as books in England except in the Sussex Edition. But it is of interest to observe how little the life of the firm depended on books arising

directly from the war. Normal publishing was so little deterred by events in Europe that not only were new volumes
added to the *Highways and Byways Series* but in 1918 the
Blue Guides edited by Findlay Muirhead were begun with
a guide to London. Novels came from Algernon Blackwood,
from " Elizabeth," who used the pseudonym of Alice
Cholmondeley for her *Christine*, from Maurice Hewlett and
H. G. Wells. Hugh Walpole came from Secker in the last
year of the war.

Stella Benson's arrival is of interest for special reasons —
among them that she is an instance of those family connexions
which are sometimes the good fortune of publishers. The
Maurices provide another. F. D. Maurice, his son Major-
General Sir Frederick Maurice, and his grand-daughter,
Joan Robinson, the economist, have all been Macmillan
authors. The two Gladstones, W. E. and Herbert; the two
Archbishops Temple; Archbishop Benson and, for a few of
his many books, A. C. Benson; Matthew Arnold and the
Wards; J. N. Keynes and J. M. Keynes; three Gwynns
— Stephen, Charles and Denis; and four Kingsleys —
Charles, Henry and the two Marys — these suggest a habit
of good inheritance. Stella Benson's connexion with the
firm was more complex. Mary Cholmondeley had come to
Macmillan's at the time of the Bentley purchase and Stella
Benson was her niece. She belonged also to the Heber
family and so to a little dynasty of Macmillan authors,
running from Archbishop Tait of the 'seventies to Edith and
Osbert Sitwell of to-day. It is, therefore, natural enough
that a manuscript offered by her should have been read with
a friendly eye, but whoever casts his mind back to his own
first reading of *I Pose* is likely to agree — and the more
readily, the greater his liking for Stella Benson's exceptional
vintage — that, in manuscript, it might have been in some
peril, or, to see the problem from an opposite point of view,
that even a good Reader, even a Reader of Morley's quality,

might have been in danger of rejecting it. In fact, by this time, not Morley but Charles Whibley was principal Reader to the firm, and Whibley, in that capacity, was fortunate among men. He combined with wide scholarship and a taste balanced and conservative enough to save him from the elderly vice of running hysterically after new things, a power, while guarding those personal likings without which criticism is emasculate, to see work not of his own school from outside his prejudices. It is extremely improbable that *I Pose* had either the body or the bouquet that would have made it his own wine, but he recognized its quality instantly and Macmillan's were Stella Benson's publishers until her too early death. In spite of the marked success of *Tobit Transplanted* she never captured the multitude, and it is unlikely that she would have done so without a coarsening of her texture, but she was of great value to Macmillan's as evidence that they were renewing their youth, and they were of corresponding value to her. It would not have been surprising if their list of novels, with the names of Hardy, Henry James and Kipling at its head, had been charged with being unadventurous, but for that very reason imaginative work which was unusual or experimental was unlikely to be dismissed as freakish if it bore their imprint. Their reputation had the merits as well as the demerits of weight, and Stella Benson, when she began, needed what they had to give as much as they needed what she brought to them.

Solid books of criticism, politics and sociology showed no signs of falling off. Morley's *Recollections*, Colvin's *Keats* and Gosse's *Swinburne* all belong to 1917. Asquith made his appearance in the list with *Occasional Addresses 1893–1916*. Cromer's last *Political and Literary Essays*, Saintsbury's *History of the French Novel*, Stanford and Forsyth's *History of Music* and Charles Whibley's *Political Portraits* are proof enough of unwarlike range. Sir Richard Gregory, so long the editor of *Nature* and the firm's adviser on science, published in 1916 his *Discovery : or the Spirit and Service of Science*, and Henry Clay's *Economics : an Introduction for the General Reader* appeared in the same year. *The Commonwealth of Nations* was edited by Lionel Curtis, whose testament of idealistic Imperialism later formed the three volumes of his *Civitas Dei*, finally gathered into one volume as *The Commonwealth of God*. Theological and devotional works not surprisingly flourished. Illingworth's *The Gospel Miracles*, H. B. Swete's *The Holy Catholic Church* and Hensley Henson's *Christian Liberty* may be remarked among them as well as various symposia on the relation of Christian belief to modern thought and research, for the editing of which B. H. Streeter was responsible. Canon Streeter was often the firm's adviser on theological subjects and sometimes it was possible to consult William Temple, Rector of St. James's, Piccadilly, who in those days had leisure to write his *Studies in the Spirit and Truth of Christianity*, his *Plato and Christianity* and his *Mens Creatrix*, all of the war period. But Macmillan's had never been poor in Prime Ministers, Archbishops, and men of science. Where these giants may almost be taken for granted, it is, in a sense, of more importance to notice, as signs of refreshment and vitality, such accessions as that of Stella Benson, and a flowing in of poetry and drama to the firm that had published Arnold and waited so patiently for Tennyson.

These were the years of Hardy's *Satires of Circumstance* and *Moments of Vision*, of new poems by James Stephens, of an edition in two volumes of Wilfrid Scawen Blunt's *Poetical Works* and a steady outpouring of Tagore. AE was already among the firm's great men ; Lysaght and Stephen Gwynn had been forerunners of an Irish group that was presently to bring new and vigorous blood to St. Martin's-street. James Stephens, not alone among his countrymen, has a gift of conversation developed beyond the point at which monologue begins. The monologue is so good, and Stephens, in common with his audience, enjoys it so ardently that he is one of the few authors of whom his publishers have reason to lament that he writes too little. But he is fertile in comparison with Ralph Hodgson, who came to Macmillan's in 1917 with a volume of *Poems*, small and flawless. A few of these verses had already appeared as broadsheets, issued by the Poetry Bookshop, and Hodgson had previously published one book, *The Last Blackbird*. Through all the years of silence that have followed its appearance, the volume of *Poems* has sustained its author's reputation. Nothing that it contained has been forgotten. " Eve," " Time, you old Gipsy Man," " Reason has moons " and all its shorter pieces are steadily reprinted in anthology after anthology, in school-text after school-text, and so would " The Bull " and " The Song of Honour " have been if it had been thought right in the poet's interest to release these longer poems from so small a volume. Though Hodgson might by the classifiers be classified as a Georgian, he has been relatively exempt from attack by the later coteries. He committed all the crimes for which his contemporaries have been most bitterly reproached : he was unpolitical and unselfpitying ; he was an elaborate craftsman whose devotion to classical models was apparent in his variants ; he did not think it necessary to prove himself original by excluding from his vocabulary beautiful words because they were beautiful or because Keats had used them ; he invented no cipher, was content to be understood, and unashamed of giving pleasure. In spite of this, he has been allowed to slip through the net of denigration by which the repute of Brooke and Flecker has been temporarily enmeshed. Few have seen him, for much of his life has been spent in Japan, and, when he has been in England, he has stood apart from literary controversy. Nevertheless, if now, as perhaps he may, he should send to his publishers, after a quarter of a century, a volume with which at last he was satisfied, it would be received, not as the work of a forgotten or unfashionable poet, but with an extraordinary eagerness and curiosity. Within his perfection of craftsmanship and the steady discipline of his self-criticism, Hodgson sings with a passionate intensity and grace that only the great lyric-writers command. No one whose output is so small can rank with the giants, but he is a poet of that rare kind whose art may live when even the poet's name is no longer remembered. His short verses will always pass from lip to lip, and they contain indications that, if he were to produce a long poem, it might well give new life to the English epic. His prosody appears at first to be of the utmost simplicity, and his rhymes to fall from heaven, but the simplicity and naturalness are those of a blackbird's song which, by the almost Meredithian break in its music, catches the listener's breath and makes his heart turn over. The same quality of resilience applied to sustained narrative or meditative verse might, a reader feels, give it a new point of departure. But that is dreaming. As yet the 1917 volume has no successor, and all that can be said with certainty is that the little book does not dry with the years. It has a miraculous freshness and ease, like a familiar stream that declares itself again at each encounter in a wood. It renews itself with the seasons of the mind and will have a springlike immortality.

A year later there came to St. Martin's-street one of the most prolific of novelists. It has recently been a custom among those whose productive energies are chiefly confined to passing the eye of mutual admiration from hand to hand to sneer at Hugh Walpole indiscriminately for his merits as well as for his faults. It is as well to distinguish between them. He was greatly ambitious, which is not a fault if ambition is directed, as his was, to leaving behind him an enduring name deserved in his works. He had generosity of

mind and real courage — for no one without courage could
have sustained so great a burden as the Herries series or have
staked upon it again and again the fulfilment of his whole
purpose. But there were aspects of his ambition and of his
generosity — something almost childishly over-eager —
which laid him open to his enemies. He wrote too much and
too fast ; he entertained too often and was alone too little ;
he lent his name and his enthusiasm to innumerable enterprises which were outside the devotion of an artist that was
properly his. In an ebullient giant of Dickens's stature all
this might have been possible without damage, but in
Walpole it produced a divided mind, a stress always apparent
to his friends, and queer spasms of distrust and self-distrust.
Why did he, having his ambition, sign the chattering good-
humoured journalism that was so far beneath his powers ?
He liked to praise and help young writers — but at the same
time he liked the response of a vast newspaper audience.
Why did he make so many wild excursions into the macabre,
knowing, as he must have known in his heart, that they led
him to damaging excesses ? Partly because, in their darker
aspects, they exercised over him an irresistible fascination ;
partly for the flatly contrary reason that he was ingenuous
about them and could give himself cold shivers with no
notion that he might be failing to communicate them. In
this and in much else he was disarmingly unselfconscious.
His work poured from him ; his enthusiasm overflowed ;
nothing deterred or stayed him ; and he accepted with
delight help from his publishers that relieved him of what
may, perhaps, be called the retardations of authorship.
Revision for him was neither a joy nor an opportunity — and
yet, such are the contradictions of human nature, he was a
genuine admirer of Henry James. Before one novel was in
the press another was half-written from which it was for
him impossible to turn aside. Gradually Macmillan's came
to have more and more concern with his proofs.

A sense of what the film-studios call " continuity " is a thing that some men have and some have not, and Walpole had it not. It is a weakness that must endear him to anyone who shares it and who knows how great and how exasperating can be the labour of counteracting it. How could he continually hark back to check names and relationships, the colour of eyes and hair, whether people were childless or had families, whether verses had indeed been written when his characters recited them, and whether all the shops would be open on the morrow of a day specifically named as Saturday ? There was once a young man who, writing a leading article in *The Times*, referred to Long John Silver's wooden leg, and was met two days later by a large tray piled with letters of amendment. Walpole was similarly rewarded, and welcomed the help, from 1922 onwards, of an experienced editor of Macmillan's, Thomas Mark.

Walpole was, above all else, a story-teller, possessed by a passion for vicarious adventure, and it is possible that only by letting himself go as he did was he able to write at all. Men of strong temperament must write in accordance with their temperament and if what seems to us indiscipline was necessary to Walpole, there is nothing to do but accept the freakish fact and to look for the good that sprang from it. What sprang from it was a remarkable speed and sweep of narrative. Walpole might become entangled in his " continuities," he might sometimes draw his minor characters with too hard and hasty an outline, but, given a scene of vigorous action or a character with whom he had become deeply familiar, he was able, as few of his contemporaries were, to combine a genuine sensitiveness of perception with the thrust and movement of an adventure story. Where he will stand when time has chosen among his works, it is peculiarly hard to guess, but the gift of narrative is one for which the world has a habit of remaining grateful. It is at any rate good to remember how Walpole enjoyed the doing of his work — and enjoyment is a quality that communicates itself down the years. He made gigantic plans and, like a boy, brought them into Macmillan's in the hope of encouragement. On September 3rd, 1925, Frederick Macmillan made this entry in his note-book :

Mr. Walpole gave me to-day, 3/9/25, the following programme for his proposed work :

1925.	Portrait of Man with Red Hair
1926.	Harmer John
1927.	Anthony Trollope
	Jeremy at Crale
1928.	Wintersmoon
1929.	The Waverley Novels
	The Mountain
1930.	Chinese Horses (Short Stories)
	Millie and Peter
1931.	Flight to Thorne
1932.	The Herries Family
	I. Under Skiddaw 1771–1832
1933.	II. The Romantic Story 1832–1870
1934.	III. Mark Herries 1870–1930

" The Waverley Novels " is clearly *A Waverley Pageant*, published by Eyre & Spottiswoode. " The Mountain " suggests nothing that he published, the books of 1929 being *Farthing Hall* (in collaboration with J. B. Priestley) and *Hans Frost*. " Chinese Horses " was the title of a story included in *The Silver Thorn* (1928). " Millie and Peter " is a little mysterious. They were characters from *The Green Mirror* and *The Young Enchanted* and appeared in *Hans Frost*, but *Hans Frost* is unlikely to have been the book he had intended. *Flight to Thorne* also is baffling, the book of 1931 being *Above the Dark Circus*. But though, in these particulars, the programme was varied, it remains a remarkably accurate foreshadowing of nine years' work. " Under Skiddaw " appeared as *Rogue Herries* two years in advance of time. The vast manuscript seems to have dismayed Frederick Macmillan when Walpole proudly laid it on his desk, and the prospect of three more historical narratives to follow it did not reassure him. Nor, it has to be confessed, did the office departments to which the author bore the tidings that day gladden him with their optimism. Nevertheless, when the book was ready, everything that could be done was done to launch it, and Walpole was justified in the event. *Rogue Herries* (1930) was spectacularly successful, and Walpole, who was always a close friend of his publishers, did not conceal his pride and joy, or they their gladness that they had been wrong in doubting his high adventure. His plans were laid for another complete group of Herries novels. He harked back to Elizabeth's time in the fifth, and a sixth, of the Civil War period, was far advanced when he died. Nothing in him was pleasanter than his frank delight in his own, and in other men's, success. Writing, publishing, even advertising, were an unfailing excitement to him. His most serious and ambitious work was, at the same time, part of a romantic game. May posterity reward his strange, complicated and yet childlike spirit ! So good a story-teller is likely at any rate to live longer than many a *petit-maître* who sneered at him as soon as he was dead.

Ralph Hodgson and Hugh Walpole are far apart, but an even stronger indication of the Macmillans' power to put out new branches from the old tree is to be found among the Irishmen. Lest it should be supposed that anything revolutionary was happening in St. Martin's-street, it may be noticed, in parenthesis, that the great solid work went on as it always had. Frederick, George and Maurice were still there. Month by month and year by year, the educational list was pruned, developed, increased. High scholarship was not neglected. In the midst of the 1914 war, even the large-scale books came out as they always had — P. M. Sykes's

History of Persia, for example, or Frazer's *Folk-Lore in the Old Testament* in three volumes, or Eden and Lockyer's *New System of Gynaecology*, also in three volumes. The firm was by no means throwing its ballast overboard while putting on new sail, but its former weakness — its too timid, too conservative, too aloof attitude towards poetry and fiction — was being converted into strength. How and why ? How, in such a matter as this, does a firm change its point of view without a reversal of general policy or a departure from its tradition ? The answer is in the difference between Charles Whibley and John Morley, and, above all, between Charles Whibley and Mowbray Morris. Morley, on his own true territory — history, politics, biography, literary criticism — was an adviser of the first rank, but he had a resistance to new developments in imaginative writing. He seems to have felt in his heart that fiction was not worth his moral and intellectual powder and shot. What is more, he and Frederick, in this matter, were temperamentally too alike. Though for different reasons, they pooh-poohed with the same pooh-poohs. Outwardly, Whibley also was on the safe side, but whereas Morley's conservatism was a by-product of radical righteousness, Whibley's had fire and light in it which enabled him to see and know himself, to mark and evaluate his prejudices, and to prevent the distinctions of aesthetic taste from being obscured by moral indignations.

Thus many things that would have been impossible became possible — among them Tagore, whose work was uncongenial to Whibley personally but whose value he admitted, and Yeats, and a brilliant Irish succession. Lysaght, Stephen Gwynn, AE and James Stephens were Macmillan authors by 1912. Yeats came in 1916. In the succession, the dates as well as the names are significant : Padraic Colum (1922) ; Sean O'Casey, Lennox Robinson (1925), Eimar O'Duffy (1926), George Shiels and F. R. Higgins (1927), Katharine Tynan

(*Collected Poems*, 1930), Frank O'Connor (1931), John Eglinton (1935), Paul Vincent Carroll (1938) and Joseph Hone (*W. B. Yeats*, 1942).

The key-name is Yeats's. The story had so painful a beginning that it has seemed best to leave it untold until, in speaking now of the year 1916, it may be begun again and more happily. Even now, it would be pleasanter to omit Mowbray Morris's and John Morley's reports, but they are, in a sense, important footnotes to the history of literature, and the fact of Yeats's coming to St. Martin's-street again within sixteen years of their being written makes some excerpts from them essential to an understanding of the development of the firm. Yeats's work had been urged upon Macmillan's by Stephen Gwynn in 1900. Mowbray Morris had ended a long report as follows :

. . . I should be sorry to think that work so unreal, un-human and insincere would be found to have any permanent value, nor do I believe that it will be found to have it, any more than Maeterlinck's will be or Ibsen's, or, in another realm of art, Burne-Jones's or Rossetti's. What its com-mercial value may be at the present moment is another question. I notice that Mr. Yeats has changed his pub-lishers three times within seven years, which looks as if they had not found him very remunerative. He has some admirers, I know, but I should judge them to be more noisy than numerous, as is commonly the case with these eccentrics, George Meredith to wit. That he has any real paying audience I find it hard to believe. He has undoubtedly a feeling for literature and a real literary gift : his poetical gift I should rate higher than Phillips's, which seems to me purely literary. There is of course the chance that he may one day grow tired of this nonsense and turn to real themes ; but if he is to go on producing verse like *The Secret Rose*, I should not, for my part, make any very strenuous efforts to secure him.

Morley had agreed :

Growing Younger

I have read through these volumes with attention, and also the two pieces joined to them. To call such a writer " one of the most important figures in contemporary literature " strikes me as amazing, but I am relieved to find the critic shrink from saying that Mr. Yeats *will ever be a popular author*. I should really at last despair of mankind, if he could be. In substance I entirely concur with M. M. The whole thing seems to me neither more nor less than a pure negation of the human understanding. Neither rhyme nor reason do I find in one single page. I can appreciate " symbolism," phantasy, and so forth, as warmly as my neighbours, though I do not value it as among the highest forms of literary art. But these books are to me absolutely empty and void. The work does not please the ear, nor kindle the imagination, nor hint a thought for one's reflection. Now and again there is the ring and the colour of a poetic phrase, but not too often. . . . Do what I will, I can see no sense in the thing : it is to me sheer nonsense. I do not say it is obscure, or uncouth or barbaric or affected — tho' it is all these evil things ; I say it is to me absolute nullity. . . .

I would not read a page of it again for worlds, and I care not how many good judges swear that " Yeats is the only man who counts." Talk of Meredith, Browning, Tennyson, etc. being found obscure when they were new, and therefore Yeats ought to have his chance ! To measure the weight and force of that, just take down *Maud* or *Lotus-Eaters*, or any volume of selections from Browning, and then read (if you can) a few pages of *The Wind among the Reeds*.

There is no saying in these rather demented days what an industrious band of admirers may not succeed in foisting into an ephemeral popularity. But I doubt if even industry can do it in this case. " You may not make money by him," Mr. G. says, " tho' I don't believe you will lose." I believe you will. His work has been well before the public, and I do not observe that the publishers who have had it in hand, have clung to it.

I should write more, but I find on re-reading M. M. that he has really said what I should say.

Having set out these reports, it is perhaps worth while to

suggest that, as Readers' reports, what is to be objected against them is not so much that their writers personally failed to share the enthusiasm of Yeats's most ardent supporters in 1900 or, indeed, that they disliked his work, as that they could not, or would not, allow his quality to penetrate their disliking. The fatal phrase in Mowbray Morris is : " these eccentrics — Meredith to wit," a phrase as falsely critical as " these romantics " or " these symbolists " or " these men of Bloomsbury," bespeaking a mind closed against imaginative writing not of its own school. Morley's self-justification on the subject of " ' symbolism,' phantasy, and so forth " suggests a like exclusiveness. Both write with the dangerous vehemence of men who feel that their citadel is being undermined.

In 1916, Stephen Phillips having come and gone meanwhile, the policy towards Yeats which had ruled at the beginning of the century was reversed. His *Responsibilities* and *Reveries over Childhood and Youth* were issued by Macmillan's and thirteen volumes of his earlier work transferred to them. He employed an agent and his own correspondence with the firm was consequently slight, but if a letter was addressed to him personally there was always a reasonable assurance that he would reply to it in time. There are Irish writers of whom this is lastingly untrue. To write to them is to write to the dead. Each mitigates the silence in his own way — James Stephens, for example, yielding with grace to capture by telephone. Yeats's method was to call. At first, when he came to see Frederick Macmillan, he wore sombre clothes, a wide black hat, eyeglasses on a broad black ribbon and an air of blank, unexpectant melancholy — " a forgotten umbrella," said George Moore. Gradually the clothes tightened, as if the umbrella were being rolled up, then lightened as if it were being changed into a parasol. By the time it was Harold Macmillan and not his uncle who received him, Yeats's metamorphosis was complete. His shirt was coloured, his tie careful, his black cloth had yielded to Irish tweed. No longer diffident or remote, he became easy of approach and gracious in his acknowledgement of whatever help was given him — particularly in the production of his one-volume *Collected Poems* and *Collected Plays*. There has never been an imaginative writer not a charlatan who has not been pleased by his publisher's interest in his work, and Yeats was delighted rather than annoyed by queries. He would sit down, pore over the doubtful line, seek and seek in his memory for a clue to the meaning that either his youthful ardour or some ancient misprint had clouded. But sometimes he himself was not available. His most esoteric work, *A Vision*, was full of conundrums which might or might not be intentional and were the harder to solve because Yeats was seriously ill in Majorca while the book was going through the press. " I don't expect many people to understand it," Yeats said. " In fact, I know only one man who *will* understand it all, and he is a doctor in Scotland."

When a complete edition was projected, his whole works were elaborately studied on his behalf, phrase by phrase and comma by comma, before being submitted to his personal care. The edition has been delayed by the war, but all of it was seen and revised by Yeats. He attended to every point that was raised, explaining his meaning where he thought it might have been missed, and writing : " For the first time there will be a satisfactory text of my work, thanks to your watchfulness and patience." Since his death, there have been published his *Last Poems and Plays*, a commemorative volume, *Scattering Branches*, edited by his old friend Stephen Gwynn, and an authorized biography by Joseph Hone.

The association between poet and publisher is of peculiar interest and reveals an unfamiliar aspect of Yeats. What made it possible to the firm thus to redeem their early mistake ? Why were they able to make so good a use of a second chance ? First, it would seem, that though, under Morley and Mowbray Morris, they had had an unquestionably blind spot in their view of imaginative experiment, this misfortune had never affected their general health. The resulting errors had, for a time, been grievous, but small in proportion to the whole activity of the firm. So great was their organization and repute and so broad their basis, that Yeats, in his later life, was willing to return as Hardy had been. Secondly, when he came, he found that the firm were still personal and had never become stiffly departmentalized.

CHAPTER THIRTEEN

Notes for the Future

" Old Spain" and other Splendours—Educational Developments—
Novelists—Poets and Dramatists—Biography, Scholarship and
History—Keynes and the Economists—The Hundredth Year

AVING emancipated themselves from Victorianism
where it was dangerous and carefully preserved the
good in it, Macmillan's were able, in the period
that followed the war of 1914-18, gradually to
adapt themselves to a new age. The three older partners
remained. Less adaptable in many respects than Alexander
had been, they nevertheless did not fail to give opportunity
to those who were to succeed them. Daniel, who was to
succeed Sir Frederick Macmillan in the Chair, devoted his
particular attention to the educational and Indian aspects of
the business for which his father, Maurice, was primarily
responsible, while Harold, entering the House of Commons
as an advanced Conservative, did what each Macmillan in
his turn had done before him — allowed his own interest
and conscience to be reflected in the firm's list. The period
is remarkable not only for the number and weight and
authority of the books, political or economic, which expressed
the thought of the times, but for the area of diverse opinion
covered by those books. In the days of theological controversy, old Daniel and Alexander, though their personal
inclination was for the teaching of Maurice and Kingsley,
had never allowed themselves to become publishers to a sect.
Now, when controversy had changed its nature, Macmillan's were preserved from becoming publishers to a party.
The outstanding book of 1919, Keynes's *Economic Conse-*
quences of the Peace, was a portent. In the same year Mac-

millan's published Marshall's *Industry and Trade* and in the next Pigou's *Economics of Welfare* which has become a classic on its own subject. Taken together, these three books are a sign of new development.

Before examining it, other aspects of the firm's activity may be noticed. The times were not propitious for the issue of collected and limited editions, but in several instances the attempt was made. The only real success was the Mellstock Hardy in thirty-seven volumes. Henry James in thirty-five, though enriched by elaborate prefaces that contained criticism of the art of fiction as candid and as scientific as any that has been written, failed. Morley's *Collected Works* found an unresponsive market and of W. E. Henley's five volumes only the *Poems* were asked for. Eden Phillpotts was not a Macmillan author. *The Three Knaves* had appeared among the Sevenpenny Novels, but nothing else had borne the imprint. Now Frederick resolved upon gathering together and issuing with a preface by Arnold Bennett twenty volumes of the Dartmoor Novels as a venture of his own. They were not warmly received. Even the Sussex Kipling, as has already been told, had little fortune. The days of such magnificence seemed to have passed.

Nevertheless lavish publishing which broke new ground in history or science was still possible. Garvin's *Life of Joseph Chamberlain*, of which the fourth volume has yet to appear, began in 1932, and will certainly justify itself. Stresemann's *Diaries, Letters and Papers* (1935), issued after Hitler's accession to power, foundered upon the public's indifference to foreign politics of the recent past, and Fortescue's six volumes of *The Correspondence of George III* were scarcely more fortunate ; but Lytton Strachey and Roger Fulford's edition of the *Greville Memoirs* (1938) out-classed all its rivals by its unexpurgated completeness and editorial accuracy, and Emily Anderson's *Letters of Mozart and his Family* is likely to stand. There were new editions

of Palgrave's *Dictionary of Political Economy* and of Grove.
A new series of *English Men of Letters* was edited by J. C.
Squire, who for a generation, as writer and critic and discerning friend of writers, had served English literature as few
others had in his time. It cannot rank collectively with the
old series, partly because the material was poorer and partly
because writers of the quality of John Addington Symonds
are not easily to be found, but it contained work of originality
and distinction — conspicuously three volumes on Americans
whom Squire had nationalized for his purpose : John
Freeman's on *Herman Melville*, John Bailey's on *Whitman*
and Edward Shanks's on *Poe*. The *Great English Church-
men* series (1927) contained studies of Thomas Arnold, St.
Thomas of Canterbury, Cranmer, Laud and Wesley.

The general rule appeared to be that, though taste had not
degenerated, the public was looking anxiously from book-
shelf to purse and buying in a changed spirit. Even highly
priced books were bought willingly if their contents and the
public's need to read them were felt to justify the price.
What could no longer be sold easily were costly books whose
value was chiefly decorative or whose material was available
elsewhere. Even Muirhead Bone's *Old Spain* was a disappointment. It was published in two great volumes bound
in pig-skin. Only two hundred and fifty copies were for sale,
each signed by the artist and by Gertrude Bone, the author of
the text. At the party given to celebrate its appearance in
1936, the colour reproductions were put to the severest
possible test by being hung on the walls beside the originals.
Plates used in the collotype process lay on the tables with
pulls of the pictures to show their various stages and the
pains taken by the artist and by his printers, the Oxford
University Press. The success of the book in fulfilling its
aesthetic purpose was unquestionable, but at a hundred
guineas a copy it was a luxury that had to be done without.
A stock of copies remained unsold. That they will some day

be bought is probable. In the end, long-term publishing on the grand scale is seldom unrewarded. But they point — and the more strongly because the book itself is of such magnificence — to one of the truths of the period : people were buying books to read, not to look at or to collect.

The art of controlling an educational series consists not only in new works but in care and maintenance. That is to say : not only must books be planned which open up new territories but existing books must be re-edited or gradually displaced. An educational publisher must have the foresight and courage to supersede himself before others supersede him, and must be willing, during periods of transition, to maintain two different, and, in a sense, rival books in the same field. Thus a *Modern French Series* and a *Modern German Series*, and new Courses in both languages, were brought into being to succeed, though not yet to drive out, the older productions of Fasnacht and Siepmann. Similarly, while the familiar *Elementary Classics* continued to hold their place, the *Modern Classics* were devised to meet the needs of pupils who were no longer required, as they had in the past been required, to study the grammatic minutiae of the texts. Abridged versions of standard works fortunately began to go out of fashion and additions to the *English Literature* series ceased. Its newer counterpart is the *Scholar's Library*, containing several of the Hardy novels, as well as other complete texts and anthologies of essays, poems and plays. The most important fresh enterprise in the educational field was *Teaching in Practice* which was by no means a replacement of anything that had formerly existed. A six-volume encyclopaedia of modern methods of teaching in Primary Schools, it gave teachers material for the courses they must undertake. It was edited by E. J. S. Lay, whose own methods of elementary teaching had set a new standard for the country. Its instant success led to the design of a corresponding *Projects and Pictures* for Infant Schools, followed by a similar set of volumes for Senior Schools.

In considering the novelists who came to Macmillan's during this period, it would be a waste of time to look for a governing principle in the firm's selectiveness. They looked for good in whatever kind, always, as long as Frederick lived, with a tendency towards light entertainment and away from what he would have considered extravagance or freakishness. Mazo de la Roche was the next novelist of any note to come to St. Martin's-street after Hugh Walpole. After two short novels came *Whiteoaks* (1929), which, with its predecessor *Jalna*, originally published elsewhere and transferred to Macmillan's in the same year, was the inauguration of a Whiteoaks series as popular as Walpole's Herries. Eimar O'Duffy's *King Goshawk and the Birds* (1926) succeeded well enough to suggest that the English resistance to satire was less stubborn than it is commonly supposed to be, and O'Duffy's death after the writing of only two more books was evidently the death of an original talent. E. M. Delafield came in 1928, Richmal Crompton in 1931, and Frank O'Connor's short stories, *Guests of the Nation*, in the same year. Edward Shanks, John Collier, Edward Thompson, James Hilton, A. G. Macdonell and Naomi Royde Smith all became Macmillan authors in the early 'thirties and Osbert Sitwell's important accession, leading on to *Escape with Me!* in 1939, to *Two Generations* in 1940, and to much else in prospect, was marked by a volume of essays, *Penny Foolish*, in 1935. An adventurous historical novel on Napoleon, *So Great a Man*, by David Pilgrim, brought in one of the oddest collaborations of recent times, David Pilgrim being John Palmer and Hilary Saunders who, under another pseudonym, are jointly Francis Beeding. As Pilgrim, they are historical novelists ; as Beeding, writers of thrillers ; independently, Saunders is the prolific and officially anonymous author of *Bomber Command* and other well-known pamphlets, while John Palmer, who succeeded Shaw many years ago as dramatic critic of the *Saturday Review*, is the author of able studies of Molière, of Ben Jonson and of the French Theatre, and is among the most devoted and learned of Shakespearian scholars.

To Macmillan novelists, Pearl Buck, a Nobel prizewinner, was added from America in 1940, her book on *The Chinese Novel* having appeared in the list during the previous year. Margaret Mitchell's famous story came to London through the New York house. In spite of the American success of *Gone With the Wind*, English Macmillan's proceeded cautiously, printing at first an edition of three thousand copies by photo-lithography. Soon they were printing thirty thousand and later a hundred thousand copies at a time. James Hilton's tales also were widely popular ; A. G. Macdonell's *The Crew of the Anaconda* was a memorable war-time thriller ; and the coming to St. Martin's-street of Storm Jameson and St. John Ervine brought valuable reinforcement to the list of fiction. There has been in recent years abundant entertainment and much good story-telling, but the shadow of the withdrawn giants, Hardy, Kipling and Henry James, falls long upon the path of those who remain.

Tennyson, Matthew Arnold and Hardy have a like tendency, in such a narrative as this, to dwarf the poets and dramatists. But Yeats is not easily dwarfed ; he, Ralph Hodgson, James Stephens and AE, have already been spoken of. Wilfrid Wilson Gibson came next after Yeats in order of time. 1922 brought Padraic Colum, who had already a reputation in Dublin, and 1925 the phenomenon of Sean O'Casey. Laurence Binyon's connexion began in 1924 when he was commissioned to compile his *Golden Treasury of*

Modern Lyrics, which would also provide part of the material for a fifth book for Palgrave's *Golden Treasury* (1926). His own work began to come to Macmillan's with *The Sirens* in 1925 and culminated in his *Collected Poems*, his last book of verse, *The North Star*, and his translation of Dante. The final proofs of the *Paradiso* had scarcely been passed by him when he died. Lennox Robinson also first came as a successful anthologist, his plays being published later on the recommendation of Yeats. John Freeman came in the same year (1925) and George Shiels two years later. With the warm admiration and support of AE and Yeats, F. R. Higgins seemed likely to become a leader of the younger Irish writers. More than a romantic belief in the fortune of poets who die young gives assurance that his *The Dark Breed* (1927) and *The Gap of Brightness* (1940) would have had yet finer successors. He was to have collaborated with Yeats in a collection of Irish ballads ; his work was rich in the promise that speaks through achievement ; and his loss was one of the most serious that Macmillan's suffered. They needed young poets. A shilling series of Contemporary Poets begun in 1934 brought Christopher Hassall, Elizabeth Belloc (Hilaire Belloc's daughter), Elizabeth Daryush (daughter of Bridges), and another Irishman of quality, Patrick Kavanagh, as well as such poets of established repute as E. H. W. Meyerstein and R. C. Trevelyan. But still Macmillan's needed young poets. In the end, the great men came to them — Sturge Moore is another example — and poets as well known as Edward Shanks, having established their names already, came to St. Martin's-street in mid-career, as Edmund Blunden did in 1941 and Edith Sitwell in 1942. It was, too, in 1941 that Edward Marsh's verse translation of Horace, possibly the best and certainly the warmest and most elegant ever made in English, was published. Hardy, Yeats and AE ; Gibson, Sturge Moore, Binyon and Blunden ; John Freeman, Edith Sitwell, Hodgson, James Stephens, Sean O'Casey — it was a group without parallel between the two wars. Still Macmillan's needed young men.

Always behind the hazardous output of fiction and verse, the great business of general publishing went on. What is to be observed in it is again not a predominant tendency but its variety and range. Although Macmillan's only previous connexion with Samuel Butler had been their refusal of his translation of the Odyssey, it was to them that Festing Jones brought his *Memoir*. Henry James's *Letters* were edited by Percy Lubbock in 1920. Samuel Alexander's *Space, Time and Deity* was one of the more formidable undertakings of that year ; J. B. Bury's *Idea of Progress* supplied a useful corrective to the then fashionable meliorists ; and Saintsbury's *Notes on a Cellar-Book* delighted Frederick Macmillan's convivial heart. Bryce, one of the firm's oldest and most distinguished friends, made his last bow in *Memories of Travel* (1923), and George Macmillan had private satisfaction in watching the success of the abridged edition of *The Golden Bough* and in launching before his death two of the greatest works of scholarship in Macmillan history — Frazer's translation of and commentary on the *Fasti of Ovid* (5 vols., 1929) and Arthur Evans's *The Palace of Minos*, the four volumes of which were begun in 1921 and completed in 1935, the year before George Macmillan's death. The 'twenties were distinguished by Mrs. Hardy's *Early Life* of her husband (the *Later Years* came in 1930), by Curzon's *Leaves from a Viceroy's Notebook* and by Ponsonby's *Letters of the Empress Frederick* which drew to itself the limelight of 1928 by a preface telling an almost Ruritanian story of how the letters had been entrusted to him by the dying Empress and how, after her death, her son, the Emperor Wilhelm II, had ransacked her rooms for them in vain.

Harold Macmillan himself made his appearance as an

author in 1927 with a contribution to *Industry and the State* by four Conservative members of Parliament. Since then his *Reconstruction : A Plea for a National Policy* and *The Middle Way* have shown the direction of his personal thought — a direction so little extreme as to leave the firm's list open to a wide variety of political and economic opinion differing from his own. About the same time there were new accessions among the historians. L. B. Namier, whose *Structure of Politics at the Accession of George III* appeared in 1929, was to become the editor of an important series of *Studies in Modern History* which owes much to its editor's lively mind and devoted scholarship. A year later Keith Feiling's *British Foreign Policy 1660–1672* began his connexion with the firm, and Norman Kemp Smith's translation of Kant's *Critique of Pure Reason* was published. *The Sovereignty of the British Dominions* was Macmillan's first work from A. Berriedale Keith.

Both the author and the subject of Stephen Gwynn's *Life of Mary Kingsley* (1932) had close associations with the firm. Macmillan's had published Gwynn's novels many years earlier, he had written on Donegal and Antrim in the *Highways and Byways* series and on *Thomas Moore* in the *English Men of Letters*. His *Masters of English Literature* has a vigour and grace rare in school books. Apart from all this he had long been a friend of Macmillan's, constantly bringing in authors and ideas — among them Yeats, and George had a special pleasure in the Mary Kingsley biography which appeared to him as a fulfilment of a double friendship. The story of the Bains, a family with close personal and business relations with the Macmillans and many of their authors, was told in *A Bookseller Looks Back*, by James Stoddart Bain.

Lord Lloyd's *Egypt Since Cromer* came happily into a list that already held Cromer's *Modern Egypt* and, in an altogether different field, John Eglinton's *Irish Literary Portraits* was a fortunate key to the firm's existing possessions in Ireland — fortunate because, provocative of strife though a book with such a title might have been, John Eglinton appears to enjoy a special immunity from the sharper venoms, having a capacity to make friends and even to criticize them fearlessly without making enemies. About the same time, there appeared *First Russia, Then Tibet* by Robert Byron — a book which suggested that its author might shine in literature, travel, politics or the criticism of art. His life was ended by war before his powers were fully concentrated but there is little doubt that in him, and in " Christopher Caudwell " (Christopher Sprigge), whose *Illusion and Reality* made its mark in 1937, Macmillan's lost two young authors with a natural inheritance in the future.

Nineteen thirty-six was a year of continuing loss. Kipling died in January, George Macmillan on March 3rd, Maurice Macmillan on March 30th, and Sir Frederick on June 1st. The three senior directors' achievement and services have already been described. Among the greatest of them was that, like Alexander before them, they had so conducted the firm that even the death of all of them in the space of three months did not disorganize it. Under Daniel and Harold it continued to live and grow, Will Macmillan retiring from active share in the business. In the following year there appeared *International Relations since the Peace Treaties* by E. H. Carr, whose *Twenty Years' Crisis 1919–1939* and *Conditions of Peace* (1942) have confirmed and enhanced a reputation founded by the short survey published in 1937. Carr is among the latest of the writers on politics and economics whose work has given a distinctive character to the firm's list since 1919 and may be recognized as constituting the major development of the modern period. Keynes, Marshall and Pigou, spoken of at the opening of this chapter, show the development beginning. Keynes had already, in 1913, published with Macmillan's his *Indian Currency and Finance*. In 1922 there came from him *A Revision of the Treaty*, in effect a supplementary volume to the *Economic Consequences*. A year earlier he had published one of his major works, *A Treatise on Probability*, which was followed by his *Treatise on Money* (1930) and *General Theory of Employment, Interest and Money* (1936). There were, too, pamphlets, tracts and essays, culminating in *How to Pay for the War* (1940), a brief prescription for an unpalatable medicine which, with slightly different colouring matter, the country has since faithfully swallowed. The firm acquired a tradition that brought the economists in cohorts — among them G. D. H. Cole, some of whose books were transferred to Macmillan's in 1928 ; George Peel with *The Economic Impact of America* ; Norman Crump with his *First Book of Economics* ; Paul Einzig with a long succession of books initiated in 1929 ; Colin Clark with *The National Income 1924–1931*, Sir Cecil Kisch, Lord Stamp, Lionel Robbins and Joan Robinson with her *Economics of Imperfect Competition* in 1933. How wide the range is, probably none but an economist can fully appreciate. It is clear that in economics, as in politics proper, the firm's policy has not been to advance any narrow doctrine but to give expression to the contemporary mind. The year 1935 provides a pretty case in point. Cole's *Principles of Economic Planning* and a volume called *Planning for Employment* by fourteen members of Parliament did not exclude from the catholic list Horobin's *The Pleasures of Planning*, a work which amiably flouted a great part of the planners' enthusiasm.

Before another war came, the firm suffered new losses. Sir Richard Gregory retired after forty-five years' association with *Nature*, and a long career as the firm's scientific adviser and as the author or editor of numerous class-books in science. Early in 1939 Macmillan's manager, G. J. Heath, died. Heath, who was seventy-five, had joined the firm as a boy of thirteen. Having been greatly responsible, under Maurice Macmillan, for its overseas development, he knew the detail of its business and of the whole financial aspect of publishing as few others have known it. At home he cultivated roses and played bowls, but his life was concentrated in the firm. As he grew older, he stayed even closer to his desk, and no one remembered when he had last been persuaded to take what other men would regard as a summer holiday. With him went out a great store of experience dating from the old days in Bedford-street, and not Macmillan's only but the whole book trade felt the loss. His son Roland Heath was already secretary to the firm when the old general manager died, and is now a director.

Little now remains to be told but events that are too near to be seen in perspective. In common with all other businesses, Macmillan's found themselves faced in September 1939 with a new crisis. On Friday 1st, Harold Macmillan addressed the staff. None knew what severity of bombing to expect. Heads of departments, it was decided, might come to the office on Monday if all was well, but others were to wait until Tuesday. The staff quietly dispersed, some having clapped their hands a little in vague embarrassment. On Monday and Tuesday, St. Martin's-street was outwardly the same and for many days thereafter. Inside the office changes began. The younger men went to the forces, to reappear now and then in their military disguise, as did many of the younger women. The firm was in special difficulties in the matter of its staff. In recent years, several heads of departments had died or retired and, in two or three instances, their seconds-in-command, who would normally have succeeded them, had themselves died prematurely. The policy of not looking outside the existing staff and of giving youth its chance had been pursued, young men had been put in key positions, and there remained no one, with enough experience of the firm's practice, by whom they might be replaced. Harold Macmillan himself gave up his directorship when he entered the Government in May 1940, and after a time, Lovat Dickson, who had won experience in a small publishing firm of his own and had joined Macmillan's in 1938, became a director.

When the process of evacuation was in full swing and many unbombed businesses were moving out of London, Macmillan's resolved that they would stay, and put heart into the staff, and into many others outside St. Martin's-street, by an uncompromising announcement of their decision. At the same time, everything that could be done was done to give protection to the staff and to the premises. A part of the deep basement holding the bulk of the stock was reinforced with girders and made habitable. Emergency exits were provided, a system of fire-guard was fully organized while such a system was exceptional and, some say, unique, and communication by telephone was established with the spotters on the roof. At first, during the daylight raids, the staff withdrew often to their refuge, but soon outgrew the habit as the rest of England did. Many had their houses wrecked or damaged ; one was killed at home ; but no one was injured in St. Martin's-street.

So the business of publishing went on. The firm collaborated with the Oxford University Press to produce a new edition of *War and Peace* in one volume. Young men brought in their account of battle in the air and of their criticism of life — Richard Hillary combining the two in *The Last Enemy* ; Eric Linklater's imaginary dialogues won a distinguished place of their own by the ease of their style and the deep seriousness that informs them ; and, as in the earlier war, works of travel and scholarship appeared without interruption. Among these were Rebecca West's *Black Lamb and Grey Falcon* ; Sir Percy Sykes's *History of Afghanistan* ; Sir Aurel Stein's *On Old Routes of Western Iran* ; a two-volume edition, greatly amplifying the earlier texts, of the *Journals of Dorothy Wordsworth* ; Romney Sedgwick's *Letters from George III to Lord Bute* ; Lord Ponsonby's memoir of his father, *Henry Ponsonby* ; and C. M. Bowra's *Heritage of Symbolism*. From the New York house came the four volumes of President Roosevelt's *Public Papers and Addresses* for 1937–41. These are evidence enough that the old principle of continuity was unshaken. An account of them and of the other books published in those years of war belongs to a chapter that shall be written on another occasion by another hand. Nor shall this volume end in a peroration, for the life of which it treats is by no means done. Its pattern is a little spoiled by Harold Macmillan's defection to the Cabinet. It would have been pleasant to have balanced two brothers with two brothers. But there is compensation in recording that politics has paid for what it has borrowed — the bulk of the Prime Minister's works having been transferred to St. Martin's-street. The thought of this would have made the two young booksellers rub their eyes a hundred years ago.

LONDON : *Spring and Summer* 1943.

INDEX

239

Index

Index

Kingsley, Charles, 1, 2, 28, 30, 35, 37, 39, 41, 42-3, 46-8, 51, 57, 58, 65, 82, 136, 210, 225 ; controversy with Newman, 71-3 ; death, 107

Kingsley, Mrs. Charles, 46

Kingsley, Henry, 51, 58, 61-2, 65, 210

Kingsley, Mary (daughter of Charles Kingsley), 107, 210

Kingsley, Mary (daughter of George Kingsley), 210, 233

Kinloch-Cooke, Sir Clement, 124

Kipling, Rudyard, 60, 61, 147-8, 150-52, 200, 209, 226, 234

Kisch, Sir Cecil, 235

" Knapdale," 66-7, 99

Landor, W. S., 23

Lane, John, 146

Lang, Andrew, 63, 103

Lay, E. J. S., 228

Lee, Sir Sidney, 201

Lee, Vernon, 60

Le Fanu, J. S., 184

Lemon, Mark, 70

Lethbridge, Sir Roper, 106, 186

Lewes, G. H., 116, 117

Liddell, Alice, 79

Lightfoot, Bishop, 30, 63

Linklater, Eric, 237

Lloyd, Lord, 233

Lockyer, Sir Norman, 69, 71, 84-5, 87

Longfellow, H. W., 60, 83

Longman, C. J., 204

Longman, T., 14, 15, 16, 20

Longmans, 14, 15, 16, 17, 132

Lubbock, Percy, 232

Luciani, Luigi, 190

Ludlow, J. M., 45

Lushington, Henry, 57

Lysaght, S. R., 212, 219

Lytton, Lord, 125

Macaulay, Lord, 182

Macdonell, A. G., 229, 230

MacLehose, James, 12, 13, 14, 16, 17, 19, 39, 53, 54, 57, 65, 69, 74, 75, 83

MacLehose, James, the younger, 39

MacLehose, Norman, 39

Macmillan, Alexander, 1, 9, 19, 23, 28 ; birth, 7-8 ; early struggles, 19, 20 ; voyage to America, 20 ; at Seeley's, 20, 21, 24, 52 ; his selection from Shelley, 21-2 ; and F. D. Maurice, 24, 28, 30, 34, 35-6, 43, 66, 126-7 ; at Aldersgate-street, 24, 25, 26 ; at 17 Trinity-street, Cambridge, 25 ; at 1 Trinity-street, 29, 30-49 ; marriage, 38, 39 ; children, 39, 82, 107, 114, 135 ; at 23 Henrietta-street, 50-67 ; Tobacco Parliaments, 50-53 ; and Tennyson, 52, 53-4, 57-8, 173 ; and *Macmillan's Magazine*, 56-61, 71 ; and American affairs, 63-4, 66 ; on copyright questions, 64, 83, 174-6, 177 ; publisher to University of Oxford, 24, 66, 68 ; Knapdale, 66-7, 99-100 ; Hon. M.A., 68 ; his creative faculty, 69-70 ; and Newman-Kingsley controversy, 71-3 ; *Globe Shakespeare*, 74-5 ; the underselling problem, 76, 177, 178, 206 ; *Ecce Homo*, 78-79 ; visits America, 82-3 ; and Hardy, 41, 54, 87-91, 92, 95, 98, 99 ; *Nature*, 85, 87 ; second marriage, 100 ; gradually delegates responsibility, 101, 135 ; Bedford-street receptions, 103-104 ; and Pater, 105-6 ; and future Indian business, 106, 186 ; and J. R. Green, 107, 124 ; visits George Eliot, 116-17 ; and Shaw, 120, 131, 132 ; and Shorthouse, 121, 122 ; and Barrie, 134 ; and Malcolm Macmillan, 135, 136, 137 ; death, 139 ; later references, 173, 192, 225, 234

Index

Index

THE END